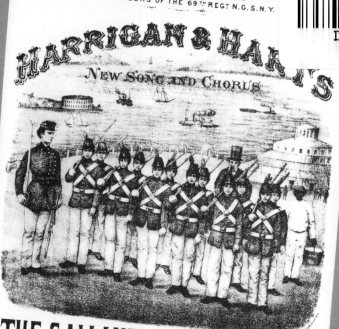

THE MERRY PARTNERS

*The Age and Stage
of Harrigan
and Hart*

Books by E. J. Kahn, Jr.

The Army Life
G. I. Jungle
The Voice
Who, Me?
The Peculiar War

THE MERRY PARTNERS

The Age and Stage of

HARRIGAN
AND
HART

by E. J. Kahn, Jr.

Random House, New York

This book is affectionately dedicated to
the memory of my grandfather,

JOSEPH PLAUT,

who remembered when.

CONTENTS

LIST OF ILLUSTRATIONS

AUTHOR'S NOTE

One afternoon toward the end of 1952, as I was walking along a New York street, minding my own business and only four blocks from my destination, a car drew up beside me and its occupant offered me a lift. I accepted. From such chance pickups true romances occasionally sprout. In this instance, I had hardly seated myself when the man next to me said, "You know, I've felt for some time there ought to be a book in Harrigan and Hart. Can you think of anyone who might be interested in tackling it?"

From somewhere in the car a voice, surprisingly like my own, uttered a fateful monosyllable. It was "Me."

Even if I were as old as my children seem to believe me to be, I could have had no first-hand acquaintance with the events and individuals touched on herein. Accordingly, the facts in this book have been brashly filched from the labors and memories of older and, on the whole, wiser people. Among the authentic historians of the social and theatrical scene whose researches I have cheerfully rifled are Herbert Asbury, T. Allston Brown, Henry Collins Brown, Barrett H. Clark, Walter Prichard Eaton, James L. Ford, George Freedley, Douglas Gilbert, Isaac Goldberg, Smith Hart, Arthur Hornblow, Robinson Locke, Frank Luther, Brander Matthews, Ward Morehouse, Lloyd Morris, Montrose Moses, George C. D. Odell, Arthur Hobson Quinn, Rebecca Rankin, Jacob Riis, Cleveland Rodgers, Sidney Rose, Cecil Smith, Sigmund Spaeth, Townsend Walsh, Arthur Roberts Williams, and James G. Wilson.

I am in substantial debt to many newspapers and magazines whose pages I have hungrily scanned, especially the late and, by me, lamented *Spirit of the Times*, *Clipper*, and *Dramatic Mirror*. From dozens of books dealing with one aspect or another of this treatise I have gleaned a useful fact or two, but it would be burdensome to try to list them all here, although their authors may feel quite differently. I owe much to Dr. William Van Lennep and the exemplary vaults of the Harvard Theatre Collection, over which he hospitably presides. I am almost equally grateful that the Theatre Collection of the New York Public Library exists and is so handy. Other branches of that institution, and also the Public Libraries of Boston, New Orleans, San Francisco, and Worcester, have done their bit to help. A nod of pleased acknowledgment, moreover, to the Museum of the City of New York, the New York Historical Society, the Columbia University Library, the American Antiquarian Society, the Historical and Philosophical Society of Ohio, and the California State Library.

Many individuals have with their patience and knowledge contrived, in one fashion or another, to offset my impetuousness and ignorance. Among these are Samuel Hopkins Adams, Lucius Beebe, Dr. Louis F. Bishop, Mrs. Bruce Bliven, Jr., Gardner Botsford, Mrs. John J. Braham, Clarence S. Brigham, Johnson Briscoe, Robert Campbell, Mrs. William Galt Chipley, Saxe Commins, Mrs. Frank Craven, Russel Crouse, Joseph Curtis, Kate Davenport, Emil Friedlander, Neil Gray, Preston Gray, Dr. Kent Roberts Greenfield, Robert W. Hill, Stewart Johnson, Harry Latimer, Alexander Lindey, Bettina Gray Liscomb, Alfred Mayo, Jean McCloskey, Major Kenneth C. Miller, Edith Oliver, Mary Reardon, Richard H. Rovere, May Davenport Seymour, William Shawn, Frederick P. Todd, Joan Toner, Sanderson Vanderbilt, Mrs.

John A. Warner, Dr. Henry W. Wells, Israel Wice, and Robert Wolf.

To a nephew of Tony Hart's, Anthony Hart Athy, and to Mr. Athy's family, I am immeasurably beholden for having been permitted access to some of their memorabilia. The list of Edward Harrigan's relatives who have furnished me with documentary or reminiscent source material is much longer. I should have been at an utter loss without the generous aid of Harrigan's five surviving children—Adelaide Ash, Nedda Logan, Nolan Harrigan, Philip Harrigan, and William Harrigan. None of these relatives of either Harrigan or Hart is accountable for my own arbitrary—and, perhaps, capricious—choice of contents.

I must reserve an especially reverent word for Ann Connolly, who has toiled long and faithfully in the dusty mines whence much of this volume was unearthed, and without whose efforts the whole project would have been far more onerous than I care to think about.

And I guess I also owe thanks, or something, to Joshua Logan, who gave me a ride that day when I could just as easily have made it on foot.

E. J. K.

Scarborough, N. Y.
June 11, 1955

THE POEM ON THE FACING PAGE is reprinted from *Slavery Days Songster*, a paper-covered booklet published in 1877 by A. J. Fisher, the purveyor also of a line of fifteen-cent pamphlets including *Bashfulness Cured* and *Lover's Telegraph*—this last a practical, self-help treatise addressed to clandestine sweethearts who wished to learn how to communicate furtively by means of hand-mirror signals flashed from windows on opposite sides of a courtyard, or by clever placement at table of napkins and silverware, "so arranged as to completely elude detection on the part of gossips, scandalmongers, etc."

THE STARS OF THE PERIOD

Hasten for seats, do not delay,
  Great artists are in town today;
And high upon the roll of fame,
  Resplendent shines their well-known name!
Refinement's air pervades their acts,
  And what they do no neatness lacks;
Reputation great they've earned and made,
  No one throws them in the shade!
In their great act, "Slavery Days,"
  Deaf'ning applause they're sure to raise.
Go and see the "Blue and Gray,"
  Clasping hands in bright array;
And the Sixty-ninth (the "gallant")
  Observe the *boys* possess *men's* talent.
Nature, Harrigan has surely blest,
  Made him "different from the rest,"
And by his own majestic sway,
  Banish, he will, all care away.
Next comes Tony, who sings so well,
  In dancing none can him excel;
Devoid of all that's stale and low,
  No rival does this artist know.
Homage should to both be paid:
  Astonishing is "The Day Parade;"
And other sketches they will do
  That are to life and nature true.
Remember, the music of excellent worth
  In the mind of Braham had its birth;
Then the manager of this great team—
  Obliging Hanley—deserves esteem!
Satisfaction, great, is given to all—
  Now don't forget this night to call.

—EDWARD AUSTIN

THE MERRY PARTNERS

*The Age and Stage
of Harrigan
and Hart*

THE BOYS
Expect
IT

In *Kim,* published in 1901, Rudyard Kipling had his title character and a native lama peer out across the Indian plains at sunset one day as a regiment of soldiers, urged on by their band, filed toward their camp. "At the far end of the plain a heavy, dusty column crawled in sight," Kipling wrote. "Then the wind brought the tune:

> We crave your condescension
> To tell you what we know
> Of marching in the Mulligan Guards
> To Sligo Port below.

Here broke in the shrill-tongued fifes:

> We shouldered arms,
> We marched—we marched away.
> From Phoenix Park,

We marched to Dublin Bay.
The drums and the fifes,
Oh, sweetly they did play,
As we marched—marched—marched—
With the Mulligan Guards!"

Kipling did not indicate whether or not he was aware that this number in the musical repertoire of one of Her Majesty's far-flung garrisons was but a slightly altered version of a song that dealt with a route of march covering less than a mile of the lower East Side of Manhattan Island:

We shouldered arms and marched and marched away,
From Baxter Street we marched to Avenue A.*
With drums and fifes how sweetly they did play,
As we marched, marched, marched in the Mulligan Guards.

In any event, it was not only on the Indian plains that the strains of "The Mulligan Guards," with or without vocal accompaniment, used to be interminably heard. In England, the Coldstream Guards marched briskly to it. In Paris, from the Rue de Rivoli to the Avenue de l'Opéra, appreciative voices chorused

Armes en bras nous marchons gaiement
De la rue Baxter jusqu'à l'Avenue A.
Les fifres, tambours, on les écoute doucement,
Quand les Mulligans marchent là, là!

In New York, the song could be heard everywhere. Newsboys, policemen, hot-corn venders, the oyster sellers at their street-corner stalls, and the hokey-pokey men, who sold ice cream, whistled it as they went about their various

* In some versions of the lyric they marched from Jackson Street to Avenue A.

chores. It was wafted across the harbor from the decks of the moonlight-excursion boats that plied between the Battery and Coney Island. It was cranked out by a hundred organ grinders and plunked out on a thousand parlor pianofortes. It was blasted out by Patrick S. Gilmore's celebrated brass band, an organization that on some occasions consisted of as many as 150 instrumentalists, headed by the great Jules Levy, a cornettist equally renowned for his elegant waxed mustache, his unwavering monocle, and his incomparable rendition of "Yankee Doodle." Throughout America, children who in other eras might have chanted "Ten Little Indians" could be found chanting a variation on that theme called "Ten Little Mulligan Guards."

In Vienna, the distinguished composer Karl Milloecker, preparing the score for a musical production, *The Beggar Student,* which was to be put on at the Casino in New York in 1883, heard a catchy tune that he promptly borrowed for his first-act finale. It was not unusual then for one musician or playwright or journalist to crib liberally and lightheartedly from the work of another. *The Beggar Student,* however, had to be revised during rehearsals in New York. Milloecker's American sponsors knew that local audiences, however tolerant of routine pilferage, would never stand for anybody's thus appropriating, as he had, "The Mulligan Guards"—a number inseparably associated in the minds of all New Yorkers who were not stone-deaf with the men who made it famous, Ned Harrigan and Tony Hart.

"The Mulligan Guards" was composed, in 1872, by Edward Harrigan, a twenty-eight-year-old itinerant actor and sketch-writer, and David Braham, a thirty-four-year-old violinist who was conducting the pit orchestra at the Theatre Comique on lower Broadway, and who was to become Harrigan's father-in-law and lifelong associate. The two men, over a twenty-year span, collaborated on more than 200 popular songs, including such classics of their type as "Paddy Duffy's Cart," "Maggie Murphy's Home," "The Babies on Our Block," "The Widow Nolan's Goat," and "Dolly, My Crumpled-horn Cow." The first public airing of "The Mulligan Guards" took place in the spring of 1873 at the Academy of Music in Chicago, where Harrigan was filling an engagement with Tony Hart, who, though not yet eighteen, had already been in show business for seven years, ever since he had run away from a reform school just outside Worcester, Massachusetts.

For fourteen years, until they split up with a rending tear that to many New Yorkers was as cataclysmic as an earthquake, Harrigan and Hart were a much esteemed and enormously successful team. It was indicative of the celebrity they enjoyed that the first public performance the aspiring duo of Weber and Fields ever gave together included a respectful imitation of Harrigan and Hart. To many out-of-towners, Harrigan and Hart were a New York landmark equal in stature to Broadway. "A visit to New York would be as incomplete to the countryman if he did not see Harrigan and Hart," declared one New England guide book in the eighties, "as if he had by some strange mistake missed going to Central Park." In New England and elsewhere, countrymen organized savings clubs, much as people nowadays do with a prudent eye toward Christmas, and when their hoards had become sufficiently robust the club members would descend en masse upon New York and, specifically, upon Harrigan and Hart. A lady writer for the Chicago *News* thought the combination was almost too good for the East Coast. "The love New York had for Harrigan and Hart," she asserted, "was one of the few beautiful American things it can be credited with."

Harrigan and Hart complemented each other splendidly. "Hart could play all the parts seven Harrigans could write," the Boston *Traveller* stated, "and Harrigan could write what seven Harts could play." (If there was any disagreement in Boston with this thesis, it appeared to be mainly of degree. The Boston *Herald* thought that "Harrigan could write all that twenty people could play, and Hart could play all that twenty Harrigans could write.") Harrigan, a stocky, serene man who had practically no interests outside of the theatre, was a prolific writer. In addition to some eighty or ninety sketches that he dashed off while working in variety theatres as a young man, he was the author of thirty-five full-length plays— nearly all of them topical farces that seem woefully dated today, but that when fresh earned wide acclaim. Not only did Harrigan act in these and sing his own songs in them, but he produced, financed, and directed them himself and put them on in theatres that he ran himself. He even wrote the text for his own programs. He assembled a more or less permanent company of supporting actors who were so closely associated with him that some of them proved to be practically unemployable when he retired, since they had never had the experience of working for anybody else. One actor who died at twenty-three was even at that age the veteran of thirteen years' exclusive apprenticeship to Harrigan.

Harrigan's company was affectionately described by one critic of the eighteen-eighties as "the jolliest lot of local trash that ever held the boards." Of the group, there was none jollier than Tony Hart, an actor hailed as the foremost genteel wench who had ever pouted across the footlights. It was not uncommon in his day for men to take female roles. There was, for instance, the tragic experience of Charles T. White, in the early eighteen-fifties the proprietor of White's Ethiopian Opera House (where, to the presumable despair of the box-office attendant, seats were priced at twelve and a half or six and a quarter cents, depending on location), and a famous minstrel. In 1890, like many another alumnus of minstrelsy, which by then had begun to fade in popular esteem, White found himself in Harrigan's company. White had for many years sported a lush, full beard, but he had to shave it off when Harrigan cast him as an old colored woman in *Reilly and the Four Hundred,* a satire on Ward McAllister's census of high society. Two weeks after the play opened, White jumped out of bed one wintry night and ran outdoors to watch the Fifth Avenue Theatre burn down. He died almost immediately thereafter of pneumonia, an illness some of his sorrowing admirers were certain he would never have contracted if the stern demands of his profession had not forced him to shave off his protective facial warmth.

Tony Hart had a round, clean-shaven face that Harrigan once likened to that of an angel on a Valentine, but he was no mere female impersonator. He could, and did, fill masculine roles as expertly as feminine ones. In one play, he had six parts—three male and three female—and in another he played both a mother and her son. "His imitation of the manners, gait, movements of the body and facial expression of a young girl was absolutely wonderful," one New York critic exclaimed after observing Hart in skirts. "We could hardly divest ourselves of the idea that the performer before us was not a female." The detective William Pinkerton, an expert at seeing through disguises, once refused to believe that Hart was a man even after being taken backstage following a performance and allowed to scrutinize his costume and make-up at close range. Pinkerton was not persuaded of the truth until Hart had pulled off his wig and let loose with a few robust phrases that could only have been learned in a boys' reform school.

One of Hart's closest friends was Nat C. Goodwin, the comedian, who in his autobiography, otherwise pretty much limited to an analysis of his own five marriages, said effusively that Hart "caused more joy and sunshine by his delightful gifts than any artist of his time." Goodwin, who had appeared with Harrigan and Hart as early in his career as 1876, before he had been married even once, went on to say, of Hart, "To refer to him as talented was an insult. Genius was the only word that could be applied. He sang like a nightingale, danced like a fairy, and acted like a master comedian. . . . His magnetism was compelling, his personality charming. He had the face of an Irish Apollo. His eyes were liquid blue, almost feminine in their dovelike expression. His head was large and round and covered with a luxurious growth of brown, curly hair, which clustered in ringlets over a strong brow. His feet and hands were small, his smile almost pathetic. His disposition turned December into May. . . . Tony Hart was the friend of all mankind and my especial pal. I have loved

three men in my life and he was two of them." Goodwin
was not the only witness to Hart's compelling magnetism.
While Victor Moore's father was lying on his deathbed,
he opened his eyes and saw a strange physician hovering
over him. "I know you're a bum doctor, but you look like
Tony Hart," the dying man muttered, and he closed his
eyes in trusting contentment.

By no contemporary of theirs were Harrigan and Hart
more highly regarded than by one of the leading theatrical
columnists of their time, Mrs. Mary Hewins Fiske, who
from 1881 until her death at the age of forty-five in 1889
presided over a department of chitchat in the weekly New
York *Dramatic Mirror,* signing herself "The Giddy
Gusher." A plump, forceful woman who wore a big man's
watch chain across her bosom, she had been a circus performer at the age of twelve (she quit when an elephant
squeezed her too hard), and a playwright at sixteen. She
became known as the Queen of Bohemia, and her funeral
oration was delivered, appropriately, by Colonel Robert
Ingersoll, the famous agnostic, who had a wide circle of
acquaintanceship among actors and other proper Bohe-
mians. She was married for a time to Charles K. Fox, the
manager of the Bowery Theatre, who once manifested his
displeasure with the orchestra there during a performance
by striding to the footlights and pelting its members with
hard rolls; her last husband was Stephen Fiske, the drama
editor of the *Spirit of the Times,* a sporting weekly that
doted upon Harrigan and Hart almost as fervently as did
the Giddy Gusher herself. Mrs. Fiske thought that Tony
Hart had a smile that would coax the birds off the trees,
and that Ned Harrigan was the Molière of the New World
and a more venerable citizen, all things considered, than

Grover Cleveland, who was President at the time of her appraisal.

Such extravagant praise for Harrigan and Hart was commonplace. People practically knocked themselves out vying to see who could flatter Harrigan most. Less than a week after the New York *Herald* had exclaimed, "What Howells has done for New England and Cable for Louisiana, Harrigan has done for New York," the old New York *Daily News* countered with, "What Dickens was to London in his novels and Zola to Paris, Mr. Harrigan is to New York in his plays." Molière was only one of a troupe of eminent playwrights to whom he was compared. The New York *Times* detected in his work echoes of Euripides, and Brander Matthews was put in mind of Plautus. At one time or another, Harrigan, somewhat to his amazement, found his name enshrined by one critic or another alongside the names of Ibsen, Goldoni, John Fletcher, Oliver Goldsmith, Aristophanes, and Shakespeare. "Ned and Will!" cried *Turf, Field & Farm,* a sporting journal, in eulogy of the two playwrights it liked best.

Having had no formal education beyond grammar school, Harrigan was not overwhelmingly impressed by being linked with the ancient Greeks, but analogies to Molière appealed to him. Fairly early in his career, he wrote a play about a hypochondriac and his adventures in the hands of a succession of quack doctors. He showed it to a relatively erudite friend, who advised him that it seemed markedly similar in plot to *Le Malade Imaginaire,* which was the last play Molière had ever written. Harrigan at once got hold of a translation of the earlier work, and compared it with his own. He concluded that Molière had handled the subject matter more adroitly, filed away his own manuscript with "A Tribute to Molière" labelled on it, and undertook the study of French. On learning that Molière had been in the habit of reading his plays to his housekeeper, Harrigan began reading his plays to his cook, generally an immigrant Irish girl of brief residence in this country who, while dutifully attentive, would not always be hypercritical. On a wall of Harrigan's study, in later years, were prominently displayed two pictures— one of them a painting of Molière's housekeeper reacting to that playwright's lines, and the other a portrait of Charles Dickens.

Harrigan was so often characterized the "Dickens of America" that toward the end of his career he used the phrase in advertisements for his own plays. The title was first conferred upon him by William Dean Howells, an ardent advocate of literary realism, who acclaimed Harrigan for devoting himself almost without exception to what was commonly known as low life—"though whether it is essentially lower than fashionable life," Howells reflected, "is another question." (Long before Howells likened him to Dickens, Harrigan showed himself to have tastes markedly similar to those of the Englishman; in a letter to his fiancée while on tour in New Orleans, he reported that he had seen all the interesting sights the place had to offer—the legislature, the prison, and the insane asylum.) It was toward the low life of New York City in particular that Harrigan gravitated. "Polite society, wealth and culture possess little or no color or picturesqueness," he once said. This viewpoint was debatable. In the three decades following the Civil War, the upper classes of the city were a mighty colorful crew, who indulged in such picturesque pastimes as decorating the oysters they served their guests with genuine black pearls, and treating their favorite lap dogs and horses to champagne. It could readily be argued, indeed, that the rich of that era were far more colorful than the poor if for no other reason than that they picked their teeth (men were more prone to carry toothpicks then than handkerchiefs) with toothpicks made of solid gold or silver or of diamond-studded platinum, whereas the humble were constrained to use mere wood splinters.

But Harrigan was unmoved by such manifestations of high-class picturesqueness. He was primarily concerned with the habitués of the slums—the newsboys and flower girls, the barbers and butchers, the Bowery toughs and South Street sailors, and the disreputable folk who hung out in the dives known as dance houses, where it was the custom for the male patrons to buy the resident hostesses a drink every time the music stopped; where the girls, who were clearly made of sterner stuff than their proto- types today, downed an authentic drink—as long as they could stay on their feet—during each of an evening's many pauses for refreshment and profit; and where a rapa- cious kind of stag line hovered, waiting for male patrons to pass out so they could be robbed or, if they were sailors, sold while unconscious to the captain of some short- handed ship.

Most of the characters who figured in Harrigan's plays were first- or second-generation Irish and German and Italian immigrants who came to New York during the nineteenth century and of whom Harrigan was in the habit of deploring, half-jestingly, that they wouldn't come to his theatre because the incidents he showed on stage were indistinguishable from what they experienced at home. In fact, though, his subjects loved looking at themselves, or farcical facsimiles thereof. Between 1875 and 1895, first with and then without Hart, Harrigan presided over four theatres in New York, gradually moving uptown as the city did and eventually getting as far as 35th Street. And as he migrated northward, he was followed by one of the most loyal claques any theatrical figure ever commanded. Twenty-three of his plays achieved runs of more than one hundred performances each on Broadway, phenomenal displays of longevity in those days. The plays, in many cases, were lambasted by reviewers, but Harrigan's audiences didn't care; they accepted them much in the uncritical fashion that latter-day claques have been wont to hail, sight unseen, the offerings of, say, T. S. Eliot. One newspaper critic, accosted by a friend between the acts at the première of a Harrigan production, was asked, "Do you think this is a good piece?" "It won't make much difference whether it is or not," replied the critic resignedly. "It's a tremendous success already."

During Harrigan's heyday, no self-respecting mayor of New York would any more have missed an opening night at one of his theatres than, in subsequent years, any mayor would have passed up the first game of a baseball season. "The jubilation at Harrigan's last night was great," the New York *Sun* observed in 1888 after the opening of *Waddy Googan,* a play about an Irish hackman in which Harrigan played not only the title role but that also of an Italian rogue, and the success of which prompted a hack driver named John McGoodrich, after whom the author was thought to have fashioned his principal character, to abandon immediately his own name and call himself forever after Waddy Googan. "But [the jubilation] was conventional," the *Sun* went on. "It was the story of other seasons all over again—a lusty welcoming by voice and hand, a cheer from enthusiastic throats, an overflow of ready praise. Here is an occasion absolutely unique in its enthusiasm. Nothing else in the city's theatrical history affords a similar spectacle: nothing else approaches it in its democratic éclat, its intense good nature."

On opening nights at any of Harrigan's theatres, the stage would be awash in testimonial bouquets. The memory of those days must make contemporary florists writhe with envy. Ladies in the boxes ecstatically flung their corsages at the cast, and even minor actors were habitually in the receipt of floral tributes bulkier than themselves. So giddily were posies passed back and forth that one Harrigan ingenue who had a special bunch of violets made up to give to a friend at a matinee found a third party giving it back to her, somewhat wilted but still fragrant, that same evening. In 1886 the New York *Herald* estimated —quite possibly exaggerating, as it was prone to do with almost any theme—that in the United States there were 10,000 actresses who averaged 125 bouquets a year apiece, a good many purchased by themselves, but the vast majority by what the *Herald* elected to call "sappy youths." The flower-giving plague was epidemic; in Vienna, the director of the Imperial Theatre banned all flora from his stage, at least during actual performances. A few American producers tried to ape this example, complaining that the artistic effect of their productions was being smothered by petals. Who could enjoy *Camille,* Lester Wallack once complained, when donkeys in the audience insisted on hurling flowers at the cast at the very moment Marguerite was dying?

At Harrigan's opening nights, the flinging of wreaths

constituted only a trivial distraction. To the assorted members of the audience—the politicians enthroned in the boxes, the dandies in the stalls, and what was called the shirt-sleeve brigade or the "peanutters" up in the gallery —the more interruptions there were, the merrier. Practically every member of the cast who was anybody had to make a speech, often right in the middle of a scene; Harrigan and Hart were sometimes called upon for several informal addresses. In *Waddy Googan,* appropriate remarks were demanded of Harrigan at his first entrance as an Irishman, and also at his first entrance as an Italian. It often took five hours for a three-hour play to lurch its way to completion. Joseph H. Tooker—a theatrical manager and former Chief Marshal of New York, who held the honorary title of Commodore because he had once commanded an excursion boat that plied between New York and Long Branch, and who declined to wear formal dress to Harrigan and Hart openings because he couldn't feel comfortable in their environment thus clothed—was reminded by the goings-on at such oratorical performances of a dramatic incident that had occurred in 1860 on Bedloes Island.

Albert E. Hicks, a notorious pirate, was about to be hanged on the island under the supervision of Isaiah Rynders, the United States Marshal for New York, who had migrated north from Mississippi, already adept with knife and pistol, and had become the political boss of the raffish Sixth Ward. Rynders—who was the chief instigator of the Astor Place riots in 1849 and who once circumvented the arrest of a Grand Sachem of Tammany Hall he had been instructed to pick up by marching into the bar of the New York Hotel, where his quarry was known to be at

bay, and remaining there, loudly announcing the purpose
of his mission and substantially depleting the bartender's
stock, until the Sachem had got a good part of the way
toward Mexico—liked to do up his hangings in tasteful
style. In Hicks' case, the marshal had the pirate escorted
from the Tombs, where he had lain on exhibit in heavy
shackles, to the Hudson River in a coach drawn by four
coal-black horses and driven by a coachman costumed entirely in black. A crowd of gamblers, prizefighters, politicians, newspapermen, and ordinary citizens who had
mustered various river craft to proceed to Bedloes Island
and witness the ceremony were then invited by Rynders to
accompany his cortege on a cruise by barge up the river.
When, after suitable festivities afloat, they finally got to
the scene of the execution, Rynders asked his victim, "Don't
you want to say something?"

"No," said Hicks.

"Oh, go ahead and talk," said the disappointed marshal.
"Make a speech. The boys expect it."

Commodore Tooker observed that the boys expected it
of Harrigan and Hart, too, and that in the case of the
theatrical pair they were hardly ever dismissed with a
gruff monosyllable. None of the boys was more delighted
with such offhand additions to an evening's planned entertainment than were those perched on the hard wooden
benches high in the musty gallery. For this privilege they
paid, in the seventies, sometimes fifteen and sometimes
twenty-five cents a head. The gallery was an airless aerie,
rank with the smell of sweat, cabbage, beer, and horses,
but there was scarcely a newsboy in New York who
would not gladly forgo a night's lodging if he could
thereby afford an evening at the theatre. When a bank

president of the day found a teen-age messenger lounging against his polished mahogany desk and whistling a popular tune, the banker is said to have rumbled reprovingly, "Boy, this is not Harrigan and Hart's."

"You're damn right it ain't. I wouldn't pay no quarter of a dollar to come here," was the boy's reply.

The newsboys of New York were regarded by some of their fellow citizens, including James L. Ford, a drama critic of the seventies, as the most discriminating critics in town. They were perhaps also the most discriminated against. It outraged them that the five-hundred-dollar annual fees all theatres had to pay to the mayor's office to obtain an operating license were used to support the Society for the Reformation of Juvenile Delinquents. The inference that this defrayal was a fit use for such funds, inasmuch as theatres contributed to delinquency and should accordingly help correct it, was mildly resented by some stage people, but it was loudly decried by the newsboys, who felt that they were hardly in as much danger of being contaminated by Harrigan and Hart as by the city's noisome pavements.

There had been no newsboys at all in the city until 1833, at which time the *Sun,* departing radically from the view of all publishers that it was undignified to peddle their wares like tea-water or chestnuts, had appealed for venders. By 1873, when the unsettled post-war economic conditions had produced 10,000 homeless children in New York and when there were fifteen daily newspapers in the city, the streets swarmed with newsboys. They were a hardy lot, many of them orphans, who went by names like One-Lung Pete, Slobbery Jack, and Jake the Oyster, and who, if they toiled unremittingly and in good voice from

four o'clock in the morning until after dark, could hope
to earn a daily income of fifty cents or so. Their devotion
to Harrigan and Hart stemmed partly from their aware-
ness that both men had briefly been newsboys themselves.

The gallery seats were unreserved, and long before
eight-thirty, when Harrigan and Hart got under way, the
sidewalk outside their theatre would be thronged with
newsboys who had quit work early and were awaiting admittance, holding the exact price of a gallery ticket in
their hands, so that at seven-thirty, when the doors were
opened, they could vault toward a favorite vantage point
without having to wait for change. Once settled on their
planks, they would remove their coats and vests and use
them for seat cushions. If they were at an opening night,
they might spend another dime on a songbook containing
the lyrics of the evening's numbers. After a Harrigan and
Hart show had been running a few days, the newsboys
were familiar with the lyrics and didn't need songbooks.
As David Braham's thirteen-man orchestra struck up the
overture, the gallery fans would attempt shrilly to fit some
of the words before them to the tunes emanating from the
orchestra pit. This sometimes resulted in a good deal of
scrapping, inasmuch as one faction would try to accommodate one set of words to a brand-new tune, while a
nearby faction would choose another set. An especially
stimulating night, from the newsboys' point of view, was
the opening of *Old Lavender,* considered in some quarters
Harrigan's most memorable drama, in which he played
the part of a boozy, philosophical, down-at-the-heels ex-
financier, and Tony Hart was cast as a dock rat. Looking
over the songbooks that evening, the newsboys came upon
a Harrigan-Braham number about them entitled "Extra!

Extra!" and expressed their appreciation of this occupational tribute by shouting, with just as much volume as
they had ever expended on a real-life headline, the various
lyrics, including one especially pertinent verse that began:

> I sit up in the gall'ry watching of the play;
> Oh, I know all the actors, and this is what they say,
> "I am King of Denmark, you ought to hear my talk . . ."

Certain rules of etiquette were sternly enforced in the
gallery, though the attitude toward most shenanigans was
lenient. Ladies were not welcome there, but even so, men
were expected to remove their hats during a performance,
and if they inadvertently neglected to do so, their hats
were knocked off them by the ushers, who in all theatres
had been equipped with long bamboo poles ever since the
Astor Place riots. (Namby-pambies did not last long then
as theatre employees, or attachés, as the staff was called;
after one drunken alderman had retreated in bloody di-
shevelment from an altercation with a stage doorman, it
was noted commendingly in a published account of the
episode that a Harrigan and Hart sentinel was not to be
struck with impunity.) Tobacco chewers in the gallery
were allowed to spit freely—since this was after all a time
when public expectoration was widely tolerated—but only
on one another. Spitting on the orchestra patrons constituted grounds for ejection from the premises. Throwing
spitballs at the white shirt-fronts of the dudes in the stalls,
however, or even at the actors, was deemed a relatively
minor offense, punishable by no more than a whack with
a bamboo pole.

There were no restrictions on noise. From the gallery,
throughout the typical Harrigan and Hart performance,

flowed a constant din of stamping and yelling and clap-
ping, punctuated by the smug declamations of a boy
who peddled lozenges and took it upon himself, as did his
counterpart in many another theatre, to explain abstruse
dialogue to any auditors who appeared not to grasp it.
Rather than take a chance on anyone's missing anything,
and having on the whole a low opinion of the comprehension of most ticket-holders, lozenge boys would carry on
a buzzing commentary almost as persistent and all-inclu-
sive as the footnotes to a variorum edition of Shakespeare.
Long after the glib sellers of lozenges ceased to be a feature
of the legitimate theatre, actors who felt that people to
whom they were telling a story had failed to get the point
would cry in exasperation, "Bring on the lozenge boy!"

The members of the gallery were not the only spectators
who competed with the actors. General William Tecumseh
Sherman, who spent the last years of his life in New
York, was a notable ally. Retired on his Civil War
laurels, he became a slavish disciple of the theatre. He
hardly ever missed an opening night anywhere, and was
so familiar a figure to the metropolitan ticket-takers that
he rarely bothered to buy a ticket, striding past them
instead with a friendly wave and occupying any vacant
seat. After a while, to avoid complications, most of the
Broadway managers set aside a seat for him. He was one
of the few non-professionals invited to attend the dedication of the Players Club on December 31, 1888. Sherman's applause was as audible as cannonfire. "When
his hands are idle," one newspaperman reported, "his
tongue wags gleefully with a running commentary." He
usually dropped in backstage after a performance; one
ingenue in the Harrigan ranks asserted years after reach-

ing character-woman age that no one had ever paid her
a nicer compliment on a performance than the General
had; she was unable to walk past his statue at Fifty-ninth
Street, she said, without feeling a twinge of gratitude.

It should not be thought that Harrigan and Hart were
the only theatrical proprietors whose offerings were continually interrupted by demonstrations from out front.
Dion Boucicault, whose achievements in the United States
included the first depiction of Negroes as something other
than buffoons, the founding of a school of Irish comedy,
and the first use of carpets on stage (he is also said to
have invented the minute steak), was like Harrigan, an
actor as well as a playwright; his special fans, indifferent
to any actors but their idol, were apt to climb on their
chairs in impromptu gymnastics whenever he went off
the stage and abandoned it to comparative nonentities.
So carelessly was the show-must-go-on tradition observed
by some folk, if not by resolute actors, that when Charles
Fox was holding sway at the Bowery Theatre, in 1853,
a sheriff who had an injunction to slap on him tried to
slap it while he was on stage. Fox, a powerful man, picked
the sheriff up and hurled him into the orchestra pit, where
he landed on a kettle drum and, to screams of approbation, shattered it with a resounding thump. Then the performance continued. (Old-time actors often found themselves in legal scrapes, and most of them retained as counsel the celebrated firm of Howe & Hummel, whose business letterhead said "Theatrical Causes a Specialty." One
night when Harrigan and Hart were performing, there
was a loud clatter backstage, audible to the topmost row
of the gallery. "What was that?" interposed Harrigan.

"Oh, probably just Howe and Hummel filing an affidavit,"
Hart answered.)

Twenty-five years after Fox dumped the sheriff amid
the tympani, the Bowery stage was the scene of another
memorable altercation. Rose Eytinge and Cyril Searle,
her agent as well as co-star, were appearing there in *Oliver
Twist,* under the management of F. W. Hofele. The week
before, they had done another show for the managerial
team of Shook and Palmer, who were under the impression that the actors owed them money and, in fraternal,
manager-to-manager fashion, persuaded Hofele to with-
hold the sum in contention from their pay. After the third
act of *Oliver Twist,* there was an exceptionally long delay,
following which the curtain rose to reveal, surprisingly,
the scenery for a show called *Our Schoolmaster.* Searle,
flushed and agitated, rushed on stage and announced to
the audience that Hofele was robbing Miss Eytinge and
himself. Hofele emerged from the wings and tried to get
in a contradictory word, but he couldn't make himself
heard. By then, the audience, warming up to the con-
troversy, was making too much noise. "There was free
fighting in the two upper galleries," the *Sun* reported,
"and a good deal of light sparring was indulged in by
those in the orchestra pit"—these last being young men
who had ripped chairs from the floor and were smashing
gas fixtures with them.

Miss Eytinge seemed to get involved in public tiffs
wherever she played. In Virginia City, Nevada, while
starring in *Camille,* she engaged in an on-stage debate
with her leading man as to why the play had been cut.
He claimed, while the audience sat enthralled, that it was
because she had to catch a stage-coach to Reno to make a

performance there. She claimed that it was because her supporting company was insufferably poor. Never before had a Marguerite and an Armand had such a quarrel. For quite a while, they argued the merits of their cases, he standing at one side of the stage, she at the other. Finally they wearied of the exchange and moved along to the last act of the play. The audience, which had been responding to their dispute with raucous cries of "Ah, pull down yer vest!" and "Stash the racket!," settled down a bit, but when Armand turned to his by now consumptively coughing Camille and cried "Live! Oh, live for me!" it could contain itself no longer and burst into howls of disconcerting laughter.

At most theatres, such departures from the script were the exception rather than the rule. When Harrigan and Hart were on display, these occurred with engaging frequency. The interruption might be sentimental in nature, as it was one night when a newsboy and his widowed mother (all newsboys who had mothers then had widowed ones) sat down front as Harrigan's guests. He had seen the boy begging on the street earlier in the day, had given him a handout, and had invited him and his mother to the theatre. Harrigan was in blackface that night, but when he made his first entrance, the boy recognized his benefactor through his make-up and began shouting his gratitude. At that the widow rose to her feet and made an emotional speech hailing all actors as angels of mercy and invoking the Lord's blessing upon the entire profession.

In 1884, when Henry Irving and Ellen Terry were visiting the United States, they took in a Harrigan play, *Investigation,* which had among other scenes the baptism

of a three-month-old colored baby in a Chinese opium den.
A real baby was used, and Miss Terry, after pretty well
breaking up one performance by leaning way out of her
box during the baptismal scene and clucking to the infant,
broke up another when she sent the child a gold locket,
which Harrigan, halting the stage proceedings long
enough, presented on stage to its recipient. Harrigan himself, on his forty-fourth birthday in 1888, was interrupted
when the members of his cast, halfway through a scene,
surprised him by presenting him with a sterling-silver
water service, while such literary figures in the audience as
the Giddy Gusher and Mark Twain clapped indulgently.
Harrigan was so taken aback that he was unable to continue for a couple of minutes, a gap that his leading lady,
Annie Yeamans, deftly filled by stepping forward and
ad-libbing a two-minute dissertation on the efficacy of
cold water as a healthful beverage.

Another night, while Harrigan and Hart were in the
middle of a song, two detectives sneaked into the orchestra,
anxious to pounce on a spectator whom they wanted to
question about a bank robbery. Their quarry was a friend
of Harrigan's, who thought he hadn't robbed any bank,
or at any rate not the particular bank in question, and
when the actor sensed from the stage what was about to
happen, he leaped to the footlights and sounded a warning. The alleged bank robber jumped to his feet and
headed for an aisle. "Get down by Mr. Braham!" yelled
Harrigan, hoping that the fugitive might escape through
the orchestra pit. But the detectives caught him in the
string section.

Harrigan's patrons included not only a sprinkling of
the underworld but most of the city's sporting set. The

first performance of *Waddy Googan* followed by only a few hours a horse race in which an entrant named Galen had been a hot tip. Half the audience had plunged heavily on Galen, but had entered the theatre before the results were known. The play contained a colloquy between a gambler and a tramp, and when Harrigan learned from a stage-door courier that Galen had been beaten, he inserted into that scene the offhand announcement that Proctor Knott had won. It brought down the house, in more ways than one. "We who had invested," a critic for the *World* announced sadly the next day, in what had started off as a review of the show, "for the first time knew that Galen had lost."

2.

KNOCKDOWN
and
SLAPBANG

Harrigan used to say that haste and strife were the two words that best characterized the New York of his time. His plays, acclaimed by William Dean Howells for their "sublime moments of absolute fidelity" and for their author's "refined perception," were full of haste and strife. One of the most popular scenes Harrigan ever conceived, the second act curtain of *The Mulligan Guards' Ball*—which was one of nine Mulligan plays that he wrote and co-starred in with Hart—took place in a dance hall whose proprietor, an absent-minded German, had inadvertently rented the premises on the same night to two

27

irreconcilably inimical factions, an Irish social club and a Negro social club. To avoid mayhem, the proprietor persuaded the Negroes to take an upstairs room, directly above the Irish. After a good deal of spirited dancing on both levels, the group upstairs broke through the floor, and the scene ended with the ceiling caving in on the Irish and with dark bodies—Harrigan used dummies—tumbling profusely down upon the stage. The audiences loved it. The newsboys in the gallery stamped their feet so hard in approbation that the folks in the orchestra cast apprehensive glances at the ceiling above *them.*

After twenty-five years on Broadway, Harrigan complained that he was getting tired of this sort of boisterousness, which one critic called "melodious rowdyism" and which Harrigan himself called, disparagingly, "knockdown and slapbang." But his audiences never seemed to share his boredom, and, respectful of their wishes, he hardly ever failed to include a generous portion of rowdyism in his productions. (A typical lithographic advertisement for a Harrigan and Hart play showed a Chinese, holding a trombone, being flung out of a second-story tenement-house window onto the head of an unsuspecting Negro strolling by below.) The closest Harrigan came to eliminating knockdown and slapbang entirely was in *Old Lavender,* where he confined himself to a near-drowning. Reviewing this play, the *Sun's* critic noted, with pleased surprise, "There is nothing dropped from the clouds to the stage." The brief variety sketches Harrigan and Hart appeared in at the start of their career frequently ended with a spirited free-for-all; this was such standard procedure that the scripts for these sketches often closed merely with a general stage direction like "Tumult with all."

In most of Harrigan's full-length plays, there was tumult galore. *The Mulligan Guards' Nominee,* a satire on the political campaigns waged by candidates for the job of alderman, contained one scene aboard the Albany night boat, in the course of which half the members of the cast threw the other half overboard. Then the boat itself exploded. In *The Woolen Stocking,* there was a sewer-gas explosion, and in *Squatter Sovereignty,* a brawl between two clans of Irishmen. In addition to flying bodies, the script called for the presence on stage of a donkey, a goat, and a flock of geese. During one performance of this show, the geese got so upset by the frenzied antics of their human colleagues that they flapped cackling into the laps of the audience; during another performance, one actor got so carried away by the belligerent nature of his role that, in the course of a wrestling match, he broke another actor's leg.

Sometimes, to heighten the effectiveness of his scenes, Harrigan would pile knockdown upon slapbang until his auditors reeled. Toward the end of his career, one critic was moved to remark of his play *Marty Malone,* "As I tottered away, I felt as if Ali Baba and his forty thugs had clubbed me with Chicago sandbags, and all the wild mustangs in all the stables on Portland Street had run over me, and all the stable boys had caressed me with currycombs, and Wagner had been sung in a boiler factory. Compared with it, the most violent cataclysms of [Charles] Hoyt are the tender croonings of a twilight baritone in the scented cloisters of the hallowed home. Harrigan is complexly terrific. The theatre should provide private cyclone cellars."

To end one act of *Reilly and the Four Hundred,* Harrigan had a fist-fight that took place while a ceiling caved in, these events occurring during a thunderstorm. Harrigan frequently put on revivals of his more successful shows. He would rewrite the plays on such occasions, and, like as not, make them even more phrenetic than they had originally been. *The Major,* one of his greatest successes, which dealt with an Irish rogue who lived by his wits and by scandalously taking advantage of the landlady of his boarding-house, was notable, when first presented in 1881, for one scene in which its title character blew up a fireworks factory by carelessly disposing of the butt of a stolen cigar, and for another scene in which a man was scalded to death by steam from a malfunctioning ship's engine. In 1885, about to revive the play and regarding it as inadequately lively, Harrigan gave it a new ending, adding a scene that took place at Coney Island. The last spoken words of the play were "Stop, thief!" addressed to the rascally major by a detective named Spotem who was chasing him across the stage. The remainder of the action was spelled out by Harrigan in terse stage directions: "Storm rises. *Omnes* chase after Major. Arabella goes in oyster boat. Monkey breaks loose from side show. General business. Cyclone. Arabella floats off to sea. Roofs blow off. General consternation."

Nineteenth-century audiences doted on consternation. Dion Boucicault had initiated the vogue for startling effects in 1857, when he contrived to simulate a fire on stage. Ten years later, in *Under the Gaslight,* Augustin Daly had unveiled the first of a multitude of actors tied to railroad tracks. "Sensation is what the public wants," Boucicault once said, "and you cannot give them too much of it." Until roughly the turn of the century, the theatre-

going public's appetite for spectacles that staggered both
eye and ear was so insatiable that some producers hardly
bothered to equip their actors with lines, instead simply
shunting them from one hair-raising predicament to another. While dialogue languished, buzzsaws and pyrotech-
nics ran amok. From one end of the country to another,
wheels screeched, and so did audiences, as touring companies equipped with treadmills and moving cycloramas
staged the chariot race from *Ben-Hur.* Dissatisfied with
the comparative austerity of conventional productions of
Uncle Tom's Cabin, grandiose producers concocted
"Double Tom Companies," featuring two Topsys, two
Evas, and an extra-long whip for Simon Legree. In a
single act of a single play put on in 1892 by Martin W.
Hanley, who for many years was a managerial associate
of Harrigan and Hart, audiences could gape at a prize
fight, a horse race, a duel, a murder, and, finally, at a giant
millstone that raced around the stage on a track and was
about to smash in the face of the leading man, lying fet-
tered in its path, when the leading lady burst out of a
house in which she had lain trussed—the house, it almost
goes without saying, was aflame—and rescued him.

Scenic designers and stage carpenters vied valiantly to
outdazzle one another. There were so many splendors on
view in *The Black Crook,* in 1866, including a breath-taking grotto full of stalactites—let alone the first public
revelation of coryphées' legs upholstered in clinging tights
—that the head carpenter, Benson J. Sherwood, won critical acclaim almost vying with that of the knees and calves.
(Sherwood was quite a spectacle himself, standing six
and a half feet tall, weighing 400 pounds, and possessing,
according to one of his notices, a voice like a thunderpeal

and an arm like a sledgehammer.) Some producers found
the stage itself inadequate as a showcase for the ingenuity
of man. In the basement of one theatre, audiences were
invited to marvel between the acts at a representation of
Mammoth Cave inside which was exhibited a large chunk
of the world's biggest painting, a portrait of the Mississippi River Valley executed by an artist named John Ban-
vard. His canvas, though not quite as massively propor-
tioned as the river valley itself, was a pretty fair stab at
duplicating the real thing; fully spread out, it was three
miles long.

Harrigan often scoffed at the public's addiction to
spectacles. In "The Old Bowery Pit," a song about the
Bowery Theatre, which resembled the Tombs and specialized, appropriately, in blood and thunder, Harrigan
wrote, "You talk about blood, it was thicker than mud,
oh, you could not see action for smoke." The Bowery
Theatre, built in 1826, had one of the most spacious stages
in New York, and on this were arrayed not only giant
spectacles but also such sensational individuals as Frank
Frayne, a skilled rifleman who used live ammunition in
his act. Frayne starred in one sketch during which—after
some preliminary scuffling with a savage dog—he saved
a man from being lynched by severing, with one timely
bullet, a rope from which the fellow was dangling. Another gripping specialty of Frayne's was, in modernized
emulation of William Tell, the shooting of an apple off his
leading lady's head while he had his back turned to her.
He aimed his rifle by means of a mirror. Frayne performed
this thriller successfully for years until, one bleak evening
in 1882, his weapon slipped and, missing the apple, he shot
the leading lady clean through the head and killed her.

Harrigan never went that far, but he was regarded as a master of scenic effects. The same year Frayne's bullet went astray, Harrigan produced *The Blackbird,* one scene of which unfailingly brought the audience to its feet, cheering deliriously and bombarding the stage with floral missiles. This scene was called "The Devil's Pool at Moonlight." Masses of rocks rose to the flies, and down them cascaded two waterfalls, terminating in a whirlpool that had a fallen tree across it. An innocent girl was lured to the summit of the cliff by a villain intent on robbing her, or worse. She resisted. He threw her into the whirlpool. For the most part, only her pale white arms were visible above its seething surface, although at intervals she would lift her head out of the water long enough to emit a blood-curdling shriek, and, presumably, to breathe. Harrigan, cast as the hero, would scramble onto the rocks, seize a vine, and lower himself to the fallen tree. Balanced precariously on it, he would lean over the pool, grab one limp white hand, and extricate the lady as The Curtain Fell.

Now and then, in a what-have-we-all-wrought? mood, Harrigan would interpolate a satirical allusion to this kind of frenzy into one of his own plays. A character in a Harrigan drama called *The Irish Cousin* was a playwright named Barney Brogan, who proudly related the details of some of the situations *he* had concocted. (Brogan declared that the only hump-backed actor of his acquaintance had got that way from holding the waves up during an interminable run of a billowy spectacle entitled *Lonely Man of the Ocean.*) At the climax of one Brogan drama, *The Blond and the Serpent,* the Serpent, a wicked character, was to tumble from a rope by which he was clinging to an airship and crash through the glass roof of a hot-house inside which the Blond was about to marry a decent farm boy. Brogan thought it would be a nice touch for this episode to conclude with the Serpent dying to the strains of the Wedding March from *Lohengrin*.

Another Brogan opus was *The Bride of the Minute*. Harrigan had a character named Sydney Dangles describe this one to a wide-eyed girl named Rose, who wanted to know if it was exciting.

"Exciting!" said Dangles. "There's six truck loads of scenery in it. A huge derrick with a large hammer to fall on the bride. A tank of real water to drown her. A red-hot furnace to roast her, and a tunnel under the East River to fall in on her."

"And she lives?" asked Rose, anxiously.

"Certainly," said Dangles. "Her lover saves her every time."

But even at the end of the very act in which Harrigan was thus moved to snipe at the inanities of his time, he himself fell back on a tried and tested formula: he had a good number of his characters toss one another into a handy river.

Playwrights frequently turned up in Harrigan and Hart shows. There was one in *Investigation,* first produced in 1884, which also included a sprightly burlesque of the balcony scene from *Romeo and Juliet*. Hart was the Nurse, as fussy and overprotective a chaperone as ever attended a junior miss; Annie Yeamans, an actress celebrated for her mugging, was a Juliet of cloying saccharinity; and Harrigan was Romeo—an exaggeratedly Irish Romeo who kept tripping over his sword, expressed misgivings about the ability of a rickety balcony to support his weight, and, at one point, delayed his pursuit of Juliet long enough to shadowbox with a spotlight that pursued him across the stage. According to the *Spirit of the Times,* the scene regularly evoked "agonies of laughter," especially when Mrs. Yeamans, a rather dumpy-looking woman, turned to her Romeo and asked archly, "Am I anything like Miss Ellen Terry?" (Harrigan's reply was typical of the quality of his jokes, a high proportion of which involved puns. "Ah, you terry-fy me," he said. "You are un-irving me.") Henry Irving and Ellen Terry, in addition to viewing this testimonial to their fame in its normal setting, encountered it during an Actors' Fund Benefit in 1884, when, after the gifted Britishers had done a strictly non-burlesque version of the trial scene from *The Merchant of Venice,* Harrigan and Hart and Mrs. Yeamans galloped onto the stage and began flailing away at their absurd balcony. (At a similar benefit, in 1888, a presentation by Edwin Booth and Lawrence Barrett of Act V of *Julius Caesar* followed immediately after a presentation by Harrigan's company of Act II of *Waddy Googan,* featuring the song "Where the Sparrows and Chippies Parade.") The chances are that Irving, at least, remembered this particular by-product of Shakespeare for quite a while; when he was departing from Harrigan and Hart's theatre after seeing it there, he was served with a summons lodged against him by an aspiring playwright who claimed he had left a couple of scripts for Irving at a stage door and that the Englishman had been remiss in not putting them into immediate production.

The playwright in *Investigation* was asked by a young girl how one should go about getting into his line of work. "You will have to do what I and Charles Dickens and all other great men of my ilk have done before you—witness

the misery of this Great Metropolis," was his advice.
Forthwith, he obligingly took her on a tour of the metropolis. They strolled along the Bowery, where, among other
colorful characters, they fell in with an Italian astrologer
—Harrigan—married to the proprietor of a Chinese
opium den—Mrs. Yeamans. (It was characteristic of Mrs.
Yeamans' versatility that in this play she also took the
part of a Chippewa Indian.) Then they met up with an
investigating committee of upstate legislators who had descended on New York from Albany to ascertain whether
the city's sooty atmosphere was caused by the emanations
from a candle factory or from a glue factory. Their escort in New York was a ward-heeler from the Fourth
Ward, played by Hart. Harrigan often satirized current
events, and his committee, as his audiences well knew and
appreciated, was inspired by a real one that early the same
year, under the chairmanship of Assemblyman Theodore
Roosevelt, had invaded New York. Its findings, issued six
months before *Investigation* was first presented, were as
hilarious as many stage comedies. Roosevelt reported,
among other revelations of municipal scalawaggery, that
the city's sheriff was paid fifty cents a head for every person convicted in the city's criminal courts—whether or not
he had had anything to do with the case—and from this
source alone had netted $26,000 in 1883; that the chief
assessor of New York real estate, on being asked to explain the criteria he applied to his task, had replied he was
guided merely by the intuitive consciousness bestowed on
him by God; and that the city's Park Commission had
been dormant for two years because it couldn't agree on a
president. The presidency was its only salaried position, it
seemed, and each of the four commissioners, whenever

they met to elect their head, had stubbornly persisted in voting for himself. This impasse was ultimately resolved when the commissioners were persuaded to rotate the presidency among themselves and split the take four ways.

Much of the subject matter in Harrigan's plays was gleaned in precisely the fashion that his playwright in *Investigation* urged the inquiring young lady to adopt. Harrigan would plant himself upon a park bench in some inelegant section of town and sit attentively there, notebook in hand, observing the peculiarities and eavesdropping on the conversation of people who strolled by or plopped down next to him. If some uncommonly appealing individual passed by—a tramp, say, or a minor politician—Harrigan would leap to his feet and take off after him, scribbling notes as he went. Every so often, a newspaperman out after a feature story would follow *him,* feverishly taking notes on Harrigan taking notes. A reporter who constituted the rear guard in one such factfinding procession observed afterward that the people Harrigan seemed especially attracted to were "types absolutely unknown to that portion of our community who live regularly."

It was understandable that Harrigan's plays should have abounded with tumult and consternation, for the irregular types upon whom his searching eye most greedily fastened were people notable for their disorderliness even in a wildly disorderly age. The post-Civil War years in New York were so conspicuous for ill-mannered behavior that one historian of that era, who survived its brawls to write of it, declared, "Had anyone said 'I'm sorry' in those days he would promptly have been locked up as irresponsible." Harrigan thought that some of the people he portrayed on stage—one critic asserted that they exhibited "every repulsive characteristic of scoundrelism and loafing"—were "painful types," but had no qualms about their dramatic usefulness for the simple reason that they existed. "I have sought above all to make my plays like pages from actual life," he once said.

Only rarely was this ambition thwarted. In 1878, there was a lawyer who hung around the Tombs, named Michael J. O'Brien, of whom it was disrespectfully said he would take a case for a pawn ticket. Not long after Harrigan himself had been observed hanging around the Tombs, pencil and paper in hand, a sketch entitled "O'Brien, Counsellor-at-Law" was advertised for the following week. Michael O'Brien waved this playbill under the nose of a judge and demanded that Harrigan be enjoined from putting on the piece. Harrigan was duly invited to clarify his intentions. "Are you really going to impersonate Counsellor O'Brien?" a reporter asked.

"No, I just thought up the name," said Harrigan uneasily. "I wanted an Irish name for a lawyer, so I called him 'Blackstone O'Brien.'"

"But, Mr. Harrigan," went on his inquisitor, "the real Mr. O'Brien says he saw you in court at the Tombs, taking in his every word and every action."

"Oh, he's terribly mistaken," said Harrigan. However, he prudently revised the sketch before he put it on.

Harrigan felt that the conventionally respectable citizens of his acquaintance were far from stimulating to an inquiring dramatist. "The average gentleman is so stereotyped," he once said, "that he has no value except in those plays where he is a pawn on the chessboard of melodramatic vice or tragic sin." A number of contemporary play-

wrights vehemently disputed this thesis, among them
Clyde Fitch, who largely confined his attentions to the
most refined percentage of society, which was often called
"The Upper Ten." Harrigan once thought that it might
be fun if he and Fitch collaborated on a play covering the
whole gamut of New York life, Fitch to write the high-
class scenes and he the rest, but nothing ever came of his
notion, possibly because Harrigan, striving to duplicate
actual life, would have had a ninety per cent stake in the
venture.

The New York *Herald,* itself enamored of rogues and
their roguery, once said admiringly of Harrigan, "He
finds his inspiration in the city-bred murderer, blackleg,
corner loafer, and in every conceivable and unnameable
product of the town." On practically every street corner,
inspiration stood, or lurked, awaiting. Criminals roamed
the streets with abandon, some of them carrying printed
cards enumerating the charges for their various services.
Murdering Mike McGloin, a versatile thug of the time,
had a price list that ranged from two dollars for a routine
beating to a hundred dollars for a murder. He demanded
nineteen dollars for breaking a leg, but only fifteen for
chewing an ear off, which he apparently judged a slightly
less arduous assignment. (With irony that any playwright would have acclaimed, McCloin was apprehended,
at the height of his career, for the relatively ignomin-
ious misdeed of trying to sell to a junk man a few
pounds of lead he had pried out of the rain gutters of a
new building.) Some straight-and-narrow citizens, de-
spairing of curbing their nefarious contemporaries, contented themselves with debating whether it was easier for
male or female pickpockets to ply their trade with im-

punity. The consensus was that female pickpockets had
the advantage, at least when it came to robbing women,
because, as one detective of the period explained in his
reminiscences, no man, however light-fingered, could ac-
cost a prospective victim with conversational gambits like
"I beg your pardon, will you have the goodness to fasten
my brooch?" or "Wait a moment, Madam, you have a
spider on your dress. I will take it off for you."

The police were not much help. Nearly every member
of the municipal force in 1872, when Harrigan and Hart
first created a stir on Broadway, was a political appointee
of the Tammany Hall aldermen who ran the city's wards.
Most policemen had had to pay to get their jobs, and to
hang onto them were expected to continue to contribute
to the Tammany exchequer. If they slipped up, they were
apt to find themselves on twenty-four-hour duty. They
were held in such low repute by many of their fellow-citi-
zens that they were obliged to equip their helmets with
solid-rubber bumpers as a defense against the flower pots,
bricks, and other missiles that disrespectful passers-by
were apt to fling at them when no more agreeable diver-
sion beckoned. It was their prominence as targets, in fact,
that had won them the nickname "cops." They had turned
up at the Bowery Theatre one day in 1845, wearing brand-
new uniforms, to try to maintain order during a fire there,
and upon the sight of their costumes a gang of hoodlums
had set upon them derisively and given them quite a pum-
meling. Their uniforms had at once been called in, and for
years thereafter the only insignia of their office that they
dared display was a modest, star-shaped shield made of
copper.

The harassment to which the police were subjected was

in large measure provoked by their own venality. An investigating committee from Albany that looked into their activities in 1894 reported that for the previous fifty years "The New York police force was, in point of legal fact, an association of criminals who each paid for their posts and received in return carte blanche to plunder the people in any fashion their ingenuity could devise." So successful were some of the police in shaking down their neighbors that half a block from 300 Mulberry Street, where Police Headquarters was located, flourished a gambling house that catered exclusively, if illegally, to well-heeled cops. Some of the police did display ingenuity in collecting fees from gamblers, thieves, houses of prostitution, and such likely sources of income. Other members of the force were not so subtle. One patrolman, who was somehow arrested and brought to trial in 1872, was convicted of having committed seventeen burglaries, within a mere six-month stretch, on his own beat.

A tender rapport prevailed, while Harrigan and Hart were in their heyday, between the police and the lawless gangs that were a feature of the city's untidy life. This was no ephemeral relationship. In 1857, for instance, when there had been two rival police forces in New York —one responsible to the mayor and the other to the governor of the State—and the two forces met in armed and bloody combat on the steps of City Hall, each faction had as its principal ally one of the two leading gangs of the day —the Bowery B'hoys and the Dead Rabbits. The Bowery B'hoys sided with the mayor's constabulary and the Dead Rabbits with the governor's. The gangs, which had a long history of bitter enmity, fought so skillfully that, of the twelve killed and 200 wounded in this particular fray, the vast majority were policemen. "Rabbit" was a nineteenth-century synonym for "rowdy," and the Dead Rabbits had got their organizational title when, as a gang from which they were spawned was in the process of dissolution, someone had thrown a dead rabbit into the council chamber. The Bowery B'hoys were a notable ornament of the then gaudy avenue to which they claimed allegiance. They were tough, swaggering young Irishmen, flashily dressed as a rule in black coats called Shanghais, low shoes, tight-fitting plaid trousers, flowery silk vests, tall bell-crowned hats, and red underwear. They wore their hair long in back and slicked it down with bear grease, which, at the end of a normal day's operations, was apt to be smeared liberally over the clothes of some unhappy citizen or other who had merited their displeasure. They were a cocky, self-assured lot; in 1852, when William Makepeace Thack-eray, aged forty-one, was visiting the United States and, standing in Union Square, expressed to an American companion a desire to visit the Bowery and inspect its cele-brated denizens, his friend pointed to a young man loung-ing against a lamppost nearby, identified him as a probable B'hoy, and suggested that the author confer with him.

Thackeray went up to him and said, pleasantly, "I want to go to the Bowery."

"Well, you can go, sonny," was the reply, "but don't stay long."

New York teemed with gangs, mainly recruited by wards, then the city's main political subdivisions. The Fourth Ward, which took in most of what is now the city's financial district, had fifty gangs in it. One of the most venerable of the groups was a West-Side outfit that called itself, with forthright explicitness, the Forty Thieves. (Its

leader's name was, disappointingly, Williams.) Not all
such organizations were devoted exclusively to crime.
Some of them were law-abiding social clubs whose members would meet after work, and perhaps climb aboard a
grocer's cart and spend an evening singing, accompanied
by harmonica and accordion. Or they might hold a dance
in a rented hall. When they did, the most rugged members of the group would customarily be assigned to the
hat committee, whose function it was to see that every
male present paid a twenty-five-cent hat-checking fee. If
a fellow tried to get in without a hat, or appeared in a cap
or soft-felt hat and tucked it in his pocket, the committee
would teach him better manners by flinging him into the
street.

The antisocial activities of some of the gangs consisted
of no more than letting off steam every now and then by
battling another gang, a contest of which the citizenry at
large took scarcely any notice. In routine scraps of this
nature, it was generally understood that fists, feet, teeth,
and paving bricks were the only accepted weapons.
Knives, clubs, brass knuckles and the like were expected
to be reserved for serious occasions. A few of the gangs
took pains to win recognition by affecting some peculiarity
of appearance or deportment. The trademark of the
Hartley Mob, a notorious band of robbers, was a hearse
in which they carted off their loot after a group outing.
The Shirt Tails dressed, as their name implied, with
studied casualness, and the Short Boys could not abide the
sight of a six-footer. The Cadets, whose title was supposed
to reflect their manliness, made a practice of courting
young girls, seducing them with promises of marriage,
and, after having shamed them, turning them over to

bawdy-house keepers—a highly lucrative sequence of events. (After a while, some of the younger girls of the city tired of seeing others reap all the profits from the abuse of virtue, and made a rather nice living themselves by becoming itinerant flower peddlers, shyly entering business offices behind an armful of blossoms, and, a few days later, blackmailing their customers by threatening to tell their wives they had been raped.)

One of the most suitably named gangs was the Plug Uglies, a tribe of gigantic young Irishmen who stomped around town brandishing a bludgeon in one hand and a brick in the other. (The conviction of one Plug Ugly arrested for assaulting an elderly man who accidentally bumped into him on the street was handily obtained when the authorities were able to submit in evidence some gray hairs from the victim's head that, several hours after the affair, had been found still attached to the young man's boots.) Among the best-known gangs around was the Whyos, whose name derived from a cry they liked to utter when they swung into action. In one Harrigan play, a character noticing the approach of another character, walking menacingly and waving a club over his head, was moved to remark, "It's one of the Whyos," and the audiences could well understand his reason for making this assumption. The Whyos hung out in the vicinity of Mulberry Bend, a few sordid blocks removed from City Hall, and none but the most foolhardy citizen would have ventured to trespass in this bailiwick without the sanction of the gang. Murdering Mike McGloin was a Whyo. His associates included some of the most eminent ruffians of the century—Hoggy Walsh, Googy Corcoran, Baboon Connolly, and Dandy Johnny Dolan, a fastidious dresser who was doubly famed as the Beau Brummell of gangdom and as the inventor of a handy, pocket-size eye-gouger.

Several of the city's gangs had such awesome reputations that, inevitably, children not eligible to gain admittance to them formed junior branches, much as the Cub Scouts today are the springboard for many an impatient lad not eligible to be a full-fledged Boy Scout. The Forty Little Thieves and the Little Dead Rabbits could hardly wait until they became old enough—or, since the gangs were not stuffy about formal regulations, tough enough— to graduate into an adult gang. One teen-age gang, the Baxter Street Dudes, occupied themselves while awaiting maturity by running a theatre of their own, which was distinctive for the professional quality of some of its props and portable scenic effects—as well it ought to have been, since the boys who ran the theatre obtained a good deal of their paraphernalia by stealing it from the stages of established houses.

The Dudes' theatre was called the Grand Duke Opera House, a name its proprietors bestowed upon it when Grand Duke Alexis of Russia happened to visit New York in 1872, the year they put on their first production. The Opera House, rather startlingly different from the imperial court of the Romanoffs, or, for that matter, from any other theatre, had a stage only nine feet across at the footlights (which were tallow candles), and an auditorium that measured twenty by thirty feet. It accommodated, with some crowding, 150 patrons. The boxes were washtubs. The entrance was a hole in a board fence on Baxter Street. The box-office prices were reasonable—ten cents for the better seats and a nickel for the remainder, with such special rates as two seats for nine cents and three for fourteen for theatre parties. These last sometimes consisted of folks from the Upper Ten who fancied an evening of slumming, and who would cautiously engage a bodyguard or two to accompany them on their excursions. There were generally policemen scattered about the audience, but they were usually too busy seeking out thieves they anticipated finding there to be able to keep a protective eye on innocent citizens.

The cast at the Grand Duke ranged in age from eight to eighteen, and the songs and sketches they enacted were cheerfully stolen, along with their scenery, from other theatres in town. "The Mulligan Guards" was one of their staple offerings. After the curtain went up one night, the manager apologetically explained the absence of his entire orchestra by advising the audience that the musicians had repaired in a body to Harrigan and Hart's, where some new songs were being unveiled that evening that the Grand Duke wanted to appropriate while they were still fresh. The audience clapped loudly in appreciation of this thoughtfulness. (In 1877, Harrigan and Hart cheerfully acknowledged this state of affairs in a sketch of their own entitled "The Grand Duke Opera House.") The opera house lasted only ten years. Some of its leading figures grew up and became preoccupied with gang warfare, and others moved along into the somewhat more legitimate theatre, among them the comedian Sam Bernard. The Grand Duke languished despite the efforts to help it of such unlikely ambassadors from the world of theatrical elegance as Lester Wallack and John Gilbert, who visited the place one night, at the management's request, and drew a large crowd of ne'er-do-wells who wanted to gape at them. (Later, the Baxter Street Dudes repaid the com-

pliment, while momentarily in the chips, by buying out
the entire gallery at Wallack's Theatre one evening, a
reciprocal gesture Wallack may or may not have relished.) One thing that contributed to the downfall of the
Grand Duke was the emergence of a neighborhood rival,
the Five-Cent Theatre, which was run by a son of Edwin
Booth's scene-painter, who served as its scene-painter,
too. Another handicap was the jealousy of youthful gangs
who had no theatre, and, by way of indicating their pique,
would throw stones at the Opera House patrons at nearly
every performance, thus discouraging attendance. But the
theatre might have endured anyway if it hadn't run afoul
of the municipal authorities, who, unwilling to excuse its
proprietors because of their adolescence, closed it down
for nonpayment of amusement taxes.

The Grand Duke Opera House was located within the
Sixth Ward, known informally as the Bloody Sixth, at a
spot called Five Points, where Baxter, Worth, and
Park Streets formed a turbulent junction. Five Points
was indisputably the most sanguinary quarter of the
Bloody Sixth, and the vilest place in town. In the fes-
tering tenements of Five Points, the heart of which
was known as Paradise Square (it had once been a park),
lived an assortment of cutthroats, prostitutes, ragpickers,
waifs, and other social outcasts, not a single one of whom
was reputed ever to have turned an honest dollar. Of 600
children in residence there in 1870, only nine attended any
kind of school. (The area, aside from a handful of lopsided shacks, is now occupied almost exclusively by court-
houses and other high-toned civic edifices.) Charles Dickens was drawn to Five Points as if by a magnet, and
said after touring it, "All that is loathsome, drooping, and

decayed is here." Harrigan described it as a place "where vice in rags held carnival all night long," and he put it on the stage. Respectable citizens who might have thought twice about walking through other parts of the city after dark thought three times about visiting Five Points at noon, and the police patrolled the area, when they bothered to at all, only in pairs.

An exception to this cautious mode of behavior was one of New York's most dashing law-enforcers, Alexander S. Williams, a policeman who did as much as any individual could to clean up Five Points, and who is best remembered as the man who gave the name "Tenderloin" to New York's recreational district. That occurred in 1876, when Williams was promoted to captain and assigned to the Twenty-ninth Precinct, which took in the area bounded by 14th and 42nd Streets, and by Fourth Avenue and the Hudson River. Williams was as concerned as any other policeman of his time with his personal financial security. On receiving news of his assignment, which placed him in gratifying proximity to most of the city's saloons, whorehouses, restaurants, theatres, dance halls, and other promising benefactors, he exclaimed, "No more chuck steak for me. Now I'll get a little of the tenderloin."

Williams, a friend of Harrigan's after they had both become prominent fixtures of the Tenderloin, was to get a lot of choice cuts before higher-minded citizens forced his resignation—including a yacht that he moored in Connecticut at a dock that itself cost $39,000. He was a familiar figure in the Broadway saloons, which he was in the habit of raiding every so often if they neglected to push a brand of whiskey in which he happened to have a financial interest. After he had been nudged off the police force, he denied having engaged in any such racketeering. He had got rich, he said blandly, from shrewd investments in building lots in Japan. He began life as a ship's carpenter and joined the police force shortly before the Civil War. He demonstrated his mettle right off by confronting two Houston Street toughs, banging their heads together, and throwing both of them through a saloon window. He averaged one fight a day for four straight years, and wielded his nightstick with such zest and effectiveness that he quickly acquired the nickname Clubber. His victims were usually booked for "resisting an officer in the discharge of his duty." According to Alfred E. Smith, who grew up in the Fourth Ward while the Clubber was cracking skulls there in the discharge of his duty, Williams was a much more highly venerated person among the Ward's residents than any United States Senator could hope to be. Williams never succeeded in converting Five Points into anything remotely resembling a paradise, but while stationed in another part of town, the East 30's, where the Gas House Gang held sway, he convincingly demonstrated to some skeptics how thoroughly he had domesticated that once unruly crew. He hung his watch on a lamp post one night and walked slowly around the block. On his return, to the whole town's amazement, the watch was still there.

A critic reviewing a Harrigan play once said that his characters had been "seized alive and spliced to the mundane drama." Considering the moral standards of many of the citizens Harrigan depicted, this would have been a foolhardy practice for him to have followed literally, but he did try it a few times, physically transplanting individuals from the streets to the stage. In the course of what the Louisville *Courier-Journal* described as "Harrigan's

plebescital researches," the playwright seated himself next
to a grimy old Irish bum on a park bench one day and, as
he inspected his companion's clothing from this vantage
point, became so enchanted with this bedraggled garb that
he asked the man to let him have it in exchange for a brand-
new outfit. The bum wanted to know why he wanted his
clothes. On Harrigan's explaining that they were to be
used by an actor, the bum became indignant. He and his
clothes, he informed his accoster, were—to use Harrigan's
customary variation of the word—*dacent,* and they wanted
no part of any disreputable acting folk. Harrigan thereupon offered the bum $25 a week, to play himself. The man
found this proposition so attractive that he suppressed his
distaste for actors and accepted it. Harrigan's only stipulation was that under no circumstances was he to invest any
of his earnings in a new suit.

Another time, Harrigan plucked a B'hoy fresh off the
Bowery and, after some perseverance, taught him to enun-
ciate a few lines with satisfactory exactness. The young
rowdy won high critical praise as an actor—though his
dialogue was so faithfully based on his own vernacular
that he actually had nothing to do beyond playing himself—but this experiment was not altogether successful.
In the theatre, Harrigan managed to control him fairly
well, much as a circus can control a gorilla behind bars.
Off-stage, the fellow kept reverting to type. After the
show one night, he went for a stroll with another member
of the company and suggested, in a disarming manner, that
they both pay a call on the Bowery B'hoy's dear old mother.
The other actor accepted the invitation, stepped inside a
dingy tenement, and presently found himself lying on the
street outside, with a throbbing head and empty pockets.

That was the last Harrigan ever saw of that particular
Bowery B'hoy, and from then on, he only used professional
actors as actors.

Discouraged though he may have been by this awkward
turn of events, Harrigan never relaxed in his hunt for
authentic costumes. If the people who wore the clothes he
and Hart hankered after couldn't always be counted on,
that made the clothes themselves none the less attractive.
Many of his plays had sixty or seventy roles, and more
than a hundred costumes. On the eve of a production, the
merry partners could be found prowling the back alleys
of New York, in search of suitable garments. They were
familiar figures on Baxter Street, lined with second-hand
clothing shops whose proprietors, Jews who had recently
arrived from Europe, were fiercely competitive. It was all
a passer-by could do to keep from being bodily dragged
inside a store. (One merchant, Harris Cohen, was so en-
vied for the firmness of his grip and the strength of his
pull that several of his rivals, hoping somehow to emulate
his magic touch thereby, changed their names to Cohen,
too.) The actors had to be careful not to canvass the same
area too often, for word would spread quickly of their odd
obsession with other people's wardrobes, and panhandlers
would come swarming around them, unbuttoning as they
approached. One resourceful bum, anticipating Harrigan's
visit to his neighborhood, sold him a disreputable pair of
trousers and then pulled them off to reveal another pair
beneath, which he offered to let go, considering the volume
of business he was proposing to transact, at half price.

"I have often followed a man or woman around the city
for hours until a favorable opportunity presented itself for
opening negotiations for the purchase of clothes," Harri-

gan once said. "No matter with whom I may be or what I
am doing, let me see a quaint costume and I will do my
utmost to secure it. My persistence in this respect often
gets me into very queer scrapes." Every now and then,
some citizen beseeched by Harrigan or Hart to part with
his hat or his vest would summon a policeman, but since
nearly every policeman in town knew the pair, these incidents were fairly easily straightened out.

Since Hart was often in need of ladies' apparel, he was
apt to have special difficulties. Once, after he had boldly
chased a frowzy woman into the heart of Five Points,
and, on catching up with her, had offered her $25 for her
raiment, he had a hard time convincing her it was only her
clothes he wanted; she had never before heard of a man
offering money just for *that*.

Some of the garments they brought back to the theatre
from their safaris were so verminous their actors wouldn't
touch them, and Harrigan and Hart were reluctantly
obliged to compromise with realism to the extent of having
them boiled and spread to dry on the roof, which after
an especially successful expedition resembled a ragpicker's
stockpile. In *Old Lavender,* Harrigan wore a coat he had
picked up in a Baxter Street pawnshop, some pants an
alert attaché of his had purchased from a beggar on Sixth
Avenue, and a pair of shoes he himself had noticed on a
Bleecker Street mason. The shoes appealed to him because
they were coated with lime. Harrigan got them after persuading their owner to accompany him to the nearest shoe
store and exchange them for a brand-new pair. Harrigan's
hat was a dented antique that one of his supporting actors
had seen in a back-street curiosity shop in Syracuse and had
bought him as a present. Harrigan was grateful not only

for the gift, but for this evidence that Hart and he had infected others in their company with their zest for the hunt. How else, Harrigan once asked, could one account for the fact that an actor, in Syracuse or any other out-of-town community, would visit a curiosity shop or, indeed, explore any axis beyond the shortest and straightest route between theatre and hotel? The *Old Lavender* role called for a wig, too. Harrigan had one made up for him in London by Clarkson, a master wigmaker, but was appalled, when it arrived, by its hygienic appearance; he rejected it and substituted for it a greasy old hairpiece that he extracted from an ash barrel on South Fifth Avenue.

For another of his starring roles, that of an elderly exslave in *Pete,* produced in 1887, Harrigan dispatched an emissary to the South, where he visited a few plantations, negotiated with some aged Negroes on them, and returned triumphantly with a trunkful of clothing that gave every evidence of having belonged to the sellers long before they had achieved freedom. Harrigan selected for himself from this beguiling wardrobe a pair of pants that was exactly what he had been looking for; it had been mended so often it was all patches.

3.

ALL

Jumbled Up

TOGAYTHER

New York in the mid-nineteenth century was so informal a community that the city authorities often didn't take the trouble to give names to all its streets, ceding this privilege to the people who dwelt or worked along them. It often happened, accordingly, that the various downtown alleys that wound in and out among the lopsided tenements and stores were christened by neighborhood gangs, whose wishes in the matter were not to be ignored. There were two dowdy thoroughfares in the Bloody Sixth Ward called, with some justification, Murderers' Alley. The habits of their human inhabitants and of the pigs that took care of

garbage disposal were not vastly dissimilar. On one Murderers' Alley, off Little Water Street, stood, until it was
demolished in 1852, a tenement house, the Old Brewery,
which enjoyed the reputation of being the scurviest hovel
in town. Behind its wooden walls huddled a seamy crew of
beggars and crooks. Miscegenation and incest flourished
to such an extent within that it was difficult to ascertain
just where any resident family, or race, began or ended. A
leading tenant, George Appo, a one-eyed pickpocket and
confidence man, was reliably thought, however, to be the offspring of a particular Irish woman and a particular Chinese
man—Quimbo Appo, who held the distinction of reputedly
being the first low-caste Chinese to settle in America. His
son George, ruggedly low-caste on his own merits, was to
earn the distinction of enriching the English language
when, testifying before a crime-investigating committee in
the nineties, he made the first recorded use of the phrase,
"He trun a scare into him."

The dubious fame belonging to the Old Brewery was
conferred, after its disappearance, upon an institution one
block away. This was Gotham Court, just off Cherry
Street, where a thousand people of assorted origins lived
in two rows of squalid tenements. Access to these was by
a pair of narrow lanes. One, six feet wide, was known as
Single Alley, and the other, because it measured a relatively spacious nine feet across, as Double Alley. (This
last was also sometimes sardonically called Paradise Alley,
and was the inspiration for "The Sunshine in Paradise
Alley," a song written in 1895.) Beneath Gotham Court
ran one of the city's principal sewer mains. There were
manholes in both alleys, and inside the tenements some of
the criminals who hung out there had cut additional open-

ings into the sewer, to obtain hiding places for their loot, or if need be, for themselves. These excavations worked two ways; while they afforded the gangsters easy entrance to the sewer, they also afforded an easy exit for its odors and for the numerous outsize rats that frequented it. Gotham Court was condemned in 1871, but another twenty years passed before it was evacuated.

Harrigan used to hang around Gotham Court as a boy, and his observations of its mixed-up population helped to inspire him when he created and named his own fictional alley, which he also located in the Sixth Ward. This was Mulligan Alley, and it, too, had a cosmopolitan flavor. The Wee Drop Saloon, run by an Irishman named Walsingham McSweeny, faced a two-story tenement, the upper floor of which was occupied by Ah Wung, a Chinese, who ran a combination laundry and ten-cents-a-night lodging house. (Harrigan meant this to be a relatively decent lodging house. There were some places in the lower wards where the overnight charge was five cents to lie down and three cents, if all the floor space was already reserved, to squat in a hallway.) Below Ah Wung's premises was an Italian junk shop. The tenement next door was given over to two Negro institutions. One was the headquarters of a social club called the Full Moon Union, which featured in its vigorous initiation ceremonies something called the Royal Burn-Alive Brotherly Grip, and the members of which, once they had mastered this violent handshake, were committed to the forthright end of throwing white folk—preferably Irishmen—off horse cars. The other was a policy shop run by Welcome Allup, whose wife, Rebecca, was one of Tony Hart's most popular roles. She was a smart, pretty, self-assured young colored woman who frequently got sent to Blackwell's Island for drunkenness. Harrigan created her and her married name in tribute to a Negro washwoman named Rebecca who hung around a saloon at the corner of Prince and Crosby Streets, and whose tin pail needed such uncommon replenishing that the other patrons referred to her as "Rebecca at the well." This real Rebecca was often arrested, too, while in her cups, and whenever the police threw her into the paddy wagon she would cry, "Well, it's all up."

There was nothing especially ludicrous about the groups Harrigan chose to assemble in close quarters. A census taken toward the end of the sixties at Five Points by an intrepid statistician had disclosed that the area then harbored only ten native-born white Americans, as opposed to 812 Irish, 218 Germans, 189 Poles, 186 Italians, thirty-nine Negroes, and a scattering of unclassifiable persons, a case in point being George Appo, the pickpocket who was half Chinese and half Irish. Reflecting on his boyhood, Harrigan once said, "Below Fourteenth Street, after eight o'clock at night, the U.S. language was a hard find." The city was flooded with immigrants. The potato famine of 1846-47 in Ireland and the 1848 revolution in Germany had caused hundreds of thousands of Europeans to embark on clipper ships for the new world, which for many of them meant simply New York. The Irish got a head start, two million of them migrating to America between 1840 and 1860; during the second half of the nineteenth century, nearly three million of them arrived. Around 1870, the Germans began to catch up; in 1882 alone, a quarter of a million of them crossed the ocean. These two groups, and, to a lesser extent, the Scandinavians, Italians, and other resettled Europeans, became,

with their descendants, a powerful influence in the economic and political life of New York.

Early November arrivals would scarcely lose their sea
legs before they found themselves full-fledged, if somewhat imperfectly informed, voters. Tammany Hall aldermen would corral them and send them to the nearest
Tammany Hall judge, carrying notes that said, "Please
naturalize the bearer." In *Cordelia's Aspirations,* a Harrigan play first presented in 1883, Dan Mulligan, a
staunch Tammany man, visited Castle Garden, where immigrants then first touched American soil—600,000 of
them that year and almost 800,000 the year before—and
he exclaimed to Cordelia, his wife, "My, my, this is the
place that swells the majority."

Until the end of the century, there were few Federal
laws governing immigration. Most of the measures that
had been enacted dealt with questions of health, and not
even these were strictly enforced. Up to 1855, it was possible for immigrants to step off a ship at the Battery and
at once become absorbed, without any fuss, except perhaps
a cursory examination at Quarantine, into the new world.
In that year, Castle Garden, where five years before one
exceptional alien, Jenny Lind, had scored a triumph, was
converted into a reception center for all aliens, and it functioned as such for the next three decades, following which
the Federal Government turned it over to the city and
eventual use as an aquarium. Incoming ships would anchor
off the Battery, and transfer their passengers to barges
for the last lap to Castle Garden. There they would be
met by a random variety of well- and ill-wishers—doctors to check them for the plague, interpreters to tell them
where they were, relatives (if they were lucky) to take

them by the hand, money changers to convert their funds (if they were lucky enough to have any) into American currency or, in not a few instances, counterfeit American currency; and the landlords of nearby boarding houses to thrust circulars upon them attesting to the splendor of their hospitality.

The Army was also represented at Castle Garden by large recruiting posters, in several languages, offering two-hundred-dollar bonuses to anyone who would sign up on the spot, and by sergeants ladling out lemonade as an added inducement. Ladies from uptown patrolled the area, on the prowl for low-wage servants. The housewives had to compete with agents from some of the disreputable dance houses, who tried to persuade attractive young girls to come right to work there and, if they got hold of any, kept them virtually imprisoned until they were too lame or too sodden to work, at which point the girls would be unceremoniously booted out into the street. *These* recruiters had to compete in turn, at least from 1880 on, with the Salvation Army, which began its American career at Castle Garden that year, when it was represented by a team consisting of one man, seven women, and a tambourine.

Harrigan and Hart, or some purchasing agent of theirs, were also to be found now and then, greeting a shipload of immigrants, hoping to buy costumes. One time, rehearsing a play in which an actress was supposed to be an Irish schoolteacher, Harrigan tried to coax pedagogical-looking cloaks off the backs of a few arrivals at Castle Garden. He was universally rebuffed; the ladies he approached had been warned about unscrupulous American schemers and were understandably suspicious of what they took to be an obvious attempt to fleece them. Harrigan ultimately got the cloak he wanted, but only by persuading a friend of his who was visiting Ireland to acquire one there. Harrigan re-created Castle Garden in several of his plays. The opening scene of *The Major* was laid there. A character in it, whose real-life prototype the dramatist had seen on one of his visits to the place, was an Irishman whose luggage consisted mainly of a heavy sack containing eighteen shovelfuls of County Connaught dirt, which he proposed to walk on when he first arose every morning in the new country, to bring him good fortune.

Occasionally, the immigrants were cruelly mulcted, even before they had set foot on American soil, by swindlers organized into smooth-functioning gangs. One such crew would row out to an incoming ship, just after it had cleared Quarantine, and, dressed in immigrant clothes, swing aboard and mingle with the passengers, ascertaining which ones had money. At Castle Garden, these confidence men would swiftly change to other clothing handed them by confederates, and then, in the guise of solicitous strangers, approach the individuals they had already found to be worth robbing. Some of these sea-going crooks were reputed to be so quick, glib, and chameleon-like that they could seduce a girl between Quarantine and the Battery and then, disguised as a guardian of public morals, blackmail her at Castle Garden a couple of hours later by threatening to proclaim her fall from grace throughout the United States.

The more prosperous of the proprietors of many of the boarding houses near Castle Garden, to which immigrants gravitated for want of any better destination, would send runners all the way to Europe, with instructions to return on the next boat and spend the entire journey—by clipper

ship, a two- or three-week one—singing the praises of this
or that New York address. Any immigrant who fell into
such a trap was not likely to escape from it with a full
purse. Every so often, a boarding-house keeper whose establishment had been proven flagrantly antisocial would
be barred by the immigration authorities from drumming
up business within Castle Garden itself, but it was usually
possible for a landlord thus enjoined to bribe a policeman
or customs official to distribute his circulars for him.

The Italian immigrants suffered worst. A pair of pious-
looking swindlers milked them for years by the simple
expedient of putting on priests' clothing and walking solemnly around Castle Garden, murmuring Latin benedic-
tions and graciously taking a collection. Further ashore,
many Italians fell into the clutching custody of some
padrone or other. The *padrones* were middlemen of Italian
origin who offered to save New York employers of ditch-
diggers, rubbish-collectors, and other unskilled workers a
lot of trouble by hiring labor forces for them on a whole-
sale basis, and who offered to save Italian immigrants a lot
of trouble by getting them jobs. It was often a simple
matter to persuade these immigrants, who were totally
unacquainted with English and illiterate as far as Italian
went, too, that there was no way they could get a job in
America *except* through a *padrone*. The *padrones* exacted
a staggeringly high commission for their philanthropic services. Some of the more affluent among them were little
better than slave traders. They would let it be known in
Italy that they stood ready to provide a proper education
for musically gifted children, and, when the parents of
promising bassos or violinists shipped them happily across
the Atlantic, they would pocket the kids' scholarship

money and farm them out to organ-grinders. Or the *pa-drones* would have signs posted in Italy, describing the United States as a land flowing with milk, honey, gold, ravioli, and other lures. When an immigrant deluded by these enticements arrived and professed bewilderment on not finding them, a *padrone* would approach him, sympathize with his disappointment, and offer him a job to tide him over until the promises of the promised land were fulfilled. The *padrone* would then sell him a set of work tools at a fantastic price, rent him a room to sleep in at an outrageous rate, and, should the poor fellow manage to save a few dollars despite these obstacles, offer to bank his money for him and then abscond with it. Considering the introduction many Italian immigrants had to America, it was no wonder that quite a number of them, not long after landing on its disillusioning soil, took to carrying around stilettos.

Once past Castle Garden, most immigrants headed straight for the lower East Side and squeezed into its tenement houses—a type of accommodation that had been designed primarily to cram the largest number of aliens into the least amount of space. There, they found themselves in an environment neither much more comfortable nor much more American than that which they had gone to considerable pains to get away from. Some of the newcomers tried resolutely to be assimilated into American life. In *Squatter Sovereignty*, Harrigan had an Irish immigrant girl reject a wooing compatriot because, after having been in the United States for all of four months, he had shown himself lamentably disinclined to become acclimated. "He doesn't even know what ice cream is yet," she said scornfully. "I'd sooner marry a Turk." But most of the immigrants clung to their familiar ways and clung together—either with people of similar origins or with others who shared with them the common bond of poverty. (When an Irish girl was arrested in 1871 on the charge of having committed adultery with her sister's husband, a Negro, the incident was considered newsworthy not so much for its interracial as its sororal aspect.) In *McSorley's Inflation,* produced in 1882, a Harrigan-Braham song about tenement-house life, entitled "McNally's Row of Flats," contained the chorus:

> It's Ireland and Italy, Jerusalem and Germany,
> Oh, Chinamen and nagers, and a paradise for rats,
> All jumbled up togayther in the snow or rainy weather,
> They represent the tenants in McNally's row of flats.

Among the immigrant groups, the Irish—or, as they were widely called, the Celts, or Hibernians—had a slight advantage. Despite the "nagers," "togaythers," and other touches of brogue that peppered their dialect, they could make themselves fairly well understood in English-speaking circles. "My district is the town of Babel," an alderman declared in one Harrigan play, "and the Irish flag floats from the top." There were a lot of Irish in New York, and they were industrious, ambitious, and aggressive. These qualities did not altogether endear them, in the post-Civil War years, to the older settlers of the town. A great deal of bitterness between the Irish and the rest of the community had been stirred up during the city's draft riot of 1863, when the lower classes, with the Irish predominating, had rebelled so vigorously against what they regarded as a discriminatory conscription law that before civic tranquillity could be restored 1200 New Yorkers had been killed in street fighting—a casualty list that was higher than that of many a Civil War battlefield skirmish. It did not make the Irish feel any friendlier toward their fellow New Yorkers when, after the termination of these municipal hostilities, one city official declared publicly, "The Irish cattle have had impressed on them a respect for order." Actually, the Irish of New York had participated as enthusiastically as most other groups in the war, and perhaps more than some, inasmuch as they were on the whole improvident and could not afford, like some of their better-off contemporaries, to buy their way out of military service. From among the ranks of the Irish immigrants in New York, a whole brigade of Yankee troops was mustered. It could be, and was, pointed out by partisans of the Irish cause that during the Civil War a number of liquor stores in New York neighborhoods populated almost exclusively by Celts had had to close down because most of their male patrons were out of town.

The antipathy of the Irish in New York to England was a determining factor in their unpopularity, too. In 1860, the Sixty-ninth Regiment, then and in later years an overwhelmingly Hibernian outfit, had refused to march in a parade honoring the Prince of Wales. This Anglophobia was intense and persistent. It reached its height at the end of 1865, when Irish-American advocates of revolution in their homeland held a Fenian convention in Philadelphia, set up a republic of their own within the borders of the United States, and resolved to embarrass, if not destroy, the British Empire by capturing Canada. Financed by the contributions of hod carriers and servant girls, an expedition actually reached the Canadian border and engaged in brief combat there, but the net effect of the movement was to provide little more than laughs—like the ones Harrigan got in *The Mulligan Guards' Nominee* when he introduced the Nightingales, a women's auxiliary of the Fenian Army which had as its goal the shipment of 10,000 flannel shirts to Canada, and which, to accelerate its work, had instructed its members to snip all the buttons off their husbands' pants. The Celts in New York calmed down a bit after their annexation of Canada proved abortive, but they continued to manifest their chauvinism whenever an opportunity arose. For some time after the Brooklyn Bridge was opened, in 1883, the Irish crossed it with distaste, simply because May 24th, the date of its formal unveiling, was Queen Victoria's birthday. And when Abram S. Hewitt, a reform mayor elected in 1886, declined to follow the practice of many of his predecessors in that office and fly the Irish flag from City Hall on St. Patrick's Day, his political goose was cooked. His successor circumspectly reinstituted the old custom.

The Irish were prominently displayed on the mid-nineteenth century stage. In the imported works of English dramatists that were put on in New York, practically all the Irish characters were blackguards or idiots, but this appraisal was balanced somewhat by the fact that the two principal American dramatists of mid-century, John Brougham and Dion Boucicault, were both emigrants from Dublin who portrayed their fellow Celts more sympathetically. Brougham, like Boucicault and Harrigan an actor and manager as well as a playwright, came to the United States in 1842, when he was thirty-two, and before he died in 1880 had written seventy-five plays, a good many of them laid in his native land. Boucicault arrived in 1853, and soon became the most celebrated local dramatist of his

time, turning out more than 100 original plays or adapta-
tions. He loved to sing the praises of the Irish. In 1875,
in an impromptu speech between the acts of his play *The
Shaughraun,* he said, "Among the various European
nations that so largely contribute to form the American
family, there are Swedes, Germans, French, Spaniards,
Scotch, Italians—all are represented. But there is one more
favored here than all the rest—one endeared to you by a
hundred ingratiating faults, a thousand redeeming weak-
nesses; one who, lying on the breast of this land, looks back
fondly to the old country. And her adopted mother is not
jealous of that love. On the contrary, her great sympathiz-
ing heart beats in unison with the same emotions, for the
American heart is strung with cords torn from the Irish
harp."

Boucicault's plays dealt for the most part with native
Irish, Harrigan's with transplanted ones. "You have done
for the Irish in New York what I have done for the Irish
in Ireland," Boucicault once told Harrigan. Joseph
Howard, Jr., a theatrical writer on the *World,* characterized Harrigan as a man waving two patriotically inscribed
banners—"Erin Go Bragh" in one hand and "E Pluribus
Unum" in the other; and to Amy Leslie, who wrote
stage chit-chat for the Chicago *News,* he was "Irish embalmed in the spices of American independence." The
character of Dan Mulligan reflected this dual allegiance.
Mulligan was so Irish that he thought Lafayette was a
Celt whose real name, until the French changed it for
self-glorification, was Lafferty; he was so American that
he razed a Sixth-Ward barber pole because it was painted
with the colors of the German flag rather than of the
Stars and Stripes.

Tony Hart was a Roman Catholic of pure Irish descent. Harrigan, though regarded by the public as a man no less Celtic than his partner or than Brougham and Boucicault, was not. There was English as well as Irish blood in his veins. He was not even a Catholic. His father was active in Masonic affairs, and the playwright himself tended to share the agnostic views of his friend Robert Ingersoll. But he played so many Irishmen on stage that he sometimes absentmindedly talked with a brogue off-stage; in the eyes of his fans he was as Irish as Dan Mulligan himself. When Harrigan died, his family was nonplussed by a couple of unknown mourners who trudged into his home and settled themselves down for a night-long, old-country-style wake; it had not occurred to them that any other denouement could have been conceived of for the career of a man who to them had long been the very image of an orthodox Hibernian.

The Irish and the Germans—or, as this group was widely called, the Dutch—were the élite among the immigrants of New York. Themselves disdained by the upper-crust Anglo-Saxons, they in turn had little use for the Italians or the Chinese. In the eighties, a joke that was considered hilarious in lower-class circles had to do with the escape from jail of a man under sentence to be hanged; his disappearance didn't matter much, the story went, because there were two Chinamen in town and either one of them would make an acceptable substitute. *The Last of the Hogans* contained a scene in which an Italian night watchman on a wharf stated his views on rats. He didn't really care for any of them, he said, but while he was on the subject he did have to confess a partiality for Norway rats, because they ate Chinese rats. "The Chinee must go!"

he exclaimed, while the audience guffawed at this refer-
ence to the relative status of the city's ethnic groups.

According to the Boston *Herald,* Harrigan's stage was
the scene of the "war of the races in cosmopolitan New
York." The co-existence of the various groups in the city
was, indeed, far from peaceful. The Irish had more respect
for the Germans than any other group, but Harrigan was
not exaggerating much when, in *The Major,* he introduced
an immigrant couple from Ireland who had felt impelled
to make the long trip across the Atlantic simply because
their son, who had previously come to America, was on
the verge of marrying a Dutch sausage-maker. One situation treated fictionally by Harrigan, but based on fact,
had to do with August Bimble, a German bandleader,
who had taken an Irish picnic job away from an Irish
bandleader named Paddy Brannigan. Brannigan got his
revenge by urging the unsuspecting Bimble to play the
Northern Irish tune "Boyne Water," which Brannigan
assured him was so beloved by all true Irishmen that the
British considered it treasonable. Actually, it was detested
by all Irish except Orangemen, and when the unwitting
Bimble ordered it struck up, the picnickers rioted and
attacked his musicians, who had to flee for their lives. Most
of the butcher shops in New York were run by Germans;
they sold their second-hand bologna to Italians and their
third-hand bologna to Chinese. The esteem in which the
various races held one another was satirically summarized
by Dan Mulligan in *The Mulligan Guards' Nominee,*
when, campaigning for alderman, he revealed that he had
been in consultation with a visiting king of the Sandwich
Islands, who had informed him that his cannibalistic subjects thought that Frenchmen were fit only for lunch, that

Italians were gristly, and that Dutchmen were the cause
of dyspepsia, but that Irishmen were universally regarded
as a dainty morsel.

One of the earliest Harrigan and Hart plays, *The Doyle
Brothers,* had a scene in which an Irish appleseller provoked a fight with an Italian appleseller. An Irish policeman pulled them apart, and then promptly arrested the
innocent Italian. The Negroes of New York—who were
of course neither immigrants nor aliens, but for all the
native-born white citizens of the city cared might as well
have been—picked on the Italians, too. South Fifth
Avenue, just below Washington Square, was the center
of Negro life in the post-Civil War years (Harlem was
then pretty much of a wilderness), and in a song called
"South Fifth Avenue" Harrigan referred to the habit
of some Negroes of ostentatiously holding scented handkerchiefs to their noses whenever they were obliged to
walk past a saloon catering to the Italian trade. Street
fights between Negroes and Italians—the former armed
with razors and the latter with stilettos—were a common
occurrence in downtown New York, and, inevitably, on
Harrigan's stage as well. There was nothing a Harrigan
audience enjoyed more than to witness a band of blackface actors, razors at the ready, advance across the stage
toward a band of Italians, chanting, in terms their op-
ponents could presumably understand, "Cutta! Soona!
Quicka!"

Harrigan's plays poked fun at all the racial groups—
he was kindest to the Irish, but was not above having his
sharp-tongued colored woman, Rebecca Allup, suggest
that if the Irish in New York thought home rule was such
a great thing, why didn't they all go back to Ireland and

rule there?—and the butts of his jokes relished it. The
Dramatic News, a weekly of the seventies, ran a piece
once purporting to be a visiting European's impressions
of New York and its heterogeneous population. He
passed quickly over the native-born Americans as un-
worthy of sustained comment. "The next two largest ele-
ments in respect to nationalities are the Irish and
Senegambian contingents," he observed. "For these, there
has been erected a theatre by Monsieur Harrigan, an
Irishman, and a bull-voiced Senegambian lady, Miss
Antoinette Hart; and here are presented only plays which
appeal directly to the races in question." At the opening
of *The Muddy Day* in 1883—this was a play recounting
the rivalry of two garbage-scow captains, one of them a
German who wouldn't dream of hiring a Celt for his crew,
and the other an Irishman whose ambition was to fill up the
harbor of New York with silt, so British ships would be
unable to enter it—the *Spirit of the Times* noted that
"Irish aldermen tried to applaud more loudly than a party
of Italian gentlemen in one of the private boxes, and exchanged glances of fun and defiance with the German
grocers and bakers in the opposite stalls."

A characteristically popular Harrigan scene was one in
The Mulligan Guards' Ball. This took place in a faithful
replica of one of the lower-ward barber shops, where, on
Sunday morning, workmen of all nationalities habitually
repaired to sit around and discuss the week's sporting
events and other important news. Dan Mulligan was there,
and he got to talking with Simpson Primrose, the colored
barber, about a story in the *Clipper*—the city's most popular weekly among the sporting and theatrical set—about
a prizefight in which an Irishman had beaten a German.

Primrose allowed as how a Negro could probably have licked either of them. At that, Gustave Lochmuller, a butcher who figured in all the Mulligan plays and whose daughter married Dan Mulligan's son, spoke up to say no German would be caught dead fighting a Negro. Primrose, resentful of the slur, lunged at Lochmuller with his razor. Mulligan interceded. "A man has no right to insult a colored man to his face," he said. It was one of the rare instances in which Harrigan refrained from having his characters come to blows.

Richard Harding Davis once wrote, in an analysis of Harrigan's work, that anybody who doubted the plausibility of some of the tumultuous scenes the playwright staged—such as one in which an incensed Irish laborer tried to kill the foreman of his work gang simply because the foreman had mistakenly listed him on a payroll as an Italian—was unacquainted with the facts of New York life. There were plenty of outlandish incidents taking place all the time, Davis said, that more than justified Harrigan's inventions, and Davis cited as one example the case of two Irish boys who had tried to blow up the statue of Garibaldi in Washington Square, merely because a passer-by had identified the sculpture to them as a portrait of a Dago. The boys had reasoned that no Dago on earth deserved so substantial a memorial. "As a historian of the war of races," Davis concluded, "Mr. Harrigan makes no mistakes."

4.
SING,
Ye
Terriers,
SING!

At the Democratic National Convention of 1920, held in San Francisco, Alfred E. Smith first became linked with the song, "The Sidewalks of New York." This association was the result of a bandleader's mistake. The Eighteenth Amendment to the Constitution had gone into effect a few months earlier, and the convention, which ultimately selected James M. Cox as its candidate for the Presidency, was the scene of some sharp infighting between wet and dry forces. William Jennings Bryan, with all the silvery eloquence his gifted tongue could muster, upheld Prohibition. Against him stood Representative W. Bourke Cockran of New York, a spellbinder of no mean stature himself. Cockran, with a great flourish of oratory, put into nomination the name of a resolute wet, Al Smith. The usual ovation followed, and the band prepared to strike

73

up a tune appropriate to the Smith cause. The bandleader
knew two things about Smith: he was governor of New
York, and he was a notorious devotee of the songs that
had been sung by Harrigan and Hart and written by
Harrigan and Braham. Forthwith, the bandleader instructed his men to play what he thought was an eminently
fitting Harrigan-Braham song, "The Sidewalks of New
York." Smith was stuck with it for the rest of his life.

In the bandleader's defense it could be argued that at
least "The Sidewalks of New York," written in 1894 by
Charles B. Lawlor, a vaudevillian, and James W. Blake,
a hat salesman, contained echoes of Harrigan and Hart.
Lawlor and Blake are thought to have been inspired,
consciously or subconsciously, by an 1879 tune from *The
Mulligan Guards' Ball,* entitled "The Babies on Our
Block:"

> If you want for information, or in need of merriment,
> Come over with me socially to Murphy's tenement;
> He owns a row of houses in the First Ward, near the dock,
> Where Ireland's represented by the babies on our block.
> There's the Phalens and the Whalens from the sweet
>   Dunochadee,
> They are sitting on the railings with their children on
>   their knee;
> All gossiping and talking with their neighbors in a flock,
> Singing "Little Sally Waters," with the babies on our
>   block.*

---

* In 1896, as a promotional stunt, the New York *Sunday Journal* commissioned thirteen leading composers, among them George M. Cohan and Paul
Dresser, to collaborate on a single song, and the best broth this bevy of cooks
could stir up was still another echo of Harrigan and Braham called "The
Babies in the Park."

Had Governor Smith been within earshot of the addled bandmaster, he could have straightened him out easily. No latter-day crooner ever had a fan more faithful than Smith was to Harrigan and Hart. Once, when Smith, then a state assemblyman, was traveling by train from New York to Albany, a three-hour ride, he ran into a friend as they were pulling out of Grand Central Terminal and invited him to share his compartment. They swiftly got into a discussion of old songs, and Smith bet his companion that he could sing from memory—or in his case, croak— the chorus and at least one verse of any Harrigan-Braham number the man could name. It was a bold pledge, because, although the total output of Harrigan and his father-in-law has never been precisely computed, they composed well over 200 songs. Taken up on his bet, Smith demonstrated that he had not been idly boasting; from New York to Albany, without faltering, he gave a Harrigan and Hart recital.

It was natural enough that Smith should have been attracted to Harrigan and Hart. His maternal grandparents could have been characters in one of their plays. They had emigrated from Ireland in 1841 on a clipper ship of the Black Ball Line, and had at first taken a room on the second floor of a dingy lodging house at Dover and Water Streets, in the Fourth Ward, directly above a German butcher shop. Their children and grandchildren grew up in the lower wards that Harrigan wrote about. Smith was born in a South Street tenement in 1873, and as a boy spent many happy hours high in the gallery looking down on Harrigan and Hart's stage. (The governor-to-be, moreover, was a promising actor himself as a young man. In the late nineties, he had a leading role in a parish-church

production of Boucicault's *The Shaughraun;* in 1915, after
his political career was well under way, he co-starred with
Jimmy Walker in a revival of the same play put on for
the benefit of the church.) In later years, Smith used to
say that his political philosophy had been shaped in part
by a colloquy he was fond of quoting from *Old Lavender*
—a scene between Harrigan, in the title role, and Hart,
as Dick, the wharf rat. The dialogue took place alongside
the clipper *Winged Eagle,* bound for Liverpool with a
cargo of flour.

> DICK: Say, Lavender, what do dey send all dat flour
> away for? Dere's an awful lot of starving people here.
> OLD LAVENDER: The millions of souls battling for su-
> premacy in the old world and neglecting their agricultural
> pursuits turn with a longing eye to this nation and cry for
> bread. The West with its prolific acres answers their calls.
> The Republic may stagger financially, civilly, or morally,
> but the Herculean energy of the American people will prop
> her up, and there she'll stand as firm as the Rock of Ages.
> DICK: Say, Lavender, dat's de way dem actors talk. I
> hear 'em when I go to de theatre and sit in de gallery.

On May 24, 1933, Smith was invited to take part in a
celebration marking the fiftieth anniversary of the opening of the Brooklyn Bridge. The occasion was an especially nostalgic one for him. On Decoration Day in 1883,
less than a week after the bridge's much-heralded unveiling, he had been standing on South Street, beneath the
Manhattan approach, when the cadenced march of a
body of troops on the structure above had given rise to a
rumor that the whole bridge was about to collapse. There
was a riot, and in the general haste to get off the sup-
posedly doomed span, ten people were killed, thirty-five
were injured, and the ten-year-old Smith, down below,

was showered with coats, purses, hats, and parasols abandoned in their flight by panicky promenaders. At the golden anniversary of the bridge, Smith elected to sing a song—one that, he lamented, had by then been forgotten by nearly everyone except himself. Since he picked it, there was no question of its being a genuine Harrigan-Hart-and-Braham creation. The number was "Danny by My Side," which had been written in 1891, long after fears for the bridge's safety (not to mention reservations on the part of Irishmen about its Anglophilic associations) had been conquered:

The Brooklyn Bridge on Sunday is known as lovers' lane,
I stroll there with my sweetheart, oh, time and time again;
Oh, how I love to ramble, oh, yes, it is my pride,
Dressed in my best, each day of rest, with Danny by my side.

Oh my, do try, to take in the Bridge on a Sunday,
Laughing and chaffing and watching the hours go by.
Moonlight and starlight, watching the silvery tide,
Dressed in my best, each day of rest, with Danny by my side.

When, in 1910, a year before Harrigan died, his admirers got together and formed a Ned Harrigan Club, Al Smith was the unanimous choice for the office of commodore in it. The avowed purpose of this group was to get Harrigan in the Hall of Fame, a goal that was never realized and never seriously contemplated. The actual purpose was to have an excuse for a series of social gatherings. Up to the entrance of the United States in the First World War, quite a few such meetings of the club were held. Joe Humphreys, the prizefight announcer, was its president and chief organizer of its festivities. Like Smith, he had been a lower-ward newsboy and a veteran of the Harrigan and Hart gallery. Humphreys disdained microphones and had so resonant a voice that he found them quite superfluous both in his professional work and at the smokers, beefsteaks, chowders, and other hearty fraternal conclaves that studded his social schedule and that were likely to be enlivened by loud group singing. Harrigan's own voice, a kind of mongrel tenor, was not exemplary either in tone or volume, but the musical interludes in his shows were so popular that a lot of people thought of him primarily as a song-and-dance man. At oyster stalls, in saloons, and on the street, complete strangers would recognize him and cry, "Sing us a song, Ned!" One time he took a few of his children to Maillard's for hot chocolate and was there set upon by an idolatrous Supreme Court justice.

"Sing us a song, Ned," asked the judge.

Harrigan declined, politely.

The judge was determined to have his song, and, Harrigan failing him, he did what must have struck him as the next best thing: the judge himself sang the whole of "Paddy Duffy's Cart."

The Ned Harrigan Club, at the time it was founded, planned to have two formal meetings a year—one on October 26th, because that was Harrigan's birthday, and the other on March 26th, because that was exactly six months away and the members could thus enjoy the maximum period of recuperation between sessions. Occasionally the Harriganites, as they sometimes called themselves, would also go for a steamboat outing in the summertime, with Commodore Smith in command, but mostly they met semiannually for dinner, five or six hundred strong, in some such roomy setting as Webster Hall or the Teutonia

Assembly Rooms. (The Teutonia had German waiters, and after they had finished serving, before the music began, Humphreys would order them out of the room, lest their lives be imperilled when Irish sentimentality got thoroughly uncorked.) Wearing paper aprons with the lyrics of some Harrigan and Braham song inscribed on them, and tall green paper hats—one observer declared effusively that when the celebrants got wound up they resembled a sea of shamrocks—they would prime themselves with beefsteak and beer and then settle back for some singing. First there would be solos, by veteran actors from the Harrigan and Hart company, if any were around, or perhaps a rendition by Commodore Smith of "The Market on Saturday Night" or "Downtown in the Old Neighborhood," or a rendition by Jimmy Walker of "The Pitcher of Beer" or "My Dad's Dinner Pail." Then the whole assemblage would raise its voices in testimonial chorus. "Sing, ye terriers, sing!" Humphreys would roar, frightening waiters two blocks off.

Irish workingmen were often called "terriers" in the late nineteenth century, as the old-timers in the Ned Harrigan Club well remembered. In *A Brass Monkey,* a play written in 1888 by Charles Hoyt, who was a contemporary and rival of Harrigan's, there had been a popular song entitled "Drill, Ye Terriers, Drill," which related the sad experience of one maltreated Celt who had been blown high in the air by dynamite while on a construction job, and who, on falling back to earth, found himself fined one dollar for his absence. "You were docked for the time you were up in the sky," the song went. The terriers who barked most vigorously at the Ned Harrigan Club dinners were in many cases one-time Irish workingmen who

had risen to higher estate and had become police officials
or sheriffs or judges or district attorneys. The warden of
the Tombs was a Harriganite, as was the sergeant-at-arms
of the United States Senate. William J. Fallon, the criminal lawyer, and Richard E. Enright, at one time the
Commissioner of Police, were members. So were such orna-
ments of Tammany Hall as Thomas Brophy, Thomas F.
Foley, Charles F. Murphy, and Jimmy Hines. So was
George M. Cohan. No meeting of the Ned Harrigan Club
was considered complete without the affectionate bellowing
of a song Cohan had written in 1907 for his *Fifty Miles
from Boston:*

> H-A-double R-I-G-A-N spells Harrigan,
> Proud of all the Irish blood that's in me,
> Divil a man can say a word agin me . . .

Cohan was born in 1878, when Harrigan and Hart were
the idols of lower Broadway, and as a young man aspiring
to emulate their success—his first play was produced in
1901, when Hart had been dead for ten years and Harrigan was in semi-retirement—was much influenced by his
knowledge of the plays-with-music they had put on a
generation before him. For the program of a Ned Harrigan Club beefsteak held in 1914, Cohan wrote: "Edward
Harrigan was a fine artist, a great writer of human
comedies, and one of the grandest men it has ever been
my pleasure to meet. Hoyt could always tickle the funny-
bone of the American theatregoer, but Harrigan turned
the same trick and got to the old heartstrings at the same
time. Harrigan inspired me when I applauded him from
a gallery seat. Harrigan encouraged me when I met him in
after years and told him of my ambitions. I live in hopes

The Mulligan Guards

THEATRE COMIQUE!
514 BROADWAY 514.

MR. JOSH HART...SOLE PROPRIETO r
John R. Topham..............Treasurer | Richard Doyle....Engineer and Gas Man
G. L. Stout....................Stage Manager | R. L. Weed.....................Scenic Artist
David Braham..........Orchestral Director | Miss Margaret Devoy.............Costumer
Nelse Waldren..Machinist and Properties

SPECIAL NOTICE.—In consequence of the very long Programme given nightly by this Company, we are compelled to say that but TWO encores will be allowed. The great number of Acts and the fatigue to the performer compel the management to enforce this notice. The good sense of our patrons will at once see the necessity of this and will please comply with it. ☞OUR PATRONS WILL OBLIGE US BY REPORTING AT THE BOX OFFICE ANY INATTENTION ON THE PART OF DOORKEEPERS AND USHERS OF THIS THEATRE.

DOORS OPEN AT 7,   TO COMMENCE AT 8 O'CLOCK.

PROGRAMME FOR THE WEEK,
Commencing March 15th, and Wednesday and Saturday Matinees

OVERTURE.......................(new).........MR. DAVE BRAHAM AND ORCHESTRA

The Evening's Entertainment will commence with the Laughable Farce, entitled the

☞ Sleep Walker ☜

Joe Parsnip..Mr. Charles White
Alf Jingle..Mr. J. F. Crossin
Doctor Bogey...Mr. J. A. Graver
FAVORITE SONGS...MISS ALICE BENNETT
CHARACTER DANCE...MISS KITTY O'NEIL

The Laughable Sketch by **PORT WINE VS. JEALOUSY!**
Wm. Carter, entitled................
Sebastian Vandergruss Beton St. John, | Simon Coriolanus...........Mr. Wm. Carter
Mrs. Anastasia Coriolanus..Miss Amy Roberts

SERIO-COMIC SONGS...............................MISS ADAH RICHMOND

☞ HARRIGAN AND HART!
In their Great Musical Sketch,

The Mulligan Guards

CARROLL and HARRIS...In their NEGRO SONGS and SAYINGS

The Celebrated Irish Comedian and Vocalist..... **FRANK MARA**
In his Great Specialties, IRISH SONGS, JIGS, ETC.

First time this Season of Harrigan's Laughable Sketch.

☞ A Terrible Example

The Terrible Example............Mr. John Wild | Mr. Theopollus Moriarty...........Mr. E. Harrigan
Secretary Duffy..Mr. Tony Hart
Jones.....} The Celebrated | Mr. D. H. Kelly | J. B. Gough.................Mr. J. F. Crossin
Smith.....} Glee | Mr. J. A. Graver | Mr. Marwood.........Mr. T. Ryan
Brown.....} Club, | Mr. G. L. Stout | Mrs. McGuigan........Mr. James Bradley

MISS ELLA WESNER in her Unequalled Character Songs and Charges!

Overture, * * **D. Braham and Orchestra**

Concluding Every Evening and the Matinees with the Emotional Local Drama, by G. L. Stout, entitled

☞ The Italian Padrone
Or, the Slave of the Harp!

Antonio Simotti, the Italian Padrone.........................Mr. E. Harrigan
Matteo Verbani, an Italian..Mr. G. L. Stout | Seppo Aldi, an Italian...........Mr. D. H. Kelly
John Alberts, a Colored Representative..........................Mr. Charles White
Lorenzo McCoy, of the Police Force...............................Mr. Tony Hart
Forty-Nine, a Wharf Waif....Mr. John Wild | George Howard, a Mechanic..Mr. J. F. Crossin
Mr. Weldon, a wealthy Merchant..................................Mr. J. A. Graver
Joe Short......................Mr. J. Bradley | Marin, Slave of the Harp....Miss Saidee Vivian
Otto Grazia, an Italian Hag................Mrs. Vivian | Bidelia Fogarty........Miss Polly Booth
Nina, wife of Seppo.....Miss Marie Gorembo | Nannette, a White Slave...Miss Kitty Tibtome

NOTICE.--MONDAY, MARCH 22nd
☞ Still Greater Attractions!
First Nights of the Sensation Irish Drama, from which the plot, action and characters of the Irish Drama performed in this house—and also the plot, action and characters from the Drama (claimed under oath as original by the man up the street) was taken,

☞ PYKE O'CALLAGHAN!

TONY HART   AS   PYKE O'CALLAGHAN
ED HARRIGAN   AS   RED RUFUS

HARRIGAN & HART

Will also Perform, for the First Time in Three Months, their Great Sketch,

Patrick's Day Parade

Which has been Rearranged, Altered and Rewritten by Mr. HARRIGAN, and will be almost an ENTIRE NEW SKETCH. Also, a New and Beautiful Negro Sketch, by HARRIGAN and HART,

SLAVERY DAYS!

In which they will Introduce New Songs, Dances and Sayings. Also,

FIRST APPEARANCE THIS SEASON OF

R. M. CARROLL AND HIS 3 TALENTED SONS

Master Benney, The General and Little Dick, they appear in the

Masquerade and McFadden Family

In which these Artists stand without equals in the World. First appearance of the Great London Sensation, the Graceful, Fearless and Beautiful Equestrienne,

LITTLE PAULINE

And her Lilliputian Performing Pony, "LOUISE VICTORIA." This Charming Little Artiste has been pronounced by the English Press "Something Unprecedented"—The Greatest Novelty witnessed in the British Metropolis for years. Her performance takes place in a Patent Ring Erected Upon the Stage.

THE CHAMPION OF THE GLOBE, FREDERICKS

Who performs the Feat never accomplished by any other Artist—that of

THROWING A SOMERSAULT UPON A REVOLVING GLOBE!

NOTICE IMPORTANT.—That Mr. John R. Murray, the popular Circus Manager, has just returned from Europe, where he has secured for the coming Tenting Season, the Wonderful

PROF. LEON & SONS

Said to have no equals in the World, in their Acts of Posturing. That Mr. Murray has brought them from Europe is of itself sufficient guarantee that they must be first-class We have secured their services for a few performances only, as they start travelling early in April with J. R. MURRAY'S GREAT RAILROAD CIRCUS. Due notice of their appearance will be given.

Also of the appearance of the **Great Cool Burgess, Rickey & Barney,** **Miss Nelly St. John, Mr. Larry Tooley, Mr. Wm. Barry,** and the Beautiful and Accomplished **Richmond Sisters.**

☞NOTICE.--MONDAY, MARCH 29TH,

After careful preparation, will be produced a New Dramatic Local Sketch, by permission of the Managers of the Union Square Theatre, entitled

☞ THE TWO AWFULS!

This Local Drama is taken from the Drama of THE TWO ORPHANS, now in the fourth month of its most brilliant career—in fact, the Two Orphans has been the only Legitimate Dramatic Success in New York this season. It will be produced with New Scenery and Effects.

To follow the Awfuls, Ed Harrigan's Great Local Dramatic Extravaganza, with New Music by Dave Braham, entitled

DOWN BROADWAY
Or, From Central Park to the Battery.

PARTICULAR ATTENTION IS CALLED to the following Original Sketches by Ed. Harrigan, which are in active preparation, and will shortly be presented:

FIFTH AVENUE HOTEL; OR, THE NIGHT-CLERK'S TROUBLES
A Beautiful French Sketch, with New and Original **THE IMPERIAL GUARD!**
Songs, Marches, Etc., entitled
Also, a side-splitting Farce, abounding in Funny Situations, and Sensation Absurdities, **BEHIND THE SCENES!**

MATINEE—WEDNESDAYS AND SATURDAYS!

Admission..Fifty Cents
Reserved Seats.............One Dollar | Family Circle..........Twenty-five Cents

Richardson and Fore, Printers, 366 Pearl Street, near Broadway.

Nedda Harrigan Logan

Harrigan and Hart in 1872

Harrigan and Hart in One of Their Earliest Minstrel Sketches,
"You 'Spute Me"

"The Gallant 69th Boys" in *The Doyle Brothers*,
Tony Hart (EXTREME LEFT) Commanding

Tony Hart, Martin W. Hanley and Edward Harrigan

Baxter Street—Design for a Harrigan and Hart Setting
by Charles W. Witham, Their Scenic Artist

MULLIGAN GUARD BALL

MCSORLEY'S INFLATION

OLD LAVENDER

LEATHER PATCH

ROGER O'ROURKE

REILLY AND THE 400

CORDELIA'S ASPIRATIONS

PETE

Ida Harrigan Logan

Tony Hart in 1870

Gertie Granville
(Mrs. Tony Hart)

Harrigan and Hart in "The Blue and the Gray"

Dave Braham

Philip B. Harrigan

Johnny Wild

Philip B. Harrigan

George L. Stout

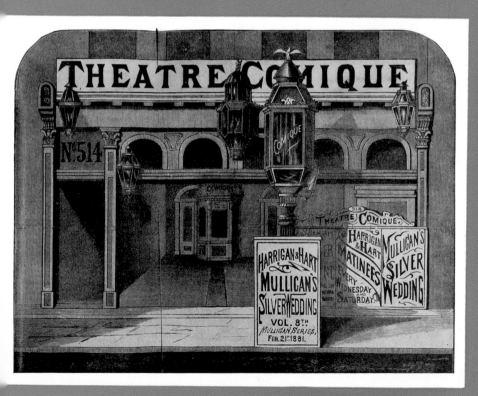

The First Theatre Comique, Broadway and Spring Street

Harrigan (LEFT) and Hart in Their Sketch
"Ireland vs. Italia"

'The Regular Army, O''
(LEFT TO RIGHT, *Edward Harrigan, Tommy Ryan, Mike Bradley,
Dan Diamond, Johnny Wild, Tony Hart*)

THEATRE COMIQUE

514 BROADWAY.

HARRIGAN & HART..................................PROPRIETORS.
John E. Cannon ....Manager.
Dave Braham ....Musical Director.
Edwd. Harrigan .Director of Amusements   Robt. Cutler....Master Machinist
William Gray.....Stage Manager   Robt. Puller...........Properties
Chas. W. Witham....Scenic Artist   Rich'd Doyle. Engineer, Gas, etc.
William Harrigan.......Treasurer   Archie Stalker. Advertising Agt.

Harrigan & Hart,

Wednesday Evening, Feb. 16, 1881.

100th PERFORMANCE 100th
Of Mr. Edward Harrigan's Comic Play, entitled

THE
Mulligan Guards' Nominee

The Play produced under the immediate supervision of the Author Mr. Edward Harrigan

Mr. DAVE BRAHAM,

Our popular director and composer supplies the public demand with fresh and original musical compositions viz.:
CANIDA I OH! DOWN IN GOSSIP ROW. HANG THE MULLIGAN BANNER UP.
MULLIGAN'S PROMISES. SKIDMORE MASQUERADE. THE SKIDS ARE OUT TO-NIGHT.
A NIGHTCAP; A NIGHTCAP.
Sparkling and original incidental music to the Play by the same composer.

THE SKIDMORE GUARD in new and beautiful uniform will muster and parade.

Regimental Roll:

Mr. JOHN WILD,   Mr. James Fox,   Mr. WILLIAM GREY,
Mr. Edward Goss,   Mr. John McCullough,   Mr. John Coffee,
Mr. Michael Foley,   Mr. George Merritt,   Mr. Fred Queen,
Mr. John Oberist,   Mr. W. Merritt,   Mr. John Meally,
Mr. Joseph Buckley,   Mr. Jas. Fitzsimmons.   Mr. Thomas Ray.

OUR CONSTITUENCY.

DAN MULLIGAN	MR. EDWARD HARRIGAN
REBECCA ALLUP	MR. TONY HART
Capt. Simpson Primrose	Mr. John Wild
Rev. Palestine Puter	Mr. William Grey
Gustavus Lochmuller	Mr. Harry Fisher
Snuff McIntosh, Humphrey Down,	Mr. Edward Burt
Caroline Melrose	Mr. James Tierney
Wetmore Cinders	Mr. William West
Oliver Bullwinkle	Mr. Edwin Barry
August Bimble	Mr. Harry Sinclair
Walsingham McSweeny	Mr. Michael Bradley
Mrs. Honora Dublin	Mr. John Queen
Major Dandeline Douglas	Mr. Michael Foley
Dick Dublin	Mr. Fred Queen
Tip Moloney	Mr. Eugene Rourke
Carl Robecker	Mr. Robert Hall
William Cromwell	Mr. John Meally
Officer Sudden	Mr. John McCullough
Officer Soon	Mr. Joseph Buckley
Officer Stop	Mr. John Coffee
Pedro Giovanna	Mr. James Fitzsimmons
Gus Lochmuller, Jr.	Mast. Emil Husel
Bridget Lochmuller	Miss Annie Mack
Cordelia Mulligan	Miss Annie Yeamans
Diana McFudd	Miss Emily Yeamans
Lucetria Crowly	Miss Mary Bird
Henrietta Dempsey	Miss Belle Mordaunt
Annetta McSorley	Miss Susie Byron
Arabella Higgins	Miss Nellie Aldine
Margery McNabb	Miss Nellie Walton

Hackmen, Policemen, Mulligan Constituents, etc., by Auxiliary Corps.

H & H   SOUVENIR   H & H

that some day my name may mean half as much to the coming generation of American playwrights as Harrigan's name has meant to me."

"Organization was always the watchword of the old New Yorker," Harrigan once said. One type of fraternal organization that figured importantly in his experience, and in his stage career, was the target company, a now extinct phenomenon that flourished in old New York for a half century. Target companies came into being in the eighteen-thirties, mainly because immigrants were refused admission into the city's existing militia groups by their choosy officers. These companies were pseudo-military out-fits, often named in honor of an alderman or other leader in ward politics—the William A. Tweed Guards, for instance—which every so often would assemble and march off for what was ostensibly a day's firing practice. Splen-didly uniformed, a company would parade through the streets early in the morning, a brass band hired for the day leading the way, and the rear brought up by a colored boy carrying a large target, on which would be prominently lettered the name of the company's patron. The outfit's first stop would always be the home of this individual, who was expected, in return for being serenaded there, to provide it with prizes to shoot for. In some instances, he would exact an assortment of clothes, hats, cigars, liquor, and other trophies from the businessmen in his neighbor-hood, in return for past or promised favors.

Then the company would move along to a pier, board a river boat, and head for some nearby picnic grounds. Often by the time it got there, its members were so drunk that, when the colored boy set up the target for them to shoot at, they hit one another more often than they hit it. By the time they returned to the city, at dusk, for a final, weaving parade through the streets, possibly setting off fireworks along the line of march, they constituted about as un-military-looking a body of men as could be imagined. Weapons absurdly askew, cigars and toothpicks in their mouths, beer steins or whiskey bottles in their hands, they would stagger homeward in a sodden burlesque of a soldierly procession. At that, their antics were not terribly much more bizarre than those of some of the allegedly more respectable military units of the city. The Ninth New York Regiment, for instance, an organization legitimately in the state militia, was not in the habit of quenching its thirst with alcoholic spirits while on the march, but when it paraded in honor of the visiting Grand Duke Alexis in 1872, its rear ranks consisted of an entire company of uniformed Negro bartenders, whose only weapons were ice buckets and bottles of champagne.

The target companies had exotic names and costumes. Those composed exclusively of Germans, who affected Prussian spiked helmets and spoke only the tongue of their fatherland, were apt to adopt some old American title like the Washington Rifle Corps or the Jefferson Riflemen. The French in New York had their Lafayette Guards, who wore bright red pants; and the Italians their Garibaldi Guards, who wore *bersaglieri* hats. There were more Irish target companies than any other kind. The Napper Tandy Light Artillery Company, conspicuous for its green jackets with yellow braid, its scarlet-striped blue trousers, and its tasseled blue caps, was a notable one. Another was the Robert Davis Pioneer Corps, composed entirely of men over six feet tall, who further enhanced their size with white bearskin shakos, not to mention red shirts, long blue coats, white leggins, leather aprons, and battleaxes. A host of target companies hailed from the Five Points area—the Liberty Guards, the Gotham Guards, the Chatham Guards, the Kelly Guards, and the Killarney Volunteers, to name a few.

Only a handful of the companies owned their uniforms and other paraphernalia; the majority of the organizations rented these, as needed, from supply houses that did a thriving business catering to their wants, and that kept in stock a suitable variety of wooden rifles (to march with), real rifles (to shoot with), swords (to strut with), targets, helmets, caps, shirts, trousers, and battleaxes. The rental charges were high, since the wear and tear on these accouterments were apt to be formidable. In addition to bullet holes, sword slashes, and similar manly disfigurements, the uniforms were sometimes damagingly altered by the wives of their wearers, who, to make their husbands look more distinguished, would embroider shoulders, chests, and sleeves with all kinds of home-made chevrons and other imaginative insignia.

Some of the target companies were occupational in their origin, being composed entirely of, say, shipwrights, bakers, or shoemakers who enjoyed a periodic outing with their fellow workers. Some of the companies were off-shoots of the volunteer fire companies that had functioned in New York until 1865, when fire-fighting became a full-time profession. Most of the holiday marksmen were recruited, however, by and for politicians. Until the downfall in 1871 of Boss Tweed (whose stature was attested to by the fact that two target companies wore his colors), it was possible to deduce a good deal of political intelli-

gence from the parade of a target company. "If during
a season of excursions the name of some well-known party
hack was emblazoned upon a new target," the *Times* explained in 1872, "it was straightway known that the pur-
loiner of tax receipts had determined to demand of the
Boss another term in the board or department to which
he had gained admission, and also, a continuance of his
street inspections. And if another target was seen with
the same name done in gold and blocked with scarlet and
with simply the addition of a 'Junior' thereto, it was like-
wise well known that the family of political hacks was
growing not only in number but in ambition and greed."

The shenanigans of these raffish martial bodies were
often criticized in less solemn vein than that of the *Times*.
Charles Hoyt, in his play *A Milk White Flag*, introduced
a preposterous regiment that was wholly made up of
officers, except for a solitary enlisted man who was the
janitor of the regiment's armory; in a prefatory note to
the play, Hoyt sarcastically called it "A tribute to our
citizen soldiers by one who would gladly join their ranks
if he knew how to dance." The most celebrated satire about
the target companies was "The Mulligan Guards," the
success of which got the organizations laughed right out
of existence. Kipling probably didn't realize it when he
had his soldiers march to the song in India; the Coldstream Guards undoubtedly didn't realize it either; but
the song to which they and many other soldiers blithely
stepped along had been composed in 1872 simply because
Harrigan considered the high-stepping target companies
to be a nuisance.

The song itself was not an instantaneous success. Harrigan and Braham, with some difficulty, persuaded a music

publisher to buy the sheet-music rights to it for fifty dollars. But when Harrigan and Hart presented it as part of their sketch of the same name, the acclaim was thunderous; and the main reason was the ludicrousness of the target company they created. (After the song, and its progenitors, had become established, Braham always incorporated it into the overture on Harrigan and Hart opening nights.) The Mulligan Guards was a three-man military organization. Harrigan led its march, as the captain of an army of one. He wore a Napoleon-type hat gleaming with gold braid, an ill-fitting military tunic with gigantic epaulets that almost reached his elbows, and a pair of pants so outsize the belt that secured them encircled his chest just below the armpits. Strapped to the belt was an enormous sword that dragged along the ground. Hart, next in line, was the army. He carried a musket, and his clothes were much too small, with an expanse of dirty white shirt showing between his tight-fitting tunic and his shrunken pants. On his head, at a precarious angle, sat a giant, motheaten, bearskin shako. Behind him sauntered the target-carrier, a colored boy named Morgan Benson, whose pompous swagger Harrigan and Hart had watched covetously as he lugged a target through the streets in a bona-fide excursion, when Benson was ten years old, and whom they had promptly engaged to perform that chore in their sketch. Later, to complement and skirmish with the Mulligan Guards, Harrigan created, and Braham composed a suitable anthem for, an all-Negro target company called the Skidmore Guards.

Benson, wearing a Confederate Army cap, toted a target that looked like an oversize lollypop and had written on it, "Mulligan Guard—Hussey, Captain." This last

represented a tribute from Harrigan and Hart to a real-
life hero, Jack Hussey, the idol of all the Seventh Ward
target companies. Hussey, a longshoreman and for some
years a gatekeeper at Castle Garden, was a native of
County Cork who emigrated to New York in 1851 and,
during an era when the city's citizens were continually
falling or being pushed into the waters that bordered it,
achieved a massive reputation as a life-saver. When he
rescued his twenty-fifth individual from drowning, Congress had a special medal struck for him to commemorate
the feat. Before he was shot and killed in a street brawl,
Hussey had fished at least one drowning person out of a
New York river annually for thirty-five years, not to mention seven horses that, at one time or another, he pulled
from the East River.

It was by no means merely the members of target companies who went on excursions. Everyone in the city did.
In the seventies and eighties, the working classes toiled
a six-day week, and they aimed to make the most of their
Sundays. They often made so much of them, especially
during the summer time, that the Monday-morning news
stories were a catalogue of violence. The author of a book
published in 1873, entitled *The Dark Side of New York
and Its Criminal Classes,* devoted a whole long chapter
to what he considered the highly apposite subject of
picnics. The Bowery emporia that specialized in treating
black eyes took on extra help for warm-weather Monday
mornings, in confident anticipation of being swamped.
The summer picnic was a New York institution—often
attracting ten or twelve thousand people to a single grassy
arena—that lasted until the nineties. There were three
principal types of picnics. One was the church social, on

the occasion of which Henry Ward Beecher or some similar pastor would lead his flock out into the countryside for an austere feast on cold corned beef, bread and butter, milk, and water, followed by a round or two of quoit-pitching and psalm-singing. A second type of picnic was that of the Upper Ten, where the celebrants would be relatively few in number, the servants many, and the menu comprised of boned turkey, lobster salad, and paté de fois gras, all this washed down with Madeira and champagne.

The third type of picnic—sometimes known, in deference to its notoriety compared to the other types, as the New York City picnic—was something quite different. It was this category that concerned the newspapers and Bowery cosmeticians. To it repaired the humblest citizens of the town, some bent on pleasure and some on mischief. The paths of these contrarily motivated groups would cross in some bosky glen. Working girls who had saved their pennies for months to buy gowns to wear to a special frolic would find, alas, that these served merely to enhance their charms in the eyes of some lurking blackguards who, after plying them with beer, or whiskey, or whiskey spiked with beer, would escort them into some shadowy woods, from which they might emerge alive but rarely, the press and the pulpit lamented, inviolate. At best, their frocks would be in tatters, especially if the dances that day happened to include a popular one called the Nine-pin Quadrille—a lusty variation of musical chairs in which the last man left without a partner was expected at the shout "Club the Nine-pin!" to be set upon by all the other participants.

New York was full of picnic groves. When Harrigan was a boy, in the forties and fifties, there were verdant

oases at 23rd Street, and open country at 42nd. (As late
as the eighteen-eighties, there was a seventy-acre riverside
farm where the East 60's and 70's are now located.)
Cheerfully climbing aboard horse-drawn stage coaches
with straw-covered floors, hordes of picnickers would head
early Sunday morning for Dudley's Grove or Alpine
Grove or Oriental Grove, on the fringe of the tiny city.
Still more would clamber aboard an excursion boat (fare
$1) and head for Hoboken, Guttenberg, Fort Lee, or
Coney Island. A scene that always went over big in the
first full-length play in Harrigan and Hart's Mulligan
series—*The Mulligan Guards' Picnic,* which had its
premiere in 1878—was the departure of a Sunday excursion boat from its dock. A couple of dozen passengers filed
aboard, handing tickets to a ticket-taker, and then a character called Lemons the Bum—played by John Wild, for
many years the team's chief supporting actor—tried to
sneak aboard without paying his fare. He was thrown off,
not too gently. Then the hawsers were cast loose, and, in
realistic fashion, the ship began to move away from the
pier. As it was drifting back, Lemons the Bum, cheered
lustily by the audience, would dash across the stage and
leap valiantly aboard the departing vessel.

The river-going picnickers usually travelled on commodious barges, towed by one or two tugboats. To the
rear of the barge was appended a skiff, manned by a fellow whose sole duty was to extricate from the water the
passengers who slipped overboard, as it was conceded
someone or other was bound to. These barges were a relic
of Hudson River history. When steamboats began operation in the eighteen-fifties, their boilers blew up with such
alarming regularity that instead of carrying passengers,

which they were perfectly large enough to do, they pulled barges on which the passengers could ride with relative impunity. The barges were elegantly fitted out, with comfortable saloons and furniture. Then, as boilers were gradually tamed, passengers began shifting to the steamboats themselves, and the barges were detached and used for hauling hay up and down the river. But when the picnic era set in, there were too few steamboats to accommodate all the prospective excursionists, so the barges were diverted once again to carrying human freight.

One reason for the spirited goings-on at a good many of the picnics was that when an organization sponsoring an outing leased the bar concession, it generally agreed in advance that its celebrants would consume a stipulated number of kegs of liquor. Rather than pay for any unimbibed stimulants, the picnickers would make prodigious efforts to drink every drop the concessionaire brought along. Another reason was that the excursionists were often joined by uninvited guests—not merely a single harmless bum like Lemons, but whole gangs of ruffians, who were not above boarding a ship full of innocent merrymakers, and, in piratical fashion, forcing its captain to alter his course and steer for some deserted beach, where, after having robbed the ship thoroughly, the gang would leap ashore and flee. No barge would have presumed to leave New York without a policeman or two aboard, but a couple of policemen were of little avail against a full-fledged raid by a gang seeking some diversionary change from cock fights or rat fights or other humdrum pleasures. When the West Houston Street gang invaded the ship *Metamora,* bound from New York to Coney Island one Sunday, its members displayed uncommon finesse. Instead of setting about them with bludgeons, they merely cried "Man overboard!" Everyone on the ship rushed to the side whence the cries had come, and while the passengers were jammed against the railings, their eyes glued to the water, the West Houston boys leisurely picked their pockets. Sometimes, the passengers would spot the rowdies as they were coming up the gangplank and would try to repel the boarders, but this could prove a costly vigilance. Before the Helvetia Maennerchor, a singing society, could cast off one sunny morning to frolic at College Point, it had a pitched battle with a raiding party. The enemy was dispersed and left howling on the pier, firing pistols at the excursionists; but by then the deck of the choral society's barge was slippery with blood and two or three of the choristers had fractured skulls.

Many of the picnic excursions were organized by politicians, who left no opportunity unseized to mingle with their constituents. Before spring was over, a conscientious Tammany man would have his summer picnic schedule all mapped out, and would know that on such and such a Sunday in late August his time, and possibly his life, would be in the hands of something like the Matthew J. Caggey Chowder Club. A typical outing was that, one tranquil Sunday in 1885, of the Thomas Albers Association, which engaged the barges *Grinnell* and *Harvest Queen,* and the tugboat *Robert Hoe,* to ferry 400 people from Clinton Street, on the East River, around the Battery and up the Hudson to Spring Hill Grove, in what is now Riverdale. The two barges were lashed together, and off Spuyten Duyvil, a reveler who had outfitted himself for the occasion in the dress uniform of the Eleventh New York Regiment, on being restrained from throwing himself off the

Harvest Queen so he could make the acquaintance of the
man in the skiff, jumped across to the *Grinnell* and tried
to dive in from there. Once more he was dissuaded. This
angered him, so he started a fight, and several dozen men
happily joined in the fray.

A brass band stationed aboard the *Harvest Queen* began to play its loudest march, hoping to distract the com-
batants. Instead, it dismayed the captain of the tugboat
up ahead, who cut loose his tow line, came about, and
pulled alongside the *Grinnell*. A handful of pacifistic
passengers leaped gratefully toward this sanctuary. Two
men and a woman proved insufficiently agile, and fell
overboard. Up to that point, fists and feet had been the
principal weapons brought into action. But now knives
began to flash. The captains of both barges hastily re-
versed their colors, to connote distress at sea. The captain
of the tugboat pulled away and, with his load of refugees,
made at full tilt for 148th Street, where a floating police
patrol was based. Thomas Albers, an alderman, bravely
remained aboard one of the barges, trying to restore order.
It was an impossible task. Pistols came into play. Two of
Albers' henchmen who had been manning a lunch counter
were shot resisting a raid on that concession. Then Albers
himself was knocked prone by a clout on the head. "This
was too much for his Christian fortitude and self-control,"
a Monday-morning newspaper reported. Losing his
temper, Albers drew a revolver and shot a man and a
boy who happened to be standing near him. Then, con-
science-stricken, Albers commandeered the lifesaver's skiff
and headed for shore, presumably hoping to flee to Canada, or at any rate Westchester. But the 148th Street
police had arrived by then, and they caught up with him

as he was pulling mightily at the oars. By the time the
police had restored quiet on the barges themselves, it was
discovered that of all the picnickers who remained on
them, the only uninjured party was the fellow from the
Eleventh Regiment who had sparked the commotion.

The organizations to which sociable New Yorkers gravitated had still other kinds of group outings; quite frequently, they went en masse to the theatre. One evening in
1887, for instance, 200 sturdy members of the Narragansett Club, a group composed of the élite among Tammany
politicians, descended pleasure-bent on Harrigan's Park
Theatre, where their favorite dramatist's play *Pete* was
on view. They brought him a basket of flowers five feet
tall, and the auditorium rocked with cries of "Ki-ki!"
and "Chagrang-chagrang!"—a couple of war-whoops
peculiar to this tribe. An outsider who witnessed the proceedings described the Narragansett contingent of the
audience as indistinguishable from a Democratic Party
convention. Richard Croker, then the boss of Tammany
Hall, was there. So was Sheriff Hugh J. Grant, the president of the Narragansett Club, and a politician renowned
as one of the only two of twenty-three New York alderman who had not made tracks for Canada three years
previous, after the board's scandalous behavior in con-
nection with the awarding of the Broadway street-car
franchise. Two organizations had been bidding for the
franchise. One, the Broadway Railroad Company, had
offered the Board of Aldermen a $750,000 bribe, half in
cash and half in bonds. The aldermen—who were destined
to become known as the Boodle Board—had figured
shrewdly that there might be some inconvenience in
liquidating the bonds, so they had conservatively accepted

the competing bribe of the Broadway Surface Railroad Company. This, to be sure, amounted to only $500,000, but it was all in cash. Grant had declined to take part in this venality, and his fellow citizens had conferred on him the nickname of "Honest Hugh." He was subsequently elected mayor, in which capacity he earned further honors by chopping down a telegraph pole at Broadway and 23rd Street, because he felt that the telephone-and-telegraph company would ruin the beauty of the city if it were allowed to get away with stringing its facilities above ground.

Another eminent Narragansett man was Commissioner of Charities Thomas S. Brennan, who had a voice almost as resounding as Joe Humphreys' and had been grand marshal of the Tammany Braves' march on Washington in celebration of Grover Cleveland's inauguration in 1885. Brennan, like Grant and Croker and Croker's predecessor as Grand Sachem of Tammany, John Kelly (who was known as "Honest John" mainly because he was less corrupt than *his* predecessor, Boss Tweed), was a close friend of the playwright's. Harrigan and Braham dedicated one of their songs to him, "The Black Maria, O!," which recounted the nefarious adventures of a typically lovable Bowery lass known as "cork-legg'd Dolly, the squint-eyed hag," who hung out at a saloon called the Burnt Rag. During the Narragansett outing to the theatre, Brennan yelled so loud that he almost drowned out the cast, and Martin Hanley, a manager usually tolerant of audience participation, was obliged to yell back, "Let her go slow, Gallagher!"

(This was a much appreciated variation on the cry "Let her go, Gallagher!" which had become famous three years earlier and was heard throughout the streets of New York. There were two versions of its origin. One had it that the phrase had first been addressed to a man named Gallagher, who, paralyzed with fear, had frozen to the handle of a safety valve on a Coney Island roller coaster. The more widely accepted version was that it had originated in the fall of 1884 at the Walnut Street Theatre in Philadelphia, where John T. Raymond, known best for his interpretation of Mark Twain's Colonel Mulberry Sellers, was playing in a show called *For Congress*. A stage-struck Philadelphian named Dan Gallagher who aspired to be an actor was hanging around backstage one night when the regular curtain man became ill, and Gallagher was pressed into emergency service. At the end of the first act, when he was supposed to lower the curtain, he got stage fright, and couldn't move. The prompter began to hiss at him, and the stage manager to mutter. Gallagher just stood there, helpless. Then, on stage, Stella Boniface, an ingenue who later became an ornament of Harrigan's company, began to giggle. Finally Sellers could stand it no longer. "Let her go, Gallagher!" he shouted. The boys in the gallery at once took up the cry, and within a few days it had spread rapidly across Philadelphia and on to New York.)

Politicians doted on the Harrigan and Hart shows, and could be found there in droves at almost any performance, whether or not a group outing was involved. Political observers in New York predicted that an election of Tammany Hall officers in 1885 was bound to be a sparsely attended and thus fairly quiet occasion, inasmuch as a revival of *Cordelia's Aspirations* was also scheduled to open that evening. By the same token, the *Clipper* expressed itself as surprised that Harrigan and Hart should have had a full house on Election Eve in 1883. That one night of the year at least, the *Clipper* declared, the ward-heelers who comprised the bulk of their claque might have been expected to forgo the theatre and attend to business in their wards.

The affinity of Democratic politicians to the stage ante-dated Al Smith by many years. Grover Cleveland, who was even named for a theatrical man—Leonard Grover, the author of *Our Boarding House*—was a close friend and fishing companion of Joseph Jefferson's. A. Oakey Hall, the mayor of New York in 1870, wrote and acted in a play, *The Crucible,* immediately after being booted out of office and somehow avoiding conviction for malfeasance in three trials; later in his career he served as a European correspondent for the *Spirit of the Times.* Hall once declared fervently that in his opinion the theatre was "filled with noble men and pure women"—a testimonial that its recipients may have looked upon with misgivings, inasmuch as its utterer was not only a man of dubious character himself but a dubious judge of character: as district attorney of New York, before he became mayor, he had left unprosecuted 18,000 indictments that passed through his office.

The site that the sachems of Tammany Hall picked out for their society's tepee, on the east flank of Union Square next door to the Academy of Music, was in the heart of the theatrical area when the building's cornerstone was laid in 1867. Actors then hung around the Square all day long, and the hotels and bars they frequented were close by. A wing of the Tammany building was a theatre for many years—occupied first by Dan Bryant's Minstrels and then by Tony Pastor—and the upper hall of the main section of the structure was also a theatre briefly, from January, 1869, to June 1870. It was advertised as "The Alhambra Palace of America," and during its first month of operations (Oakey Hall composed and delivered the inaugural address for its opening night) grossed $40,000, an enormous sum at the time. But it rapidly went into a decline, despite the efforts of a number of managers to keep it going with practically every type of act available —trained canaries and trained dogs; a man who ate, smoked, and drank while immersed in a glass tank filled with water; living statues representing Lord Byron and Harriet Beecher Stowe; a burlesque of *Richard II* called *Bad Dickey;* and one of the most repetitiously advertised performers of history, a "great and natural curiosity" who was billed as "A Prince Royal of Persia, His Royal Highness (Genuine) Prince Sadi D'jalma. Professionally termed the Boneless Man! Boneless! The man without bones!"

The love the politicians had for Harrigan's plays was in no wise reciprocated by the plays themselves. Not long after the exposure of the Boodle Board, a few of whose members were caught before they could reach the Canadian border, Harrigan and Braham came up with a couple of songs called "The Aldermanic Board" and "The Boodle," a chorus of which went:

> It's money, my boys, makes troubles and joys
> In politics, church, or the law!
> The worship of gold, a story quite old—
> A story twice told is a bore!
> Now soldiers may cry, "We're willing to die,

For liberty joyous and free!"
Oh, say to yourself, I'm fond of the pelf,
The Boodle, the Boodle, for me!

And a writer on the gossipy weekly *Town Topics* reported, after attending a performance of *The O'Reagans* in 1886: "A brutal alderman sat beside me and roared when Mr. Wild remarked with all his power that the politicians had stolen all the stars from the American flag and were now wearing the stripes. The brutal alderman did not believe him, of course, but it might be that if anyone in life had passed this same jest to him, he would probably have committed homicide or mayhem. This is the soul of Mr. Harrigan's peculiar talent. He sees the life he is a part of and translates it as a commentator, rather than a critic."

When Dan Mulligan beat out his German friend Lochmuller for the job of alderman in *The Mulligan Guards' Nominee* (he at once asked to be known as "Tiger"), it was a campaign of such flagrant dishonesty that the ballot boxes were stuffed with practically everything on stage, including Mulligan himself. He was trying to hide there to avoid paying off a number of citizens he had persuaded to vote for him. (In 1876, New York had a large cage that was trotted out on Election Day, and into which voters suspected of chicanery were shoved until the polls had closed, so they couldn't cast illegal ballots more than once.) Mulligan had a campaign song, "Mulligan's Promises," which went, in part, "You'll be sure of a synacure from our next Alderman." In a sequel to *The Mulligan Guards' Nominee* called *The Mulligans' Silver Wedding,* Harrigan unveiled his winning candidate in all

his aldermanic glory, and some of his appointments to
sinecures were catalogued—his defeated rival Lochmuller
to be German interpreter at Castle Garden, his pal
Walsingham McSweeny to be horse doctor for all ash-
cart animals, and other deserving constituents to count
the sparrows in Central Park, inspect lampposts, and
chase hats on windy days along Fifth Avenue, all at fat
salaries.

In still another of the Mulligan plays, Harrigan had Dan
Mulligan gaze at a bottle of whiskey set out on his parlor
table, and observe solemnly, "There's the lever that moves
the machinery of a great political party." And in another
scene, Mulligan and his wife were visited by a flock of
other aldermen, who, after suitable refreshment, all dozed
off.

"Whatever will I do?" Cordelia Mulligan asked her
husband. "The aldermen are all sound asleep."

"Lave them be," said Dan. "While they sleep, the city's
safe."

The New York *Daily News* thought Harrigan's political satire was as trenchant as that of Thomas Nast, whose
stinging cartoons of the Tammany Tiger had done much
to bring about the deflating of Boss Tweed. The *News'*
analogy was a bit unfair to Nast. The Tammany politicians couldn't abide his drawings, but for Harrigan, no
matter how he needled them, they had nothing but affection. They often visited him at his home, and they felt
so at home in his theatres that they even puffed cigars
while sitting happily in their boxes, in open defiance of
a no-smoking edict that they themselves had had enacted.

When the Tammany Braves descended upon Washington for President Cleveland's first inauguration, they

were accompanied by the band of the Seventh Regiment
of the New York State National Guard. Harrigan and
Hart were honorary members of the Seventh. From time
to time, the regiment, or a large component of it, would
march in formation to their theatre, where its men could
usually hope to be rewarded by some such special dialogue
as Dan Mulligan's remarking that one of the first things
he planned to do on becoming an alderman was to go to
Albany and have the Mulligan Guards supplant the
Seventh in the State Guard. The bond that linked the
regiment and Harrigan and Hart had been forged in 1878,
when the Seventh Regiment Music and Drama Association needed some costumes and props for a show it was
putting on, and the actors supplied them. An intimate
and enduring relationship existed ever afterward. Harrigan's colored valet was engaged by the Seventh's commanding officer as a cook during summer layoffs at the
theatre, and the assistant director of the regimental band
conducted the music at Dave Braham's funeral.

At least once a year, from 1878 on, the regiment,
which, like most of the militia, concerned itself much more
with social than military affairs, would buy out nearly the
entire house at Harrigan and Hart's. The soldiers themselves would perform between the acts, after the last act,
and often during the acts. Once, every man, to the despair
of the actors, came equipped with a kazoo. In 1884, for
example, the regiment arrived 600 strong. Harrigan and
Hart, to show their appreciation of this patronage, had
flags draped over the doorways, and over the proscenium
arch hung a replica of the regimental badge, in dazzling
gold, red, and green, with the regimental motto, "Pro
patria et gloria," resplendent on it. The men of the Seventh
were overcome with gratitude. The play was delayed in-

terminably while they emitted Sisses and Booms and Ahs, egged on by a private named Waldo Sprague who acted as their cheerleader, and while they shouted, in unison, "Here—we—are—again." When Dave Braham came out to strike up the overture, he was greeted with a thunderous "Ah—there—Dave—old—boy!" Next was a raucous "Good—old—Tony!" as Hart made his appearance. The applause that greeted Harrigan was even louder. As he stepped on stage, Waldo Sprague leaped into an aisle, and yelled "One—two—three!" Whistles and screams and pounding feet shook the house. "When a Seventh Regiment man sees Harrigan," a dazed observer for the *World* said afterward, "his affection breaks out in joyful roaring that would make the bull of Basham consider himself a very asthmatic fellow indeed." That night, according to the *World,* the ovation tendered Harrigan lasted three minutes and forty-two seconds.

5.

A GENTLEMAN'S SON OF CORK ROW

The easternmost point on Manhattan Island is Corlears Hook, a bulging outpost that now lies under the shadow of the Williamsburg Bridge. Named after Jacob Van Corlear, an early-seventeenth-century Hollander who ran a farm there, the place has had a colorful history. In the mid-seventeenth century, a tribe of Indians fleeing from some homicidal white men tried to obtain sanctuary at Corlears Hook, and were promptly slaughtered by their hosts. In war, the spot has served as a fortification, having given the Hessians a fine view of the East River during the Revolution; and in peace, as a font, having once been the principal site for the immersion ceremonies of the city's Baptists. There are still a few old gaffers around town, moreover, who firmly believe—as a host of New Yorkers believed in days past—that somewhere beneath Corlears

Hook lies buried the treasure, or part of the treasure, of Captain Kidd.

Corlears Hook was a landmark of the old Seventh Ward, which, if it cannot indisputably be said to have harbored Captain Kidd, without a doubt harbored more home-grown river pirates than any other local headland. In the middle of the nineteenth century, 450 of them made the Hook their base of operations, fanning out from there to hijack various fetching cargoes that drifted by. Many of them were gangsters who had been chased out of the adjoining Fourth Ward a few years earlier, when the residents of that neighborhood had made a concerted effort to clean it up; and who, in emulation of the over-optimistic Indians before them, had sought haven in the Seventh, where, in their case, the welcome sign was out at saloons like the Tub of Blood and the Lava Beds.

The Hook was a favorite hangout, too, of the city's notorious dock rats—a pack of homeless boys, aged six to fifteen, who lived under the wharves and made ends meet by pilfering. The dock rats, one of whom was graphically portrayed by Hart in *Old Lavender,* were expert swimmers, often finding it expedient to take to the water to evade an onrushing policeman. Many of them learned to swim in a four-foot-deep water hole in Corlears Park— the garden spot of the Hook—which was locally designated a pond but was actually the mouth of a sewer. Their big day of the year was the first of August, when they celebrated Launching Day, an occasion on which, it was tolerantly conceded in the neighborhood, the dock rats had the right to throw anybody they could catch hold of into the river.

The lower East Side is almost exclusively colonized by

Jews nowadays, but a hundred years ago it was a predominantly Irish neighborhood—so much so that the area surrounding Corlears Hook, inhabited mostly by seafaring men and their families, was known as Cork Row. Practically the only non-Irish within paving-stone's throw were itinerant sailors who holed up between voyages at the "flag-houses" near the water, so-called because their proprietors solicited their clientele from one nationality or another, and hung out the appropriate sovereign colors to identify the particularity of their hospitality. It was in this aqueous and largely Hibernian atmosphere that, on October 26, 1844, at 31 Scammel Street, a block west of the Hook, Edward Green Harrigan was born.

In the early eighteenth century, some Harrigans from County Cork migrated to Canada, where their impact is presently commemorated in the name of Cape Harrigan, on the coast of Labrador. (The playwright set foot in this ancestral northland only once in his life, but he was proud of his affiliation with it and by way of indicating this had a succession of Newfoundland dogs as pets for his children.) William Harrigan, Ned's father, was the son of a County Cork fisherman who had gone to Newfoundland to join the family clan at the start of the nineteenth century. William was born at Carbonear, thirty miles northwest of St. John's, and had an appropriately briny upbringing. At the age of twelve, he shipped out as a cabin boy on a Yankee clipper. His parents had raised him as a Catholic, but at sea he began to swing over into the spiritual orbit of his ship's captain, a New England Protestant in whose cabin the boy got much of his secular education, too. From then on, William was a highly unorthodox Irish-

man. When the Henry Clay Lodge of the Masonic Order
—composed mainly of seamen, carpenters, and other salty
lower East-siders of New York—was founded in 1852, he
became a charter member, and he was Master of the Lodge
for a while.

He was unconventional in other ways, too. He claimed,
for instance, to be the only Republican in the Seventh
Ward—a distinction that, considering the political orienta-
tion of his neighbors, he may very well have enjoyed. He
was a thrifty, stern, and crotchety man. After his death,
his family discovered that his tombstone, which he had
ordered himself some years earlier for ultimate display at
the Greenwood Cemetery in Brooklyn, spelt his name with
only one "r." To be sure, this could have been a stone-
cutter's typographical error, but the surviving Harrigans
preferred to interpret it as one last testimonial to old
William's orneriness.

In 1829, when William Harrigan was in his early twenties and was first mate on a square-rigger plying between
New York and Liverpool, his ship tied up at Norfolk, and
there he met and fell in love with a seventeen-year-old
transplanted New Englander named Ellen Ann Rogers.
She was the daughter of Matthias Rogers, of Charles-
town, Massachusetts, and she also had a maritime her-
itage. Her father had died in 1813, when she was only
a year old, while he was serving as a gunner aboard the
Chesapeake during its famous fight with the *Shannon*
off Boston—the fight in which the *Chesapeake's* commander, Captain James Lawrence, allegedly cried to his
crew, as he himself lay dying, "Don't give up the ship!"
Matthias Rogers' four sons also died during or as a direct
aftermath of the War of 1812. Their widowed mother, her

savings in a calico bag sewn to her whalebone corset stays, took her only remaining child, the infant Ellen Ann, and sailed with her to Norfolk, where she ran a boarding house for transient seamen. It was extremely popular with New Englanders, who were delighted to have an establishment in Norfolk that served clam chowder, baked beans, codfish cakes, and other Northern delicacies.

A year after Ellen Ann first met William, her mother died, and the girl went to New York, where, in 1830, she was reunited with Harrigan and married him. He gave up the sea then, and went to work as a calker at Webb's Shipyard, on the East River between Corlears Hook and Delancey Street. He became a naturalized citizen and a notably chauvinistic one; of ten children he and Ellen Ann had, all but four of whom died in infancy, one was named Martha Washington and another Washington. The survivors included two girls, Martha and Mary; and two boys, William and Edward. Aside from one brief interlude, they grew up in the house on Scammel Street— a two-story, red-brick building with a mansard roof, which was a cut above most of the homes in the area.

The exception was a brief interlude, in the late eighteen-fifties, when William Harrigan decided impulsively to become a farmer. He bought a nine-acre place at Meads Basin, New Jersey, northwest of Paterson, and moved his family there for three weeks, after which he concluded that New Jersey was impossibly arid and returned to the familiar, damp riverfront of New York. His mother, a prim County Cork woman who had clung to her old-fashioned Irish ways, was living with the Harrigans and their children at the time, and young Ned was given the task of escorting her to the farm. He drove a wagon

out there containing his grandmother and her featherbed. No possession was dearer to Irish women of that era
than their beds, as the boy was to take note of years later
when, for his play *McSorley's Inflation,* he wrote a song
called "The Old Featherbed:"

> In the County Mayo, long, long ago,
> Me father himself took a wife;
> 'Twas all understood he would do what he could
> To provide for me mother through life.
> His father, old Dougherty,
> Gave all the crock'ry,
> His table to eat of their bread;
> Her mother, God save her,
> Said all she could lave her
> As a token of love was her old featherbed.

Ned's grandmother, even with her own old featherbed secure beneath her on the wagon, was leery of the
trek into the Jersey hinterlands. As they were crossing
a marsh near Newark, she suddenly cried to the boy,
"Stop the horse!"

Harrigan did, and the old lady nervously fumbled with
the front of her dress and finally pulled a worn cloth bag
from her bosom. "Do you see this, Ned Harrigan?" she
said severely. "Well, I have eighty dollars here, and I'll
never have to ask your father to bury me. Drive on!"

During Ned's childhood, one of the most exalted and
influential bodies of men in New York was the city's corps
of volunteer firemen. The fact that the senior William
Harrigan was for a while foreman of Engine No. 19 enhanced his reputation no end along Cork Row. The city

was then divided into five fire districts, and when a blaze broke out, the first official alarm would be given by a sentinel posted in one of several wooden watchtowers that overlooked the squat buildings around them. The biggest tower, at Spring and Varick Streets, was sixty-five feet high, and commanded a view all the way from the Battery to the remote environs of 34th Street. It housed a bell that weighed 10,000 pounds, and according to the number of peals its giant tongue rang out, the volunteers would converge on one district or another. The firemen were a colorful lot, in their scarlet shirts, high black boots, and black leather helmets, and on occasion would combat a fire even more gaudily accoutered. One night in the eighteen-fifties, for instance, some of the members of the Lady Washington Light Guard, a target company recruited from the ranks of Lady Washington Engine No. 40, were taking part in *The Patriots of '76,* a lavishly costumed show produced by P. T. Barnum, when the big bell clanged. The whole cast dashed off stage, and a few minutes later the fire was being tackled by a host of guardsmen still got up as Indians, Hessians, militiamen, and, in one instance, Molly Pitcher.

The identities of the various fire engines in town were as familiar to schoolchildren then as those of various movie stars are today. Engine No. 4, for example, a vehicle elegantly painted in gold and white and berthed on Mulberry Street, was known far and wide as the Mulberry Ghost. There was one machine called Old Wreath of Roses and another called Old Rover; when one of these machines effectively quelled a fire, it was not unusual for impressionable adolescents of the town to smother the praiseworthy engine with kisses. When a long gap had to be bridged between hydrant and fire, water would be pumped along from one engine to another, and if a machine fell behind during this relay operation, it was said to have been "washed." Engine No. 15, which enjoyed the proud repute of never having been washed, was affectionately known as the Old Maid. The volunteers who manned the machines ranked much higher in popular esteem than soldiers, policemen, or congressmen, and were a potent political force. Nine of New York's earliest mayors got elected to that office largely owing to having earned, or purchased, the endorsement of a fire company. Harrigan once put into Dan Mulligan's mouth the observation that he valued an honorary discharge from the Volunteer Fire Department of New York City, signed by Boss Tweed, much more highly than a discharge from the Army of the Potomac. Tweed's own political career is said to have been given its principal impetus when, in 1849, at the age of twenty-six, he wangled the job of foreman of Engine No. 6. Almost at once he became a man to reckon with, and he was a much admired figure as he charged into action, wearing a white coat and issuing orders to his men through a silver-plated megaphone.

In the eighteen-fifties, Tweed's engine company had its headquarters on Henry Street, only a block away from Scammel, and the Harrigan children would look on with awe and delight as the company's ponderous engine, sometimes called Big Six and sometimes Old Tiger, was hauled off to tussle with a fire or, as not infrequently happened, with another fire engine. (Engine No. 6 had a snarling tiger's face painted on it, and from this, as well as from a tiger used as the emblem of a political organization of Tweed's called the Americus Club, stemmed the felinity of Tammany Hall.) The fire companies were extremely competitive, and now and then, in their anxiety to beat each other to the scene of a blaze, two companies would meet head-on in some narrow street and stage a pitched battle there, while the fire they had set forth to douse raged on undeterred. Tweed's engine company had one particular adversary, Engine No. 41, informally called Old Stag, and quite a few structures burned to the ground in Harrigan's neighborhood while the crews of Old Stag and Old Tiger, arriving concurrently at some intersection like East Broadway and Chatham Street, would forget all about fires and come to bloody grips with knives, paving stones, and pistols.

It was not just the competitive spirit of the volunteers, let alone the tindery construction of most of New York, that contributed to the high incidence of total destruction by fire of so many of the city's old buildings. Sometimes when the volunteers did get to the scene of a fire swiftly and unbruised, they would find that partisans of a dilatory engine had clamped barrels over the area's hydrants and were indisposed to remove these obstacles—unless compelled to by force—until the firemen they wanted to fight that particular fire turned up. The hydrant-seizers often consisted of a delegation of Bowery B'hoys or some other sturdy gang, and even when the volunteers could dislodge them from the water supply, it was usually only after such a struggle that they were too exhausted to engage in much further physical exertion.

The gangs were fond of fires partly because amid all the hullabaloo these evoked, not to mention all the covering smoke, it was a relatively simple matter to break into nearby establishments and make off with some of the contents. Many of the volunteers themselves, indeed, were not above a little random looting, and it was as a result of this prankish addiction of theirs that New York finally got, in 1865, its first full-time, professional, non-voluntary firemen. A bill to demobilize the volunteers and substitute a paid force for them was under consideration by the state legislature in Albany when a department-store fire broke out in New York City. Three volunteers were killed, while fighting it, when a wall collapsed on them. Afterwards, their bodies were recovered, and on each one was found a brand-new overcoat with the price tag still on it. Impressed by this intimation that the volunteers, though brave, were a mite irresponsible, the legislature passed the bill.

The older of the two Harrigan boys, William, was a volunteer fireman for a spell, and at the age of eighteen went off to the Civil War with the New York Zouaves, a regiment made up mostly of Irish firemen from the city, who insisted that their bright-red fire-fighting shirts be incorporated into their military uniform. Ned Harrigan was neither a fireman nor a soldier himself, although he was occasionally accorded the honor of fetching water for Boss Tweed's engine, but he was an enchanted and observing bystander. "I knew almost everything about the city that it was possible for a boy to learn," he once declared as an adult. His formal education was modest. He attended public school up to the time he was fourteen, and had no further instruction until he later hired his own French tutor. But he had cultivated a taste for reading. Emerson and Whitman came to be great favorites of his, and throughout his life he gobbled up the works of the world's playwrights. In addition to Molière, he was especially attracted to Shakespeare, Sheridan, Beaumont and Fletcher, and to two French chroniclers of the bourgeoisie a generation ahead of him—Emile Augier and Eugène Labiche. "Shakespeare and Labiche are my greatest friends," Harrigan was quoted by the *Dramatic Mirror* as confiding to it in 1891.

Harrigan's interest in the theatre began to develop long before he had made these friends' acquaintance. Practically the only schoolboy composition of his that has weathered the years is a three-line verse—if it is verse— that went:

> Win I am a man
> I don't give a damn
> But will be an actor.

A succession of teachers complained to his parents that instead of concentrating on his studies in school, he appeared to be chiefly preoccupied with composing parodies of popular songs and dialogues for minstrel shows. His mother was not upset by this intelligence. She had become fond of music while a girl in Virginia, and not only entertained her children by teaching them Negro spirituals, but, while the senior Harrigan was at work, would borrow her husband's best beaver hat, slap it on her head at a rakish tilt, and do a minstrel walkaround for the children in the front parlor. The age of minstrelsy was just then coming into flower; the first minstrel show the city had ever seen had been put on as recently as February, 1843, when a tambo-and-bones outfit called the Virginia Minstrels had invaded New York. One of its members was Dan Emmett, later the composer of "Dixie." Almost every fledgling actor with serious theatrical aspirations was interested in minstrelsy in those days, including Edwin Booth. When Booth was seventeen, a year after his debut as an actor, he entertained the audience at an informal gathering in his home town, Belair, Maryland, by corking up his face and executing a passable blackface routine, and as a mature tragedian, it has been said he would sometimes relieve his tension while waiting in the wings for an entrance during *Hamlet* or *Othello* by breaking into a jig or shuffle.

Harrigan *père's* reaction to all this was quite different from his wife's. He had little use for the amusement world, and feared that his son's predilection for it might stand in the way of the honorable career he had picked out for him—that of becoming a longshoreman. To please his father, Ned dutifully headed for the docks, after making a few ineffectual stabs at being a printer's devil and a newsboy. From the age of fourteen to eighteen, he served as an apprentice calker in a waterfront shipyard, cementing wooden hulls by pounding a mixture of tar and oakum into the cracks between their planks. Lexicographers have never yet agreed on the derivation of the word "hokum." H. L. Mencken has gone no further than to report impartially several of the extant theories. One is that it stems from the fusion of "hocus pocus" and "bunkum," alias "buncombe." Another is that a retired sea captain, a cockney managing a music-hall in London, coined the word inadvertently when he advised a comedian to plug up a hole in his act with "a bit of oakum," a word he aspirated. There are still other folk, most of them related to Harrigan, who insist that "hokum" was one of his few lasting contributions to literature and language, and who point to the raw materials that figured conspicuously in his calking days as justification for their claim.

An apprentice calker worked a sixty-hour week in the fifties, but in whatever spare time Harrigan had he continued, when his father wasn't looking, to dabble in the theatre. He was a rapt auditor at the New York, the Bowery, and Niblo's Theatres, all located not too far from his home. When he was four, the first of a series of plays by Benjamin A. Baker about New York low life had been unveiled at Mitchell's Olympic Theatre—the *Mose* plays, whose central character was a volunteer fireman, portrayed for many lucrative years by Francis S. Chanfrau. There is no question but that Harrigan must have been influenced by some of these—*Mose in California, Mose in France, Mose in China, Mose in a Muss,* and so on—or at any rate by the first of them, *A Glance at New York*. He learned from their success, if nothing else, that audiences would pay, and applaud, to gaze at a reflection of their own lives. The stage Mose was patterned faithfully on a quondam fireman of the Lady Washington company, Moses Humphreys, who had a formidable reputation for toughness and was acclaimed as the King of Five Points. He had been deposed in 1836, after being licked in a street brawl with a contender for his throne, Henry Chanfrau, who was, coincidentally, the elder brother of the actor. The fight began as a private quarrel between Humphreys and Chanfrau, but, Five Points being the kind of arena it was, was quickly joined in by what was subsequently estimated to be a minimum of 100 auxiliary contestants. On being dethroned, Humphreys, like other kings who have lost their crowns, left his country. He went to Hawaii, where his loss of face would presumably not be widely known.

One of the theatres Harrigan patronized, the Bowery, had the indulgent policy of letting kids in the audience perform between the regularly scheduled acts. At sixteen, Harrigan availed himself of this privilege and, while Pierce's Original Campbell's Minstrels were catching their breath, declaimed a monologue he had composed on the flyleaves of a school book—a parody of a political stump speech. The management of the Bowery was impressed with the boy, and offered him a contract, but his father would have none of it. Ned resignedly confined himself to amateur theatricals. In the cellar of his home, while his father was out, he presided over informal entertainments billed as "Ned Harrigan's One-Man Show," in the course of which he displayed his versatility by singing, dancing, and tackling almost any musical instrument he could get his hands on. Physically, there was nothing terribly pre-possessing about him. He was of average height and weight; even as a boy, he had a rather prominent nose and chin. These, along with a tendency toward pudginess he then had, were to become more marked as he got older. His voice was nothing to make a choirmaster stop and listen twice—it has been described as sounding like a cross between a brogue and a twang—but so enthusiastically did he use it that he was in great demand as a participant in neighborhood wakes, oyster suppers, picnics, and other social gatherings.

When Ned was eighteen, his parents had a falling out. They got divorced, and his mother slipped discontentedly off to Staten Island, where she lived out her life in unhappy solitude. William Harrigan soon married again, this time taking as a wife a rather formidable New England widow of Methodist persuasion, who bore her new husband three more children. Ned's relationship with his stepmother was not dramatically uncomfortable, but it was strained, and he spent little time under his father's roof thereafter. Some years later he wrote a poem containing the quatrain:

> Mother's sick, ah, that's tough,
> You say you're her only kid.
> Don't use the old woman rough,
> You might get a stepmother instead.

It is not precisely clear at this date where, for the next few years, he did hang out. One reconstruction of his movements has it that at eighteen, apparently not so much on account of his stepmother as on account of wanderlust, he boarded a schooner bound for New Orleans as a deckhand, carrying with him a banjo that he had bought at a pawnshop for five dollars and had hidden from his father. This seems dubious, since the Civil War was then in full swing, and it would have been odd for a healthy eighteen-year-old New Yorker to choose New Orleans for his destination.

But he must have spent the war years somewhere, and there is no indication that he spent them in New York or any other Northern community. And the school of thought that clings to the New Orleans theory has, to back it up, a graphic account Harrigan sometimes related when he was older of how, as he was returning to New York in a couple of years, aboard a clipper ship loaded with lumber, the combustible vessel caught fire off the coast of Florida. Its crew of thirty or so, this story goes, was made up mostly of natives of the Caribbean, who got panicky and headed for the lifeboats. They were dissuaded by the first mate, who met them at the davits with a loaded revolver and shouted, "Get back, you sons of bitches, and work the pumps!" In ten minutes, they had put the fire out and saved the ship; and Harrigan used to cite this adventure as an example of the virtues of discipline when an unruly cast got out of hand during rehearsals.

Be all that as it may, Harrigan definitely headed out to sea, with California as his destination, in the mid-sixties. His journey was interrupted unexpectedly when he took ill with a tropical fever off the Atlantic coast of Panama, and was dumped ashore there by a hard-hearted ship's captain. After being nursed back to health by some natives, who took him in and doctored him with herbs, he made his way across the Isthmus, boarded a north-bound vessel, and, late in 1866, finally arrived in California. He still wanted to be an actor, but by then had resignedly come to think of himself as a dock worker by trade. With that gloomy conviction in mind, he debarked at San Francisco, a community slightly more civilized than it had been a generation previous in the Gold Rush days, but not much.

Harrigan was twenty-two, and up to then had never been within a couple of thousand miles of San Francisco, but in after years, when he became successful, the city forgave him his tardiness and even, on more than one occasion, bragged of him as a native son. By 1894, the San Francisco *Call* was calling him "the old San Franciscan," and the *Post's* obituary headline for him was "Veteran San Francisco Playwright Is Dead." California was the Texas of its time. Its attitude, at least toward Harrigan, was pretty well summed up by a West-Coast theatrical paper that once explained, "The fact that he began his dramatic career in San Francisco is sufficient reason for California to claim him with considerable pride as a self-made, self-educated, and very creditable product of her prolific soil."

Harrigan's first San Francisco engagement was a one-night, unpaid appearance, early in 1867, in an obscure auditorium called Dashaway Hall. With a song or two, he was supposed to provide a change of pace from the scolding exhortations of some local missionaries of the Father Mathew temperance movement, who had taken over the house for a recruiting session. Father Mathew was an Irish priest who had lived from 1790 to 1856 and toiled so steadfastly against spirituous liquor that he became known as the Apostle of Temperance and won a pension for his efforts from Queen Victoria. In this country, in the middle of the nineteenth century, countless zealots marched under his austere banner, after having taken a renunciatory pledge in the presence of a clergyman; and there even sprang up a Father Mathew Temperance and Manufacturing Company, which for a time did a thriving business in the sale of two varieties of "temperance bitters"—one made without alcohol and the other, strangely, with. Harrigan had no particular sympathy with the cause, but he was grateful for a chance to perform, under any old auspices, and nine years later he wrote a song entitled "Sons of Temperance" and dedicated it nostalgically to the Father Mathew Total Abstinence Societies. Possibly by way of connoting his imperviousness to their preachings, however, he subtitled the tune "S.O.T."

Launched as an amateur actor, Harrigan was still several months short of attaining professional standing. His stage ambitions had been heightened by the taste of applause that greeted him at Dashaway Hall, but the ful-

fillment of them was something else again. The only
person who encouraged him unequivocally was an itinerant phrenologist he consulted, who informed him,
upon payment of a small fee, that his creative and per-
ceptive faculties were quite singular. Harrigan was impressed, and resolved to become a character actor. He
presented himself hopefully to the managers of a number
of San Francisco variety houses—or melodeons, as these
were generally known—but the managers, possibly because they neglected to finger the contours of his skull,
were stolidly unreceptive. Meanwhile, to earn a living,
he was working as a dock laborer in a Vallejo shipyard,
across the bay. He roomed in a boarding house, and in the
evenings its tenants would often join in song. His fellow
harmonizers kept urging him not to give up on the theatre,
and finally a delegation of lodgers escorted him one evening to Butler's Melodeon, a basement variety hall in San
Francisco, where auditions were being held.

Wearing a new linen duster and straw hat he had purchased for the occasion, and carrying his battered banjo,
Harrigan announced himself timidly to the stage doorman. Harrigan was never a terribly assertive young man,
and when that sentinel slammed the door in his face he
was for returning at once to Vallejo. Not so his entourage.
One robust stevedore declared loudly that if the door
wasn't re-opened instantly, he would be happy to kick
it in. The doorman, hearing this threat, may have been
reminded that theatrical personages were, in those days,
capable of prodigious displays of temperament. Not long
before, in a playful rumpus among some minstrels outside the Bella Union, a nearby melodeon that was entered
by way of a saloon, a scuffling end man had been stomped

to death. In any event, Harrigan was admitted. He had composed a song for the tryout, an autobiographical ditty relating the trials of an Irish boy who wanted to go on the stage, and he accompanied himself with his banjo. The management, no doubt influenced mainly by his performance but just possibly swayed a little by the glowering faces of his burly retinue, gave him a job. The night he opened, the dock workers from his lodging house turned out in exuberant force and showered the stage with bouquets of ravelled oakum.

The bill of fare at San Francisco's variety houses in 1867 consisted of a mixture of singing, dancing, acrobatics, minstrelsy, and drama. Harrigan worked in and around San Francisco from the fall of that year until June, 1870, playing the Bella Union, the Olympic, Gilbert's Melodeon, and the Pacific Variety Hall, in addition to Butler's Melodeon. He shared the stage with such bygone luminaries as Joseph Murphy, who went west with the Forty-niners, soon became known as the greatest bones soloist among minstrels, and ultimately amassed a fortune of $3,000,000, more than any stage contemporary of his was thought to have had, or even dreamed about; Maggie Moore, who subsequently settled in Australia, where her husband, J. C. Williamson, became that continent's leading theatrical producer; and Lotta Crabtree, or plain Lotta, the one-time child star, in whose memory a fountain still splashes in San Francisco. In a single evening, Harrigan might be called upon to perform in both blackface and whiteface; to appear as a Swedish servant girl, a Chinese laundryman, and a tough Irish landlord; to dance in clog shoes; to don the conventional chin whiskers and belly pants of a Dutch comedian; and, for the grand minstrel finale, to come out in satin knee britches and tail coat, ruffled shirt front, stockings and slippers, and a kinky-wool wig. These multiple demands furnished him, of course, with invaluable training as an actor. He was also frequently called on to write sketches, as the more literate actors were matter-of-factly expected to do wherever they were engaged. He came to think of it as no Herculean accomplishment to turn out, week after week, sketches with titles like "Irish Comicalities," "Jessie at the Bar," and "The Finnegans." This last inspired one of his colleagues, whose name has eluded history, to come up with a sketch of his own entitled "Finnegan's Wake."

Harrigan never wielded a calking iron again. The switch from oakum to hokum was permanent. Between engagements in San Francisco, he played Sacramento and a host of mining towns in California and Nevada—Dutch Flat, Gold Ridge, Angels Camp, Hangtown, Silver City, Jackass Hill, Fiddletown, Celestial, and Virginia City among them. Few of these communities had theatres. Companies of actors passing through them would put on a show under any roof that was available, in some cases a school building, in others an empty store or saloon. It was a precarious way of life. These impromptu auditoriums were in many cases constructed in large part out of cloth and paper, and fire was a constant threat. The actors, moreover, were rarely on salary. They generally split up an evening's take, if there was anything to split. The miners who comprised their audiences were men of strong opinions and impulsive reactions. If they liked a show, they would fling nuggets of gold at the stage, sometimes considerately embedding these gratuities in apples, so that any actor struck by a flying nugget would not be injured. If they disliked a show, they were not above bombarding the stage with low-value stones that they threw unpadded.

When welcome rewards were forthcoming, the actors would often pause in the recital of their lines long enough to crawl about the stage on their hands and knees feverishly harvesting fruit. When a performance was less felicitously received, the actors had to scramble with equal energy to find enough to eat. One time, after Harrigan had managed to round up a dollar or so and had ordered his first square meal in several days, he noticed a down-and-out prospector observing him with such piteous hunger that he invited the man to share his feast. In New York, long afterward, a corpulent fellow came around to Harrigan's stage door, identified himself as the beneficiary of this treat, and asked Harrigan if he remembered the incident. "Of course I remember it," replied Harrigan. "You're the guy who ate all the potatoes."

Another time, Harrigan found himself in such straits that he was prepared to give up his banjo to obtain the wherewithal to eat. Having determined to make this grave sacrifice, he entered a gambling joint, where he had the good fortune, or good sense, to approach a man whose luck was flourishing. Harrigan sidled up to him and inquired politely if he would care to buy a second-hand banjo, in playable shape. The gambler didn't shift his glance from the gaming table. Without uttering a word, he picked up a stack of double eagles—the six-sided twenty-dollar gold pieces then in circulation—and handed them over. Then he waved away the proffered banjo. Harrigan never learned this philanthropist's name, having been too dazed and too famished at the moment of incurring his bounty to try to ascertain it. Twenty years

later, when he himself was well-heeled, he resolved to
pay the man back if he could. By that time, Frank James,
Jesse's brother, had reformed and was honorably employed
as a doorkeeper at the Standard Theatre in St. Louis.
On the theory that the James boys were widely acquainted
in gambling circles, Harrigan, while passing through
Missouri on a road tour, commissioned Frank to track
down the benefactor, but James never did get his man.

Harrigan was completely independent of his father by
now, but on one occasion, while he was playing Virginia
City with a partner named Alex O'Brien, the fact that
he was William Harrigan's son got him out of a nasty
predicament. Actors had long been having trouble in Virginia City. Several years before, the whole profession had
been held in low repute there, and had been ruthlessly
picked on by the local papers. This had resulted from the
papers' being deprived, for a while, of all theatrical advertising, and *that* had resulted from Mark Twain's kick-
ing Adah Menken's dog. Twain was the editor of the
Territorial Enterprise when Miss Menken blew into Virginia City with her celebrated Mazeppa act, in which,
seemingly half-naked in flesh-colored tights, she careened
about the stage tied to the back of a prancing horse. The
actress's dog bit Twain, Twain kicked the dog, Miss Menken got sore, the manager of the theatre she was appearing
in stopped advertising in the *Enterprise,* and the *Enterprise* got mad at all theatre people. It was a vicious circle,
and a vicious dog, too.

Harrigan and O'Brien were about to retire for the night
in their second-story room above a saloon when a be-
devilled husband of the neighborhood chose to assassinate
his wife's lover across the hall. The actors were the only

witnesses, and some friends of the slayer's, later that evening, elected to dispatch them, too, to forestall any troublesome testimony that might ensue. Breaking into the actors' room, guns poised, they shone a light on the young men's faces.

"Hold on!" one of the intruders said. "This one here looks like someone I know. You couldn't be Bill Harrigan's son, could you, kid?"

Harrigan nervously, but gratefully, acknowledged the relationship.

"Leave 'em alone," said the man to his companions, and, to Harrigan, as he was departing, he said, "Tell your old man Oily Jimmy sends his regards."

Harrigan realized then who his savior was. It was an exile from Cork Row in New York who, wanted there for a couple of murders, had prudently removed himself to the even less law-abiding West. Years later, Harrigan received a message backstage in Manhattan one night, scribbled on the margin of a theatre program. "Can I see you?" it said, and it was signed "Oily Jimmy."

The criminal, it developed, had gone straight and needed a job. Harrigan knew what to do about that. He called on his friend Thomas Byrnes, Chief Inspector of Police in New York.

"Could you use a man who knows every crook west of the Mississippi?" Harrigan asked.

Byrnes had been having trouble with transients, and expressed warm interest. Oily Jimmy was soon taken on the force as a detective.

Alex O'Brien, a comedian and dancer, was the first of two partners with whom Harrigan worked out west. Billed

as Harrigan and O'Brien, they played a lot of mining
centers together, and also several San Francisco engagements. But O'Brien was a notable lush—or, as the species
was then sometimes known, lushington—even in an era
when hard drinking was commonplace, Father Mathew
notwithstanding. The collaboration of Harrigan and
O'Brien foundered in San Francisco when O'Brien got
so out of hand that Harrigan felt obliged to commit him
to a home for inebriates. He carted him there on an open
wagon, holding him down by sitting on his stomach, while
O'Brien howled and kicked so vigorously in protest that
a crowd of spectators quickly assembled along their line
of march, cheering them on gruesomely by waving flags
and singing patriotic songs.

Having delivered O'Brien to his asylum, Harrigan repaired at once to a saloon, to compose himself, and there
fell in with another actor at loose ends, Sam Rickey,
whom he had met at Butler's Melodeon some months
before while they were both employed in a minstrel show.
They resolved to pair up. Harrigan made this decision
despite the fact that Rickey was a notoriously carefree
fellow whose devotion to and capacity for alcohol eclipsed
O'Brien's. Rickey's press notices were to include such
dubious tributes as "the truest type of Bohemian known
to the stage" and "a career of terrible dissipation." During his career, he got to Australia at one point, and there
his habits were so unrestrained even by the standards of
that soggy continent that some friends of his mercifully
contrived to have him imprisoned for a month, hoping
the experience would sober him up. After a couple of
weeks, the friends stopped in to see how he was coming
along. They found the jail awash with liquor Rickey had

had smuggled in, and not only was he contentedly besotted, but so were all the other inmates and the warden,
too.

Rickey, who began acting in the early sixties at Pioche,
Nevada, had been born Richard T. Higgins, but like
many other theatrical people of his time had assumed a
professional name. Nowadays stage folk do this mostly
for euphony; a century ago they did it less for that reason
than because their calling was not in terribly high repute
and they wished not to inflict discredit on their families.
Thus, George Washington Sloan became, for professional
purposes, George S. Knight; an O'Flaherty cloaked himself as Stuart, a Sheridan as Fredericks, a Thomas as
Lingard, and Higgins as Rickey. A few years older than
Harrigan, Sam Rickey had been a drummer boy in the
New York militia, and during the Civil War was a bugler
in a cavalry regiment. Harrigan thought he was the funni-
est man he had ever seen on stage, and other contemporaries of Rickey's acclaimed him as the greatest Irish
comedian of them all. Not only did he excel in both Irish
and German dialects, but he was an uncommonly gifted
dancer. He had a quick, jerky stride and a peculiar way
of throwing back his head when he rendered a song—
mannerisms that Harrigan borrowed from him and that
became an integral part of *his* professional technique.

Harrigan and Rickey, calling themselves the Noted
California Comedians, worked together until 1871. Their
principal offering was *The Little Frauds,* a German-
dialect sketch built around a song called "Little Fraud,"
that concerned a baker boy and his coquettish *Fräulein.*
For six years after they parted company, Rickey continued to be featured on variety bills around the country,

sometimes appearing in sketches he had written—presumably out of his own experience—entitled "Bad Whiskey" and "Taking the Pledge." But ultimately he became too irresponsible for managers to take a chance on, and for several years he wandered the streets of New York as a bum, cadging handouts from actors he knew. He died in 1885 at the Wards Island Charity Hospital, where in his final delirium he alternately hummed snatches of "Little Fraud" and reminisced about the Battle of Chickamauga. The only vehicle to follow the hearse in his funeral procession was Harrigan's coach.

The last spike of the transcontinental railroad was hammered in place in 1869. The fare from San Francisco to New York, a seven-day journey, was $140 in currency, or $116.50 in gold. Neither of the Noted California Comedians had anywhere near that amount of capital in any form, but they decided to work their way east along the tracks, earning their fare from depot to depot, if they could, by playing engagements wherever the train stopped. They took with them a third man, Otto Burbank, a veteran actor who had played in England and Australia, and had toured all over the United States with Griffin & Christy's Minstrels. At times, the trio found the response to their brand of culture so tepid that they were compelled to make several eastward hops in cattle cars. Once, when they were embarrassed for cash and Rickey was powerfully thirsty, they pawned one of the only three pairs of pants they had among them. They took turns wearing the remaining two, a system that worked out fine until Burbank, assigned the mission of ferrying Harrigan's pants to Rickey one evening while Harrigan was at a theatre and Rickey at a boarding house, disappeared with both pairs. Rickey, unfazed, made his way to the theatre wrapped in a blanket, and from the evening's proceeds both men were able to purchase new trousers. It took them five months to cross the country, but they finally made it, and on November 21, 1870, they presented *The Little Frauds* in New York at the Globe Theatre, at 728 Broadway. The attainment of their goal, a New York engagement, inspired Rickey to reach unprecedented heights of insobriety, and Harrigan reluctantly bade him good-bye, got a job with Manning's Minstrels, and once more headed west.

6.

HARRIGANANDHART

A century ago, variety artists were even less inclined than their successors are today to be independent performers. Travelling about the country, as they frequently had to do, it was pleasant to have company; it was equally pleasant on stage, where it often proved to be true that two mouths could contrive to be better fed together than either one could by itself. There were, to be sure, successful single acts, like those of Alfred Miller, the Great Gum-Elastic Man; James Messenger, the Unrivalled Cannon-Ball Performer; and Herr Schulze, The Man with the 100 Faces, who, eschewing costumes and make-up and using only lights and shadows, did take-offs of all the popular beard styles of that bristly era and of Charles Dickens, the Prince of Wales, the Crown Prince of Prussia, a Drunk, and a Teetotaller; and whose impersonations also included "the Choleric, the Sanguine, the Learned, the Stupid, the Glutton, the Miser, the Proud, the Humble, the Misanthrope, the Hypocrite, and Divided Feelings—or to laugh and cry at the same time."

Herr Schulze and a contemporary of his who earned his living by doing somersaults on a revolving globe had no need of companionship on stage, though they may have been lonely in boarding houses. A great many vaudevillians, however, found it easier to obtain engagements in tandem. A case in point was that of two actors who for many years played with Harrigan and Hart—John G. Sparks, who classified himself professionally as a "character comedian," and Joseph M. Sparks, the more prominent of the pair, who was the only actor Harrigan would permit to understudy his parts and who called *himself* a "character dialect singing comedian."

In 1877, John Sparks, a native of Hartford, was employed at Owney Geogheghan's, a saloon at 103 Bowery that was one of the scurviest joints along that extensive and crowded avenue. It was a hangout much esteemed by unprincipled beggars, who knew they could discard their superfluous smoked glasses and crutches in that understanding environment, and it was so regularly the scene of gang brawls that Geogheghan, a thoughtful host, kept a large supply of police clubs on hand, to pass out among his steady patrons in the event of a skirmish. (This disorderly tradition was maintained right up to and throughout Owney's funeral, a ceremony enlivened by the presence of two Mrs. Geogheghans, each of whom, unaware until then of the existence of the other, sought to assume what she thought was her rightful spot in the funeral procession. All the way from the Bowery to Calvary Cemetery, two hacks bearing the rival widow Geogheghans jockeyed for a position directly behind the hearse, while their tearful occupants exchanged ringing maledictions.)

Sparks' duties at Geogheghan's consisted of serving drinks, dancing jigs on the sanded floor, and putting on the gloves with any patron who wanted to fight and who didn't outweigh him by too palpably much. He found this job taxing, and decided to seek employment on the stage. But whenever he went around to talk to a variety-house manager, he would at once be asked who his partner was, would have to confess shamefacedly that he didn't have any, and would find himself back at Geogheghan's, absorbing leather. Presently he caught on, and when the proprietor of the Volks Garden, a few blocks away, inquired whether he belonged to a team, he answered affirmatively. What team?, the manager persisted. "The Sparks Brothers!" the applicant replied on the spur of the moment. He was provisionally hired, the only stipulation being that he turn up with his brother. Not having one, he did the next best thing. He scurried up to Hartford, got hold of a bricklayer there named Michael J. Hennessey who hankered to be a character dialect singing comedian and had taken part in amateur theatricals, and prevailed on him to become his brother Joe. They made out fine from then on.

When Harrigan, as one of Manning's Minstrels, arrived in Chicago in the summer of 1871, he was equally anxious to find himself a partner. The fact that both Alex O'Brien and Sam Rickey had been rather unstable associates didn't deter him; he had been happier working with them than as just another member of a touring minstrel troupe, or even than as—to cite one eulogy pinned on him by a theatre where he did a solo act in the spring of 1871 —"the great Dutch comedian." While Harrigan, then twenty-six, was having his shoes shined in Chicago one afternoon, he bumped into a sixteen-year-old singer who was also looking for a partner. They joined forces at once, and for the next fourteen years their fortunes were so intimately tied up that Harrigan's children were to grow up thinking there was a peculiar word in the English language called "Harriganandhart."

The boy Harrigan ran into at the shoeshine parlor had been known professionally for several years as Master Antonio, a name that had been thrust upon him by a theatre manager in Providence, Rhode Island, a community that has long had a thriving Italian colony. His real name was Anthony J. Cannon. Born in Worcester, Massachusetts on July 25, 1855, he was one of five children—two boys and three girls—of Anthony Cannon and his wife, née Mary Sweeney. Both the Cannons were Irish immigrants from County Mayo. The father was a laborer who, after his son Tony became successful, retired and lived to be ninety-three, ascribing his longevity to whiskey. He had a rich, unadulterated brogue, and an uninhibited way of sizing up people and situations—a trait that endeared him to Harrigan and Hart, who would walk around New York with him and take careful note, for subsequent use on stage, of his comments on the passing scene.

One time early in their career together, Harrigan and

Hart were momentarily at liberty. Hart decided to take advantage of the lull and visit his family in Worcester. Harrigan, in New York, got the team a booking a couple of days later, and sent a telegram, addressing Tony by his real name, to the Cannon family home. But Hart, a man of incorrigibly unpredictable habits, had stopped off en route without telling anybody. The message addressed to "Anthony Cannon" was, accordingly, received and opened by the senior Anthony Cannon. "Come to town immediately. Ned," it read. Tony's father, having no idea his son was supposed to be there, could make no sense out of this admonition and threw the wire away. Two days later, Harrigan sent a second telegram. "We open, Tony, on Monday," it said. "Why don't you come? Ned." Again the senior Cannon got it. Along the way, Western Union had dropped the commas. The elder Hart was a man of limited education, who had little use for commas, explicit or implicit, and the next thing Harrigan knew his partner's father had arrived in New York, red-eyed and swathed in black, to attend what he confidently expected to be his son's wake.

The only repute the junior Anthony Cannon attained as a youngster was that of a thoroughly bad boy. At the precocious age of nine, he announced that he was giving up school for the stage. His parents, who considered the theatre a dreadful environment even for grown-up children of, say, thirteen or fourteen, threatened to put him in a state reformatory, a few miles outside of Worcester at Westborough, but this prospect was not enough to make him recant or reform. By the age of ten, he was the terror—for his size—of the neighborhood, and the kindest reminiscence any of his neighbors could think of in after years about his behavior during this period was, "He was up to all sorts of jokes." One sort of joke he engineered was pulled during a performance of a melodrama that Tony staged in a neighbor's barn. He wanted to play the leading character, who was a thief and whom the boy thought himself eminently suited to portray. But a boy whose father owned the barn wanted the main part, too, and property rights prevailed. Tony found himself in a minor role, that of a sheriff whose only big moment came toward the end of the show, when he was called upon to pretend to hang the leading man. Tony became more and more resentful of his relative insignificance as the action progressed, and when he got to the hanging scene and had his neighbor securely strung up, he vengefully kicked out a soap box that the leading man, in the interests of safety, had specified must remain beneath his feet. The object of Tony's ire was on the point of strangling when the victim's father rushed into the barn and saved him. The Cannons were quickly apprised of their son's mischievousness, and a few days later they shipped him regretfully to Westborough.

Reform schools were raw institutions in those days. The word "rehabilitation" was practically unheard of. Around the time Tony matriculated at Westborough, that institution came under the scrutiny of the state authorities. Their interest had been aroused by a recital of abuses made by visitors to the place. One man declared that after he had heard a boy in an adjoining room whimper, "Don't whip me," he had then counted forty-six distinct and audible blows, which it developed had been delivered by a thick leather strap eighteen inches long. The superintendent of the reformatory declared that his institution was no more strictly administered than many an ordinary school, and that besides he and his assistants were obliged to resort from time to time to defensive measures; just a while previous, he noted, one of his charges had proposed splitting a staff member's head open with a brick. The superintendent promised, however, to keep corporal punishment within bounds; a week after this avowal, a boy who had inadvertently spoken a word in the yard during what was supposed to be a silent period was whacked so soundly that his skin was torn off in twenty spots. It was understandable that Tony found this atmosphere uncongenial. Fortunately for him, the administration, while severe in some respects, was lax in others, and after languishing there several months, he slipped through an unguarded portal one night and, with all his worldly goods wrapped in the conventional handkerchief, hiked to Boston.

By earning a few pennies here and there as a singer, bootblack, and newsboy, Tony soon got to New York, stopping off at Providence long enough to be named "Master Antonio." He sang and danced in saloons for a while, being paid, or not, as the whims of the patrons dictated. Then he was taken on by a touring circus as a lemonade boy. This struck him as an eminent opportunity for theatrical advancement, since like all eleven-year-old boys he had a highly romantic concept of circus life. The circus taught him how to make ice-cold lemonade with neither lemons nor ice. But he was soon disillusioned, not merely by that discovery but by becoming aware that even the stars of the outfit led such a marginal existence that they had to cook their own meals. He quit the circus, and shortly afterward was hired by Billy Arlington's Minstrels, with whom he travelled from place to place until, in 1870, at a rather mature fifteen years of age, he hooked up with another touring company that was known as Madame Rentz's Female Minstrels.

This organization, while it did have some females among its personnel who engaged in minstrelsy—a trade deemed so unseemly for women that some theatres would rather stay dark than permit a female-minstrel troupe to illume their stage—had no Madame Rentz. It had got its name simply because its boss, an ex-partner of Tony Pastor's named M. B. Leavitt, had hoped to capitalize thereby on the international renown of a European circus called Rentz's. Leavitt was charmed, as Arlington and other entrepreneurs had been before him, by the appealing, delicate façade that sheathed Master Antonio's tough inner core. He looked like an innocent cherub, he was the soul of affability, and he had a marvelously sweet voice. He also had one special song, a sad, sentimental number entitled "Put Me in My Little Bed," that he could deliver in incomparably touching fashion. Dressed as a cute little girl, tripping daintily on stage, he would dip a curtsy or two and go into his act. By the time he was through, according to Leavitt's presumably authentic memoirs, his audiences would be bathed in tears.

Master Antonio stayed with Madame Rentz's Female Minstrels until, in the summer of 1871, they fetched up in Peoria, Illinois. In the troupe's hotel there, he was assigned to share a room with a selfish musician. The management had provided only one towel for the two of them, and the musician, grabbing it first, dirtied it all up. When his roommate went to wash up, he became aware of this untidy state of affairs, and resourcefully fashioned himself a towel by cutting a couple of square feet off a clean white counterpane in the chamber. The management, on finding this out, said nothing to the occupants of the room but added $5 to the troupe's bill for the mutilated spread. Leavitt, in turn, said nothing but deducted $5 from the boy's pay. Master Antonio said nothing, either, but at the next town, Galesburg, he quietly decamped and went to Chicago, where he had his shoes shined and met up with Ned Harrigan.

Tony had seen Harrigan and Rickey do *The Little Frauds* when their professional paths had crossed that of Arlington's Minstrels, and Ned had sniffled through Tony's "Put Me in My Little Bed." It was quickly agreed by both of them that Tony would make an ideal *Fräulein* in Harrigan's sketch. Harrigan soon got them an engagement at a Chicago establishment he had played in with Rickey. This was the Winter Garden, which, despite its elegant name, was actually a bleak and cramped auditorium on the third floor of a dilapidated office building. The ground-floor tenant was a quack doctor who periodically quarrelled with his landlord. When he did, he would express his wrath by spraying a hose on the stairs leading up to the Winter Garden, making the ascent to it so slippery and perilous that performances would have to be cancelled. The doctor was in a benevolent mood when the new team got set to make its debut, so the actors didn't have to worry about him. They were worried, though, about how to bill themselves. Harrigan's name, they felt, should come first, since he was the older. (Throughout their partnership, Tony called Ned "Governor.") But they didn't like the sound of "Harrigan and

Cannon." They were mulling over this predicament one afternoon while descending from the third-floor loft along satisfyingly dry treads, in the company of a musician they'd been rehearsing with. As the three men left the building, a panhandler approached them. The sixteen-year-old boy gave him a dollar, and his friends were much impressed.

"Say, you sure got a big heart," the musician muttered.

"That's the word for you, Tony!" exclaimed Harrigan. "Hart! Tony Hart! Harrigan and Hart!"

Calling themselves The Nonpareils, Harrigan and Hart headed back east and decided to try their luck in Boston. They got a spot there on the opening bill of the season at the Howard Athenaeum, then one of the city's leading variety houses and destined later to become, as the Old Howard, New England's controversial citadel of burlesque. Like most variety houses of the time, the Athenaeum was patronized exclusively by men. Practically the only women in the audience, aside from a few patently unrefined types, were waitresses who served whiskey. (It was Tony Pastor who finally succeeded in breaking down the resistance of refined ladies to this form of entertainment, and he did it only by appealing to their possessive instincts and offering them bonbons, dolls, flowers, bags of coffee and of flour, sacks of coal, sewing machines, silk dresses, hams, and hats—in addition to free admission.) The Nonpareils were so unheralded when they made their debut at the Athenaeum, on August 14th, that the theatre program described them as "Harringan and Hart." They scored a big success. Booked initially for two weeks, they were held over for nearly two months, and their starting joint weekly pay of $75 was doubled.

Within less than two more years, they were to reach the $250 salary bracket, just about the top for any pair of vaudevillians of the period.

The pay that most actors got then was, by twentieth-century standards, niggardly. An accomplished, experienced performer might receive as little as $25 a week, and an impressively billed leading man no more than $50 or $75. But the really big stars of the era fared much better. Francis S. Chanfrau had earned $200,000 from his *Mose* plays. Edwin Booth and Joseph Jefferson were demanding, and getting, as much as $600 a performance. (While touring in Boucicault's *Rip Van Winkle,* Jefferson for a time had an agent who, at the end of the first act, would march into the box-office and scoop $600 from the till, even if the till held no more than $601. If by any chance it held less, the agent would previously have advised the management, there might very well be no second act.) John Brougham had the gout from eating too much expensive food. Perhaps the fanciest liver of them all was Joseph Kline Emmett, an American of Irish descent who made a fortune as a German-dialect comedian. From the proceeds of a succession of shows relating the adventures of a lovable buffoon called "Fritz," Emmett bought an $80,000 estate that he occupied only six weeks a year, gave his wife $100,000 as a birthday present, and paid $5,000 for a champion Saint Bernard. Emmett thought the first two litters sired by this dog were inferior specimens of the breed, so he shot the lot of them, even though a less fussy fancier had offered him $1,500 for a single puppy. (Emmett's son and namesake, also an actor, was subsequently prevented from shooting his own wife on a San Francisco street when an eight-year-old girl took his gun out of his hand.) When the senior Emmett went on tour, usually accompanied by his wife and at least one superior Saint Bernard, he would stride up to hotel desk clerks and throw down on the counter before them his calling card, which had inscribed on it, "The best of everything is not too good."

The Athenaeum was under the management of John Stetson, an entrepreneur celebrated for a fiery temper, a mistrusting nature, and a magnificent ego. (He once sent a company out west, under the supervision of a man named Sharp, whom he suspected of being too big for his britches. Stetson subsequently went to Chicago to check up on his deputy. He found the troupe playing in a theatre that bore a sign outside saying, "Matinee 2 Sharp." Enraged, Stetson had it altered to read "Matinee 2 Stetson.") Stetson was pleased with the crowds Harrigan and Hart were attracting to the theatre, but he was quite put out to learn that they had received several offers to play in New York and Chicago and were minded to accept one of these. Resolving that if he couldn't have them, nobody would, he tipped off the reform-school authorities to the fact that Tony Hart of The Nonpareils was none other than Anthony Cannon, still carried on their roster as a runaway.

The reformatory didn't much care if it never saw the boy again, but now that the issue had been raised it felt constrained, in the interests of law and order, to retrieve him, and it applied for a court order directing that he be restored to its custody. A hearing was held. Hart, who was barely sixteen, was at first for trying to win over the judge presiding, a man of Celtic origins himself, by singing "Put Me in My Little Bed" to him, but he was persuaded by Harrigan to let the team's senior partner do a solo act. Harrigan did practically everything except sing and dance. He told the judge that Tony had always been a dacent boy at heart, as anyone could tell merely by glancing at that innocent young face; that the lad would shure never have got into a jam in the first place if it hadn't been that his parents—through no malevolence, God bless their kind old Irish souls, but merely due to a certain lack of sophistication—had fallen somewhat short of a sympathetic comprehension of the honorable, venerable profession of acting; that the boy had just got started on what bade fair to be a long and prosperous and praise-worthy career that was certain to bring merriment and mirth and maybe even a refreshing tear or two to count-less hard-working citizens in search of an evening's respite from their cares; and that he himself, as an older man of irreproachable deportment, would personally vouch for young Cannon's good conduct thereafter. "I will make a man of him, and the reformatory will not," summed up the twenty-six-year-old Harrigan in a voice quivering with emotion.

"Take him along with you," the judge told him.

Harrigan and Hart elected to strike out for New York, and they opened at the Brooklyn Academy of Music on October 9th, an event that got pretty much lost in the shuffle, owing to the public's greater concern over the Chicago fire, which had occurred the day before. Still, the actors would undoubtedly have been much worse off if they had picked Chicago. After a week at the Academy of Music, they moved on to New York City. (Brooklyn was then not a part of New York City. It was simply Brooklyn.) They appeared at the Theatre Comique, at

514 Broadway just south of Spring Street, which had not long before come under the proprietorship of Josh Hart. One of the shrewdest variety managers in the country, Josh Hart was also active as a journalist. He was publisher of the *Dramatic News,* a gossipy weekly that came out for several years during the seventies, and of *Truth,* a not terribly veracious weekly of the eighties, whose chief historical distinction may be that Howe & Hummel were listed as members of its editorial staff. There was a newsy flavor to many of Josh Hart's theatrical ventures. At the time Harrigan and Hart came under his aegis, he was feverishly making arrangements for a timely sketch—he put it on early in 1872—with the encyclopedic title of "Chicago, Before the Fire, During the Fire, and After the Fire." A feature of this panoramic spectacle was the presence on stage of a genuine, steam-emitting steam engine, a small-scale facsimile of the engine that, immediately after the fire, had hauled to Chicago a trainload of emergency provisions dispatched to its charred inhabitants by Jim Fisk.

At the Theatre Comique, Harrigan and Hart presently fell in with a plethora of other two-man acts, many of whose members were eventually absorbed into their company—Goss & Fox, Tierney & Cronin, Queen & West, Diamond & Ryan, Barry & Fay, Quilter & Goldrich, Foley & Schaeffer, the Sparks Brothers, and Wild & Gray. Of all these, the most memorable combination was that of Johnny Wild and Billy Gray, as gifted a pair of Negro impersonators as their time could boast. In Harrigan's plays about the Mulligans and their environment, Gray was regularly cast as the Reverend Palestine Puter, chaplain of the Skidmore Guards (after becoming *au courant* with Molière, Harrigan was immensely pleased when one critic described Puter as "a colored Tartuffe"), and Wild as Simpson Primrose, the barber, who would stand for no nonsense from white folks and said, when asked to advise a lady what refreshments she should serve at a bon-voyage party, "Tell her t'order free dozen quarts of 'Promroy Sec' fo' de intellectual French an' colored people. Let de Dutch an' Irish drink whiskey. We'll hab wine!" Gray, born Cornelius O'Donnell in Philadelphia, was an alumnus of Bryant's Minstrels, and had a relatively short career. When he died in 1882, he was only thirty-eight. His talent for mimicry was so outstanding that Harrigan acclaimed him the best actor who ever appeared in his company, and gave weight to this evaluation by juxtaposing, on a wall of his home, identically framed portraits of Billy Gray and Edwin Forrest, whom Harrigan rated high among actors who had *not* been in his company.

In the popular mind, however, Gray was overshadowed by Wild. Like the majority of actors who portrayed the immigrant families in the Harrigan and Hart shows, Wild was an immigrant himself, if by a narrow margin. He came to the United States from his birthplace, Manchester, England, in 1844, when he was a year old. He was prominent on Broadway for thirty years, and among his fellow players was regarded as a unique specimen of off-stage uprightness. He was a notable family man, for one thing, having ten children. For another, he was conservative about money; before he was forty, he had saved enough to buy a 130-acre farm near Albany, which, with a sober eye on retirement, he christened "Idlewild." What was still more, he was exceptionally studious; from 1852 on, the year *Uncle Tom's Cabin* first came out in book form, he read that stimulating volume at least once every six months.

By the public, Wild was recognized as one of the first actors to have depicted a Negro on stage in any other fashion than as a shuffling, slack-jawed, bug-eyed, superstitious, dim-witted ne'er-do-well. Along with Simpson Primrose, Harrigan created for him many other roles patterned after the urbane, self-assured, and sometimes prosperous Negroes who in the late nineteenth century dwelt just below Washington Square. Their type had never been seen on the stage before, and Wild capitalized on the innovation. A typical role of his was that of Esau Coldslaw, in *The Last of the Hogans*. Coldslaw was a Bleecker Street faro dealer as well as a church deacon and the big wheel in a social club called the Knights of the Mystic Star. ("Our aim am to lift de ignorant savage of Africa into de sunshine of knowledge.") In the part, Wild, emulating the sartorial customs of South Fifth Avenue, was dazzlingly arrayed in a silk high hat, lemon-yellow gloves, a giant sunflower boutonniere, and a lavish sprinkling of diamond accessories. No matter what kind of Negro he depicted, he was singularly lifelike. "John Wild's Negro is a Negro and not a white man with a charcoaled face," one critic who had been nurtured on minstrel shows observed with grateful respect.

Wild was a handsome man with luxurious mustachios, clean-chiselled features, and a peculiarly droopy set of eyelids, which gave him a sad, spaniel-like expression. He had a trick of focussing his mournful gaze aloft at the gallery, which delighted its occupants no end and made them such slavish disciples of his art that some of his colleagues occasionally referred to him snappishly as

"Gallery-eyed Johnny." His professional career began in 1859, when he was sixteen and was driving a carry-all between Harlem and High Bridge. At the Harlem terminus of his run, one day, he took in a picnic and met Billy Arlington, née Valentine Burnell. Arlington had a banjo with him, and Wild had a yen to do a jig, so they collaborated on an informal divertissement. They got a rousing hand, and Arlington suggested that they pursue further theatrical glory together. Wild said he would discuss the matter with his mother, who, after the seemingly inevitable fashion of all mothers, threw up her hands in horror and told him never to mention the subject again. So *he* ran away. He got hold of Arlington, who had meanwhile recruited a magician named White to swell their ranks. As "White and Arlington's Minstrels," the three of them set forth to traverse the country. It was one of the most circumscribed tours in the history of the theatre. It began in Tuckahoe and foundered one week later in Mount Vernon, less than five miles away.

Wild returned contritely to his mother, but then Arlington reappeared with fresh blood, a smooth-talking song-and-dance man named Oscar Searles, who gave an irresistible account of the profits that were waiting to be reaped in upstate New York. While his mother's attention was distracted, Wild took off again. Arlington and Searles and he had played two fairly profitable weeks in that promised hinterland when, somewhere in the vicinity of Schenectady, Searles absconded with the profits. Wild bummed his way back to New York and vowed to his mother he would never again set foot on any stage. A few weeks later Searles stopped by, begging forgiveness, though pleading poverty. By way of redeeming himself, he told Wild about a three-dollar-a-week opportunity as a song-and-dance man at the Art Union, a modest institution at Broadway and Broome Street. Wild was undone by this mention of hard cash, took the job, and for the next dozen years toiled in a vast number of variety houses, circuses, minstrel units, and carnivals, until he finally hitched up with Billy Gray and checked in at Josh Hart's Theatre Comique.

It was indicative of the high opinion Harrigan and Hart had of Wild that after they became their own bosses, and he became one of their hired hands, they made a polite gesture to ensure that he would stand alone at the head of their payroll. Normally, the top salary they gave anyone was $150 a week; Wild's salary was $151. This discrepancy now and then peeved their leading lady, Annie Yeamans, a $150-a-week performer who was mainly cast in what were known as "eccentric-old-woman parts." Mrs. Yeamans had a rubbery face that lent itself beautifully to mugging, a kind of acting in which she was unexcelled. A critic for the New York *World* once declared, "Mrs. Yeamans is as much an artist in her own particular way as Duse, absurd as it may seem to use the name of the Italian tragedienne in this instance," and added, "Harrigan is admirable as Dan Mulligan. His impersonation is flawless." Three days after this was printed, another critic for another New York paper, the *Sunday Mercury,* demonstrated that he read the *World* trustingly, if carelessly, when *he* declared, "Mr. Harrigan's impersonation of Dan Mulligan . . . is absolutely flawless. His art is as true as that of Mme. Duse."

In 1872, when Mrs. Yeamans first performed with Har-

rigan and Hart, she was only thirty-seven, but in experience she was old enough to be their mother. (In point of
fact, she was old enough to be Hart's mother regardless
of experience.) She was a native of the Isle of Man, but
had travelled a most non-insular course for a Manx-
woman or anybody else, having already performed in
Australia, China, Japan, Java, Malaya, and all over the
United States. Her father was an opera singer named
William Griffiths, who took her to Australia in 1845, when
she was ten. She went on the stage with him right away,
and for six years performed with a mercurial travelling
company that changed its program every night, shifting
from grand opera to farce or Shakespeare or vaudeville,
according to the mood of its manager. They journeyed
over broad stretches of desert from one rural settlement
to another by horse cart, living in tents, carrying their
own water, cooking over open fires, and subsisting largely
on mutton. They would buy a sheep from time to time,
consume its edible parts as they moved along, and, when
they had polished it off, buy another sheep. Their audiences were composed mostly of miners, some of whom
hadn't seen a white woman for a year or more. A good
many of the miners had hit it rich, but were puzzled as to
what to do with their money. They chewed one-pound
notes, in affected disdain of tobacco or gum; and they
bought champagne by the case and then grandly cracked
open the bottles without bothering to remove the corks.
The sight of a handsomely costumed young woman in her
early teens electrified them; after almost every performance, some miner or other would come around and offer
Annie's father a sack or two of gold if he would give his
daughter in marriage the following day.

Resisting these blandishments, the girl remained true to her profession, but when she was sixteen she switched to J. H. Rowe's American Circus, which was also touring Australia, and as a member of which she became an adept wire-walker and equestrienne. That same year, she succumbed to the relatively humdrum suit of an American in the outfit, Edward Yeamans, a clown and acrobat. She married him, and within the next ten years they had three daughters, Lydia, Emily, and Jennie, all of whom were to belong in later years to the Harrigan and Hart entourage. Jennie made her stage debut at two in Australia, and mainly because of this precocious start, was known for much of her adult career as Little Jennie Yeamans. For a while she was married to Charles Dillingham, the producer. Lydia, who ultimately ended up as a music-hall singer in England, and Emily, who became known as an especially good Samaritan because of her penchant for taking underprivileged newsboys on summer excursions to Coney Island, were twin Topsys in the first Double-Tom company to interpret *Uncle Tom's Cabin*. They were coached by Jennie, a veteran single Topsy before she was ten.

Mrs. Yeamans left Emily and Lydia in Australia with their grandparents during much of their childhood, and with her husband and Jennie joined another American circus, Dick Risley's, which had an ambitious itinerary that took in Batavia, Singapore, Hong Kong, Peking, and Yokohama. The Yeamanses survived a cholera epidemic in Shanghai, but were stranded in Yokohama when the circus disbanded. But they found another circus there; it had some props and a few animals, and lacked only performers. Aside from a couple of hired Japanese hands,

the Yeamans family constituted the entire personnel. The
father tumbled and joked, the daughter danced and sang,
and the mother did trick horseback riding, walked the
slack and the taut wire, acted a half dozen parts in a
dramatic interlude, and, at the termination of the regular
program, tended an after-theatre bar. The nomadic clan
turned up in San Francisco in 1865, and a year later had
made its way to New York. Ned Yeamans died two years
after that, but his hardy widow went on acting right up to
her death in 1912, living long enough, and remaining versatile enough, to write her own daughters' obituaries for
the papers.

Harrigan and Hart and their principal associates were
usually thought of as an unvarnishedly Irish aggregation,
but there was certainly nothing terribly Celtic about the
origins of either Wild or Mrs. Yeamans. Nor was there—
unless a boyhood apprenticeship to the harp can be counted
—about those of David Braham, whom Harrigan and
Hart also met when they arrived at the Theatre Comique,
where he was conducting the pit orchestra. Braham, like
Wild an Englishman, had the formal, reserved manner
of so many of his tribe. He wouldn't dream of letting the
composition of some rollicking Hibernian schottische delay
his afternoon tea, and his son-in-law, though only six
years his junior and his professional intimate, felt the
need to apologize, while he was courting Braham's
daughter, for calling her father "Dave."

The musical world has known many Brahams, let alone
Brahms. One of them, John Braham, an English tenor
who lived from 1777 to 1856 and may have been a cousin
of Dave Braham's forebears, had a reputation in his time

equal to Caruso's. In Dave's immediate family orbit,
there was practically a musicians' federation of Brahams.
His father was a musician, his brother was a musician,
one of his sons was a musician, and four of his nephews
came to enjoy musical celebrity of a sort in the United
States—John Joseph and Harry, violinists; Albert, a
cornettist; and William, a tympanist. Of the quartet, John
and Harry were the more prominent. John, some of
whose compositions and arrangements have been published
under the title of "Braham's Wandering Fiddler," presided over the pit orchestra at the Boston Museum in
1879 for the first American performance of Gilbert and
Sullivan, a presentation of *H.M.S. Pinafore.* At the
height of the Gilbert and Sullivan craze in this country,
he joined forces with a visiting English impresario to
sponsor Braham and Scanlan's Boston Miniature Ideal
Opera Company, which consisted of 100 child singers who
put on a romping interpretation of the imported operettas.

John collaborated occasionally with Harrigan on songs,
when his Uncle Dave was unavailable. So did Harry
Braham, who became a conductor himself and sometimes
took over for his uncle in the pit at the Comique. Harry's
chief notoriety was cacophonic. In 1880, he was leading
the orchestra at Tony Pastor's theatre when he was
smitten with an eighteen-year-old girl named Helen
Leonard, who was making her stage debut there in *Pinafore.* Helen Leonard shortly became Lillian Russell and
Harry Braham became—rather hastily, since she had
found herself pregnant—the first of her three husbands.
Their child died in infancy, and soon afterward Miss Russell scandalized New York by running off to London with

Edward Solomon, a comic-opera composer. Braham sued her for divorce in 1883, and after his decree came through, Miss Russell married Solomon. Harry Braham was a man of violent temper, and Solomon, by contrast, a fellow of exceptionally mild mien. When a biographical movie about Lillian Russell was being made in 1939, its producers, perhaps feeling that an excessive quantity of husbands might make their subject seem unacceptably flighty, arbitrarily decided to eliminate Harry Braham from the story of her life. They were loath, however, to dispense with his charmingly cyclonic temperament. They solved their dilemma with typical Hollywood resourcefulness by designating gentle Edward Solomon Miss Russell's first husband and endowing him with Braham's volatility.

David Braham, a bespectacled, professorial-looking man with a floppy mustache and, like most of the Brahams, red hair, was born in London in 1838 and lived there until he migrated to the United States at sixteen. In his teens, he was determined to become a professional harpist, but he switched to the violin after a disheartening experience in the English countryside, where, on his way to an engagement, he was curtly informed by a stage-coach driver that he was welcome aboard the vehicle but his bulky instrument was not. He became a talented violinist, but never achieved—nor indeed aspired to—concert stature. He composed most of his songs on the violin, rather than the piano. Sometimes he would cover the wall of a room with music paper, and pace the floor sawing off a new tune, while his son George—in the family tradition, he was a violinist, composer, and conductor himself—

stood to one side and scribbled down the notes his father fiddled.

On arriving in this country, Dave Braham quickly got a job in a New York orchestra that accompanied Pony Moore's Minstrels. In the next few years he led Robinson's Military Band and conducted the pit orchestras at Canterbury Hall and Mechanics Hall. In 1864, he moved along to the Theatre Comique, then called Wood's Theatre, and under the management of William Horace Lingard, a protean man who was an accomplished female impersonator, the lyricist for *Captain Jinks of the Horse Marines,* and, in 1867, the much acclaimed renderer of Lingard's Great Statue Song, a quick-change routine in which, with only a few seconds' pause between metamorphoses, he transformed himself from Mayor John T. Hoffman to Governor Horatio Seymour to Horace Greeley to Benjamin F. Butler to Ulysses S. Grant to President Andrew Johnson.

Popular songs were more often sung by the people a century ago, when mechanical amplification of professional voices had not yet become rampant, than they are today. "The short-lived bits of music, coming and going with the freedom and irresponsibility of wild flowers," Harrigan once wrote in a rather flowery dissertation on music, "helped to lighten the toil of the working people and were, and are now, potent peacemakers at many a gathering where they calm the angry passions of the poor, admitting sunshine into many a darkened life. Virtue, disguised as music, enters the home of poverty, and holds temptation at bay with the gentle weapon called the popular song. Make songs for the poor, and you plant roses

among the weeds." As a composer, Braham had a conspicuously green thumb. In the seventies and eighties, it
would have been a rare experience to stroll past a row
of tenement houses on a summer night without hearing
one or another of his melodies being soothingly intoned
within. Braham never wrote any of the words to his music,
and until Harrigan came along had a flock of collabora-
tors. He composed special numbers for Little Jennie Yeamans when she was a child star, and for Major Tom
Thumb when P. T. Barnum had him on display. In 1874,
before the authors of "Sweet Adeline" were born, Braham
wrote a barroom ditty entitled "You're the Idol of My
Heart." Most, but not all, of his tunes, were original. That
same year, Braham and Harrigan were much criticized in
military circles for turning out "The Regular Army, O!"
an enormously popular tune that spoofed contemporary
recruiting methods and was alleged by one Regular Army
officer, Captain Charles King, a novelist as well as soldier,
to have grievously curtailed enlistments; but actually the
composers had merely appropriated and revised an old
soldier song that troops sniping at the Indians out west
had been chanting themselves for quite some time previous.

Just as Harrigan was frequently to be compared to
Dickens and Molière, so was Braham asserted by his contemporaries to have his special foreign counterparts.
Mozart and Offenbach were most frequently mentioned.
(In unison, Harrigan and Braham were often likened,
by their most ardent fans, to Gilbert and Sullivan. It was
regarded as something of a triumph for the Americans
that in 1879 they got their *Mulligan Guards' Ball* on view

in New York less than a month ahead of the incoming, and in theory hotly competitive, *Pinafore;* and the *Spirit of the Times* was fond of referring to its local answer to the invading Sir Arthur Sullivan as "Sir Dave.") Braham was no less flattered than was Harrigan by such analogies, and he did his best to add weight to them. In 1883, by his choice, the overture preceding one Harrigan and Hart production consisted of nicely blended excerpts from the works of Offenbach (selection from *La Belle Hélène*) and of Braham (quadrille from *McSorley's Inflation*).

In 1859, David Braham married Annie Hanley, an immigrant from Dublin whose father had been an army officer. They had eight children, nearly all of whom, in one way or another, were in due course to take part in Harrigan's theatrical enterprises. Dave, Jr., for instance, played many parts originated by Hart in revivals that Harrigan put on after Tony's death. Young Dave abandoned the stage for farming when, after spending eight solid years in a non-Harrigan play, *Checkers,* he concluded that he had had enough on realizing one night that he had the first act confused with the third. George Braham succeeded his father as Harrigan's musical collaborator. George also exhibited considerable prowess as a walker. Heel-and-toe competitions were prevalent in the seventies and eighties; six-day walking races drew the same crowds to Gilmore's Garden that six-day bicycle races were to draw a couple of generations later to Madison Square Garden. (A popular Harrigan and Hart sketch in 1878 was something called "The Great In-Toe-Natural Walking Match.") When George was in his late teens, Harrigan

would now and then take him to a saloon and supplement
his theatrical earnings by wagering that his boy could
lick anyone in the house in a heel-and-toe sprint to the
next saloon.

George Braham naturally shared in the winnings, but
he found this experience, however profitable, a bit debilitat-
ing. He preferred betting on horse races. This led to serious consequences for him one day in 1891, when *Reilly
and the Four Hundred* was playing. George, then first
violinist in his father's orchestra, was involved in a fiery
romance with a girl in the show, Emma Pollock, whose
rendition of "Maggie Murphy's Home" in it was so universally applauded that it was her theme song ever after.
Miss Pollock had given George a ring as a token of her
affection, he had pawned the ring to bet on the usual sure
thing, and the sure thing had, as usual, faltered. During the
run of *Reilly,* it became Emma's sentimental custom to
stand near the footlights for her big number and smile
fondly down upon her lover. After George had hocked her
ring, he realized that she would undoubtedly notice it was
missing when her gaze took in his moving hands. As the
first chords of "Maggie Murphy's Home" were struck up,
he suddenly doubled over and began playing his violin,
after a fashion, in his lap.

"What's the matter?" whispered his father. "You drunk
or something?"

"Pain in my shoulder," George whispered back. "Can't
raise my arm."

"Fiddlesticks," said his father aptly, gesturing angrily
with his baton. "Pull yourself together and get that fiddle
up."

George stalled, feigning breakbone fever, until the song

was finished. The following afternoon, he cajoled Harrigan into accompanying him on an interminable tour of saloons, and, by walking his legs off, or at any rate his heels and toes, earned enough to reclaim the ring before that evening's delivery of "Maggie Murphy's Home."

The oldest of David Braham's children was Annie Theresa, the future Mrs. Harrigan, who was born in 1860, in Greenwich Village. She grew up to be a handsome woman, slightly heavy-set, but with striking white skin and large black eyes, which gave her a Spanish appearance. She had a paradoxical nature. As a girl she called herself "Sober Annie" and as a woman was called by her family "the Duchess," but despite these intimations of extraordinary gravity, there was a lighthearted streak in her. She liked to play the banjo, with a verve that was far from ducal, and although her husband cared little for horse racing, she generally managed to spend an exhilarating week each summer at Saratoga, where she was often to be found at the track in the company of Lillian Russell, against whom she held no grudge despite Cousin Harry's difficulties. Annie ran the business end of the Harrigan household, signing all the checks, sitting at the head of the table, and carving the fowl; but she forgot all about sending one of her children to school until, when he was nine, a prowling truant officer reminded her of her remissness.

For the most part, though, Annie Harrigan was a serious-minded woman, and was so widely recognized as such that when a member of the Seventh Regiment, during one of that outfit's uninhibited outings to her husband's theatre, ventured to drop a piece of ice down her back, his action was enshrined for a while in the annals of the organization along with other military feats of uncommon daring. Mrs. Harrigan's role in her husband's professional affairs was anything but passive. When one of her sons decided to become an actor at the age of seven, his father started him off at a salary of $10 a week. The boy informed his father one day that he was sorry, but he had just had a proposition from Charles Frohman, at $15 a week, and would have to give notice—unless, of course, the senior Harrigan was prepared to meet this offer.

"Who has inculcated you with these excellent business principles?" Harrigan demanded.

"Mama," said the boy.

Harrigan was accounted astute at casing a house. Peeking at the audience just before curtain time, he could in one swift glance estimate the box-office gross for that performance, his associates believed, within a couple of dollars. They credited his wife with being able to estimate it within a few cents. Backstage, it was conceded that her authority ranked on a par with her husband's, and more than once she gave evidence of ranking first. One time, after a dress rehearsal, an ingenue began to lament that a red-satin gown she had been instructed to wear clashed horribly with some crimson upholstery Harrigan had picked for his stage furniture. Harrigan thought of a simple enough way out of this predicament. He told the girl to turn in her red gown and get fitted the following day for a blue one. The next morning, though, before she could do this, she got a note from Mrs. Harrigan, advising her to sit tight. "I fell in love with the gown you mention and will not have stage settings in red at all," the message said. Overnight, to help the actress out, Annie had had the furniture re-upholstered.

Another time, Mrs. Harrigan had a brief set-to with her

husband's chief property man. It had been this chap's habit, in keeping with the practice of his trade, to charge Harrigan somewhat more for every prop he bought than the stuff had really cost. Harrigan had let him get away with it, but one day Mrs. Harrigan descended upon him, brandishing a bill he had turned in. On examining it closely, she had calculated that he had charged her husband $5 for fifty one-penny whistles. "Every prop man gets his ten per cent, but you mustn't go over that," she told him severely, and added that as punishment for his sins she would—as she did—have the offending document framed, with the pertinent entry underlined in red, and displayed backstage to embarrass him until she was convinced he had permanently mended his grasping ways.

Harrigan had first met Annie Braham shortly after coming to the Theatre Comique, while visiting her father at the composer's home. Annie was twelve then and Ned was twenty-eight. Three years later, Dave Braham and some other friends of his decided it was high time Ned got married. They went to considerable pains to arrange a party at Braham's home and invited a young lady they were sure would make a perfect mate for Harrigan. When their prospect entered, done up like a coryphée, Ned was at first nowhere to be found. His host discovered him a few minutes later, eating bacon and eggs in the kitchen with fifteen-year-old Annie. Harrigan always got on splendidly with younger people. He had teamed up with Tony Hart when Hart was sixteen, and in November, 1876, when *she* was sixteen, he married Annie Braham.

In the early eighteen-seventies, there were a dozen theatres in New York, and several of these were converted church buildings. This fact must have been galling to many of the city's ministers, since they believed in wide separation between church and stage. Henry Ward Beecher, for instance, an exceptionally sophisticated reverend, confessed while orating at a banquet given in Henry Irving's honor at Delmonico's in 1885 that he had never set foot inside a playhouse until two years before, when he was seventy years old. Beecher conceded that he had found the theatre surprisingly inoffensive and that he wished he hadn't waited so long to make its acquaintance.

Many of Beecher's fellow clergymen never conceded anything in their running battle with the stage—except, inferentially, that they found it a mighty handy whipping

159

boy to have available when no other theme for a ringing sermon seized their imagination. So many churchgoers were afraid of offending their ministers by entering a theatre that for a while a number of entrepreneurs, among them P. T. Barnum, labelled the places where they presented shows along with other divertissements "museums," having found that people would cross a threshold thus identified on the theory that they could thereby avoid violating at least the letter, if not the spirit, of what they feared might be divine law. One of the sturdiest irreconcilables of the cloth was the Reverend Thomas de Witt Talmage, who, like Beecher, officiated in Brooklyn, on which they more than any two other mortals were responsible for having had pinned the nickname, "the city of churches." Talmage was something of an actor himself. His sermons were spiced with dramatic flourishes, as were Beecher's, who once enlivened a dissertation against slavery by pretending to auction off from his pulpit a lovely young octoroon girl. But for all Talmage's artful reliance on gestures and rhetoric, he had no use for the profession that employed these devices on weekdays. A chauvinistic Brooklynite, he was partial to describing the city across the East River as "the modern Gomorrah" or "Satan's Circus," and he called the New York stage "the mother of harlots." Sarah Bernhardt took this last personally, and retorted, with comparative restraint, that Talmage was a fool.

Unlike Beecher, too, Talmage *had* been to the theatre at an early age—just once, when he was nineteen. But he excused this lapse from grace as the kind of innocent mistake any youngster might make. In maturity, he vowed that he would never step inside a theatre's portals unless it were to scourge the premises with the torch of salvation.

He urged his flock to follow his example and not only to shun the stage, but to avoid all off-stage contacts as well with actors and actresses. In the twentieth century, stage folk are often to be found in elegant parlors; indeed, some of the most elegant parlors around are their own. It has not always been so. A yellow-fever epidemic that struck New York in 1795 was thought by many estimable burghers to have been inflicted by God as a sign of his displeasure that some acting folk were cavorting in the city. Thanks in part to the incantations of Talmage and his ilk, many actors continued to be regarded as not much better than the plague. In New York, a century later, one convent gave as its sole reason for rejecting the admission of a prospective student the calamitous circumstance that her father was an actor. (Harrigan did manage to get one of his daughters into a convent, but the girl was nearly expelled when, at the age of twelve, she was directed to compose an essay on some outstanding religious personage, and she innocently turned in a eulogistic paper about the one she had heard her daddy praise most highly—Colonel Bob Ingersoll.) In 1878, when a city-wide committee was organized in Philadelphia to fight yellow fever—still considered an enemy only less formidable than the stage itself —the peppery Rose Eytinge was playing there and volunteered her services. They were declined; the committee officials said they wanted no help from the likes of her or any of her breed. Impenitent, she insisted on contributing anyway, and wrote sarcastically to the papers, "If these godly men will consent to receive my mite, I shall pass it through a chink and, as a further precaution against their being contaminated, will agree to have the money fumigated."

It was thus understandable that one noted theatrical

contemporary of Harrigan's and Hart's, William A. Mestayer, should have got such an inferiority complex that he tried to improve his social status by billing himself in private life as a direct descendant of William the Conqueror. He carried a full-length portrait of the kingly William on the road with him, and spent many hours in his dressing room alongside it, practicing regal poses before a mirror. After a while, he fell into the clutches of a phony antiquarian who, for $200, sold him a sheaf of fraudulent papers proving that Mestayer was the Duke of Normandy. Elated, Mestayer ordered himself a set of ermine-trimmed robes, but he had barely got this ducal garb when an unfeeling relative of his disclosed that he had an elder brother out west, a sheep farmer who, if any Mestayer was to be a duke, appeared to have a primogenital edge on the title.

Harrigan was less often picked on from the pulpit than many of his peers. When he was once, by a clergyman who thought he ought to be permitted to harangue the playwright's audience during intermissions, Harrigan explained politely that the scheme was impracticable, because his patrons were accustomed to Dave Braham's music then and would brook no substitute. There were a couple of reasons for Harrigan's relative immunity. For one, his plays, though dealing with coarse people, were singularly free from sex and profanity. Al Smith observed admiringly that the playwright had never penned a single "damn," and William Dean Howells, in a treatise on comparative literature, was moved to say, "The comedies of Edward Harrigan are much decenter than the comedies of William Shakespeare." For another, during much of Harrigan's career the business end of his theatrical enterprises was managed by a man who many people thought *was* a clergyman. This was Martin Hanley, often known as Father Hanley. Endowed by nature with a singularly ministerial countenance, Hanley enhanced this asset by reversing his collars. Strangers who came upon him beaming benignly in a theatre lobby would sometimes inquire who the priest was, and sometimes an attaché would jokingly reply, "That's Father Hanley. Harrigan is very religious, and the Father always opens the entertainment with a prayer." Hanley occasionally joked himself about his affectation (he was apt to preface a routine handout by saying, "The archbishop and myself decided . . ."), but all the same he genuinely liked being taken for a man of the cloth. When the press described him as "ecclesiastical" or alluded to his "holy calling," it was almost, but not quite, enough to make him give out free passes. He was so set up once when a shoeshine boy addressed him as "Your Reverence" that, although normally as tight-fisted as any other theatrical manager, he tipped the boy a quarter.

Hanley was born in Tipperary in 1843, and came to the United States with his family when he was three. David Braham's wife was his sister, so he, too, was linked to Harrigan by familial ties. His theatrical career began when he was fourteen and served as supernumerary at the Bowery Theatre, and at one time or another he was an actor, musician, and agent. (The life of a theatrical agent in his day was a trifle more strenuous than it is now. Hanley often had to function as an advance man for his clients, and as such, like as not, would find himself putting up posters in anticipation of their invasion of some rustic community; on the road, accordingly, he always carried overalls in his trunk.) At fifteen, Hanley became associated with the

Ravels, the inimitable family of French acrobats and pantomimists who were known as "dancers upon earth and air." Prominent in Europe in the late eighteenth century and at Napoleon's court, the Ravels had first appeared in the United States in 1832. There were five of them at that time, four grandsons and a stepgrandson of the patriarch of the clan—François, who died at the age of ninety-four, but then only because he was severely injured in an accident while performing.

A swarm of Ravels graced the American stage. One of them, Jimmy, became a clown, and achieved the distinction of making a sucker out of P. T. Barnum. Jimmy had got hired by Barnum on the strength of a fairly simple, but engaging, act: he waddled hither and yon around the stage, wearing a tailcoat with oversize tails, and wherever he turned, a marvelously faithful duck clung to his heels. Ravel was a big success, and he asked Barnum for a three-year contract at $75 a week. Barnum said he could get twenty clowns for that outrageous price, and fired him. But then he learned that children were inquiring fretfully what had become of the funny man with the duck. Barnum had a lot of low-salaried clowns experiment with a lot of fowl, but none of them could contrive to make a duck heel. The children's demands became more and more insistent. Reluctantly and wrathfully, Barnum summoned Ravel and gave him the contract he'd asked for. After it was signed, the clown triumphantly revealed the secret of his act; it had consisted in nothing more arcane than buying a fresh fish every day and stuffing it into one of the tails of his coat. Barnum was so mad he didn't speak to his rehired employee for the whole three years.

(Barnum's belief that there is a sucker born every minute

was first voiced after another experience in which he himself was hoodwinked. This time, he paid a Long Island farmer a large sum of money for an animal that was supposed to be the world's only cherry-colored cat. After buying it, Barnum discovered that it was nothing more than a dyed black cat, but, having invested rather heavily in it, he went ahead and exhibited it nonetheless at his Museum. In deference to Broadway's biggest hit show, the cat was informally dubbed by the rapidly proliferating suckers of the public "the black crook.")

Another gifted Ravel was Jimmy's cousin Marietta, a great-granddaughter of François, who joined the family troupe as a child. A plump, curly-haired, and hot-tempered young lady, she won considerable acclaim both as an acrobat and an actress. (Once, testifying in court at the trial of two male Ravels, who had been arraigned for beating up a non-relative backstage, Marietta re-enacted with such verve her own role in the incident—she had kicked upon a locked dressing-room door to find out what all the commotion was about—that the judge on the bench pronounced himself flabbergasted by her footwork.) Martin Hanley married Marietta Ravel in 1862, and he subsequently managed road tours of several plays in which she was starred, including *The French Spy, Wept of the Wish-ton-wish,* and *The Broken Sword.* It was during an upstate New York engagement of this last in 1867, Hanley maintained in later years, that the use of the word "chestnut" to connote "tired old joke" came into vogue. In the second act of *The Broken Sword,* an actor impersonating a garrulous old man recited the story of a murder, in the course of which he kept referring to a hickory tree, and every time he did this a comedian would interrupt with "No, *chestnut,*

believed that the best way for a man to have a healthy head of hair was to let the air get at it. Both Hanley and Cummings were fastidious dressers, and neither would have dreamed of aerating his head by so unfashionable an expedient as going hatless, but together they hit upon what seemed to them an excellent compromise; they commissioned a tinsmith to insert ventilators in their stovepipe hats.

Hanley was industrious, shrewd, and far-sighted, as any self-respecting business manager ought to be. Once, when Harrigan was planning to take a large company to California, he was dismayed to learn that transcontinental rail fares had just been raised substantially. He rushed apprehensively to Hanley's office. Hanley blandly opened his safe and pulled forth forty-six round-trip tickets to San Francisco, which he had bought, at the old rate, on a hunch that a fare increase was in the wind. Hanley was the nearest thing to a press agent Harrigan and Hart ever had, and in touting them managed to attract a more than modest share of attention to himself, too. The New York *Press* hailed him as "the most ingenious explainer of modern times," and the *Dramatic Mirror* judged him "tactful as Talleyrand, enterprising as P. T. Barnum, fervently patriotic as Daniel O'Connell." He inaugurated the gracious and appetizing custom of treating drama critics to a tasty supper during intermissions on opening nights. (They had plenty of time to eat hearty: the New York *Clipper,* which like the *World,* apparently equipped its reporters with stopwatches, once complimented Harrigan and Hart for their abnormal speed in having the scenery of *Squatter Sovereignty* shifted in a mere twenty-seven minutes between the first and second acts, and an almost equally good thirty-one between the second and third. These lengthy pauses were considered no special hardship by male patrons, who left their seats then to smoke and drink, but they were tough on women, who by custom remained in their places during intermissions.) Like Harrigan and Hart, Hanley was a special favorite of the *Mirror's* ebullient Giddy Gusher. One time, he shared a paean of hers with Harry Sanderson, who was Tony Pastor's business manager. After commenting rhapsodically on their energy, honesty, executive ability, fidelity, tranquillity, and serenity, Mrs. Fiske began to get really warmed up. "Favored by Fate are these two men," she wrote, "happy in their homes, prospered in worldly affairs, popularly esteemed by everyone, fond of their Gusher, and wildly loved by her in return. What more can mortal man have?"

The Theatre Comique, called by the *World* a "bright little spot that shines like an oasis of light amid the surrounding gloom of lower Broadway," occupied premises that had originally been used as a synagogue. It was directly across Broadway from the St. Nicholas Hotel, which just before the Civil War was a favorite meeting-place of the city's pro-South residents; during the war, they set the hotel on fire to demonstrate their dissatisfaction with its general environment. The brightness of the Comique was attributable partly to a huge calcium light that burned at its entrance, so glaring that stage-drivers cursed as they steered their jittery horses past it, and out-of-town tourists blinked in awe. Inside, there was a smallish auditorium, attractively decorated in white, red, and gold, with a seating capacity of 1,400. Conveniently abutting the orchestra level was a saloon; between the acts, thirsty patrons could obtain drinks by opening a window that connected the foyer with this establishment and yelling their orders through the gap. The building was first transformed into a shrine of entertainment in 1862, when it was known as Wood's Minstrel Hall. Four years later, the name was changed, in quest of dignity, to Wood's Theatre, and the following year, in 1867, William H. Lingard, the Great-Statue-Song man, dubbed it the Theatre Comique, a name borne by theatres all over the country in the nineteenth century. In 1871, Josh Hart became its proprietor.

During Hart's regime, there were six evening performances a week, beginning at eight o'clock, and Wednesday and Saturday matinees, beginning at two. The bill of fare was as varied and robust as that of most of the restaurants of the time. Things would usually get under way with a blackface act—Johnny Wild and Billy Gray often had the lead-off spot—and then there would be a series of brief sketches interspersed with dancing or juggling or singing acts that were put on down front while sets were being shifted, and that were known as the olio. The evening would close, after three or three and a half jam-packed hours, with a somewhat lengthier sketch called an after-piece, which might run as much as forty minutes. For the week commencing December 21, 1874, the first item—following the usual overture by Mr. David Braham and orchestra—was Big Gun and Little Gun, a blackface sketch with Charles White and Billy Carter. Then came a singer, then a clog dancer, and then Harrigan and Hart's New and Original Irish Sketch, written by Mr. Harrigan, with New and Original Music by Professor Dave Braham— "Patrick's Day Parade." Next were some serio-comic songs, a blackface sketch written by Wild and White, and an original Irish specialty, "Going Home Again," written by Harrigan for the team of Diamond and Ryan. Following this, Wild and a man named William Gaylord put on a burlesque of a trapeze act; following that Miss Kitty O'Neill did a Character Dance; and following that came "The Skidmores," another Harrigan sketch in which practically everybody present performed—Harrigan, Hart, Wild, White, Carter, Gaylord, and a half dozen others. A troupe billed as The Le Calvin Brothers were next in line, with a magic act (the program said it was "the marvel of all the scientific men of the Old World") in which one *un frère* Calvin was mystifyingly wafted from one sealed crystal casket into another.

By now it was time for the afterpiece, a dramatic episode that often throbbed with topical allusions. (Within a few weeks, for instance, of the unveiling of Alexander Graham Bell's first telephone, Harrigan and Hart unveiled a sketch of their own called "The Telephone," in which they not only featured the strange new gadget but also featured the redoubtable Charles Diamond, who in his own way was equally miraculous, since he had the unique facility of simultaneously being able to sing, dance, and play the harp.) On this occasion, Harrigan and Hart were right on top of the news. Kalakaua, the King of the Sandwich Islands, was at that moment making a state visit to Washington, and was due in New York on December 23rd to receive a civic welcome in the course of which he would diplomatically attend both Protestant and Roman Catholic church services and take a sleighride in Central Park. In his honor, Harrigan wrote a tropical afterpiece called "Fee-Gee," in which the author played a County Sligo

man who had somehow become a cannibal king, and Tony
Hart played the monarch's favorite offspring, Princess
Mutton Chops.

It has been said that some of Harrigan and Hart's con-
ceptions are virtually incomprehensible to the latter-day
mind. The only known extant text of "Fee-Gee," written
in Harrigan's galloping scrawl, is difficult to decipher, although there is no mistaking one scribbled exhortation
from the island king to his subjects:

> Fee-Gees, hear me screech,
> Go to Brooklyn, hear Talmage preach.

But it is clear that both P. T. Barnum and an elephant
were among the characters depicted, along with a Brooklyn missionary named Peter Heathentamer, portrayed by
Wild. It is doubtful whether His Majesty Kalakaua got to
see this testimonial. It is even more doubtful whether he
would have understood it. Indeed, there remains evidence
that even the steadiest Harrigan and Hart patrons may
have been confused by the action. They certainly must have
been if they bothered to read the printed program for that
week, which contained what purported to be a synopsis of
"Fee-Gee's" plot. This went precisely as follows:

> SCENE 1.—A wet and dark night on the Fee-gee
> Group of Islands. In-can-tation Seen over a Missionary
> Chowder-pot. Midnight Song and Chorus of real vicious
> Cannibals. Old Probabilities wrong again. Storm clears up.
> King Luncher and populace clear Savages up Stage. King
> invited to the Feet, but declines. A delicate dish brought
> in, a real Prince for the King to eat. Princess Mutton
> Chops, the King's daughter, presents the King with a bill
> of particulars. The King not very particular about what
> brand of whiskey he drinks, invites his constituents to a

ball. They drink, knowing the Bill will be settled by the
Manager—who has a whole Hart. And at the end of
Serenade two Flats pushed on. Then we come to (Scene
2.) a Grove similar to Dudley's. Princess Mutton Chops
and Prince Dainty on the Lover's Ramble. Steady company's conversation publicly overheard. Prince Dainty,
with a but, illustrated how he would Basely knock a batal-
lion of National Gamesters. They tell, in a Duet, the
beauties of the "MUFFIN NINE," and, mutually exit to
Ball ground—a diagram of which is Scene on canvass in
the next view. A WILD tamer of Heathens, with an extra
Edition of tracts appears; in Addition to him his Christian
Wife, according to Hoyle, makes a Pair. They rhyme for
a while—the Meter of which is Gas. A distressed High-
burnian (BERNARDO), who keeps a nursery in a cradle.
These three characters, with the aid of two Indians, finish
this scene. Scene 3.—Showing the Mutual Base-ball
Ground. The game is over and pools closed. King Luncher,
who was Barred out, offers the Barkeeper Chin Music.
Sheridan's ride Illustrated. Good news. Barnum Friendly
to the Cannibals. Ministerial Cremation. Irish won't Burn.
Thrilling Situation. Saved by a Child, who is afterwards
eat for a Dessert. Ab-original pictures. The Savage in the
act of listening to the Boom of the jubilee guns. The sequel
heard for the usual prices. Scene 4.—Ward School in the
Tropics. Compulsory education. Peter Heathentamer.
First lesson to the untutored Savage. He-then a-la Brete
Hart, more cunning than the Christian, will swallow anything but Chin. The consequence. After which Bernardo,
and Princess Mutton Chops with Mrs. Heathentamer and
child—rebuilt by property man—walk out for an Airing.
Prince Dainty's meeting with Bernardo, have it out. Death
of Bernardo, who is materialized in the next scene—which
is—Scene 5th and Last. Showing Ball-room in King
Luncher's Palace. No pivotters allowed. Grand March of
Dresses which are sure to be mentioned in the morning

papers. Should the reporters fail, the inhabitants of the
dresses wear mourning for a month. Arrival of the "Gang."
The Prince braces in. The Committee Kick. Can't go back
on one of the B'hoys. Take your partners for the first set.
Forward four. Supper ANYTIME.

Many of the sketches that variety-house performers strew
so lavishly upon their stages were brash burlesques of the
repertoires of higher-class theatres. The radiant success
of Jenny Lind was the harbinger of Lotta Crabtree's
Jenny Leatherlungs; Tony Pastor's answer to Gilbert and
Sullivan was *The Pie-rats of Pen-yan;* and when all the
romantic actors of America were sighing piteously as the
sentimental lovers, Pauline Deschappelles and Claude Melnotte, in Lord Bulwer-Lytton's tremendously popular
Lady of Lyons, all the vaudeville artists were doing take-
offs of it. In their *Lady of Lions,* Harrigan played Claude
Meddlenot and Hart Paw-line Dishoffils. On one raffish
stage or another could be seen *Much Ado About a Merchant of Venice, Julius the Seizer;* or *The Charge of the
Hash Brigade.* George L. Fox did an outdoors *Hamlet;*
his Dane, on the chilly parapets of Elsinore, was not only
melancholy but shivering, and was costumed therefor in a
fur cap and collar and heavy mittens. Nat Goodwin, eager
to top his rivals, began burlesquing burlesques.

A much-employed script in the variety houses was a
sketch of indeterminable authorship that went by the name
of either *Razor Jim* or *Clams.* This had to do with a man
who, incensed because his daughter had become infatuated
with a self-centered actor, hired a Negro to assassinate the
fellow. The proposed victim was called Edwin Booth. The
actor impersonating Booth would be shown grandly de-
claiming some high-flown lines of Hamlet's or Claude

Melnotte's, as the hired killer approached and prepared to do him in. But so oblivious would this egotistical Booth remain to any petty distraction that he would go on soliloquizing even while the Negro assaulted him with knives, razors, and bullets. The climax came when the exasperated assassin lugged a howitzer on stage and fired it point-blank at Booth, who calmly extracted a black croquet ball from beneath his cape, dropped it on the floor, and continued his speech.

Firearms of any calibre were popular on the stage in the seventies, possibly as a hangover from the Civil War. So were military drills. Harrigan and Hart put on a whole succession of martial sketches after "The Mulligan Guards"; at times, their stage resembled a parade ground, if a rather dishevelled one. They even had their own military expert to train the actors who marched in their formations. He was Major John Edmund Burk, a veteran of the Duryea Zouaves who, after the war, planned to be a jewelry manufacturer but was so adept at the manual of arms that Tony Pastor persuaded him to exhibit this prowess on stage instead. Major Burk, when not drilling the Harrigan and Hart troops, did an act of his own. First, simulating an attack on an enemy standard that was planted on stage, he would pepper it with musket fire. Then, after grandiosely acting out the despair of a soldier whose principal ammunition is exhausted, he would fumble with his belt, draw a pistol, and, pistol in one hand and fixed bayonet in the other, fight his way upstage and fall gasping at the standard in a gallant and glorious climax.

A much appreciated Harrigan and Hart burlesque was *The Two Awfuls,* with which they nipped at the heels of one of the biggest hits of the early seventies, *The Two*

Orphans. The latter, produced first by Albert M. Palmer at the Union Square Theatre—it opened the same night "Fee-Gee" did—was an adaptation by Hart Jackson of a French tearjerker about a pair of homeless Parisian waifs, one of them blind, who got into a succession of hair-raising jams. It was an instant success; scarcely had it begun its run when a couple of American playwrights announced that they just happened to be at work on dramas entitled, respectively, *The Orphans* and *Two Lives.*

The beleaguered foundlings' chief tormentor was a horrid crone called Mère Frochard, who was shortly to be duplicated in wax at the Eden Musée. When Mrs. Marie Wilkins, who portrayed this monster, asked at an early rehearsal how she should interpret the role, Palmer suggested that she mold herself in the image of Mother Mandelbaum. This was quite an image. Frederika Mandelbaum, one of the most famous female crooks in the history of New York, was a swarthy, two-hundred-and-fifty-pound, puffy-cheeked, triple-chinned woman who, until she fled to Canada in 1884, was the city's principal fence. According to A. C. Wheeler, who wrote drama criticism for the *World* under the pseudonym Nym Crinkle, she was "a terrible afrite that rose out of the vase of society and for a long time hung upon our atmosphere with a sullen and portentous purpose."

Mother Mandelbaum had started off fairly modestly as a door-to-door peddler of stolen goods that small-time gangs had filched off delivery trucks. At the zenith of her career, she operated a sumptuous establishment at the corner of Clinton and Rivington Streets and there trafficked in the loot from the city's swankiest burglaries.

She paid Howe & Hummel a $5,000 annual retainer to keep her from being annoyed by legal trivia, and so effectively did they earn this keep that the police ruefully referred to her headquarters as "an institution for the prevention of conviction." Mother Mandelbaum did not often go to the theatre, but when she heard that the most villainous character in the city's most talked-about play was supposed to resemble her, she made an exception. She engaged a box at the Union Square, encrusted herself with diamonds and other suitable vestments from her warehouse, and, escorted by some of the city's most eminent thugs, lurched out of Rivington Street and sallied uptown. She didn't sit through the play. After one act, she pronounced Mère Frochard a vulgar burlesque and huffily departed.

The stealing of theatrical material was as commonplace then as that of any other commodity. Thanks in large part to the efforts of Dion Boucicault, Congress had passed a copyright law in 1856, but it was a fairly innocuous statute, prescribing nothing worse than modest fines for violations of it, and it was feebly enforced. Across international borders, no holds were barred. Unauthorized editions of Charles Dickens' books had been published all over the United States, without the author's receiving a penny. (There was blood on British hands, too. In 1886, Harrigan produced *The Leather Patch,* a play about an old pair of pants. A man had sewn some money into the seat of them, his wife sold the pants to an old-clothes dealer, and the action centered around the husband's efforts to regain his trousers. In 1889, a nearly identical play was not only produced but copyrighted in London by an Eng-

lish dramatist.) Mark Twain was one of the few writers
who ever tried to put a stop to this sort of thing. Learning
of the illicit publication in Canada of one of his books,
he announced that he was heading directly there to confront the responsible parties. "I go north to kill a pirate,"
he said. "I must procure repose *some* way." But an appeal
to his social conscience deterred him; he changed his plans
when informed that bootleg editions, which were generally
low-priced, represented the only chance many poor people
had of getting hold of his work.

Outright piracy of dramatic texts was so rife that the
Dramatic Mirror periodically ran a whole column devoted
to the practice, called "Under the Black Flag." Its readers
were kept posted, for instance, on the nefarious activities
of a Chicago man who characterized himself a "dramatist
and dealer in manuscript plays." He issued a printed catalogue listing 233 plays, including nearly every successful
production of the immediate past, and he offered his clients
their choice of the text of any one of these for a modest
five dollars. He was only one of a number of operatives
in the field. One play pirate, according to "Under the
Black Flag," sued a rival pirate for having pirated his
own pirating tricks. No decision was reached. The judge
who heard the case dismissed it after professing himself
too bewildered by the litigants' contentions to render a
rational verdict.

All this was tough on playwrights. When one Harrigan show was put on for the first time in Pittsburgh, four
years after its première in New York, a Pittsburgh critic
reported sadly that, in one underhanded production or
another, he had already heard every note of every song in
it and every word of every line worth stealing. Another

time, a brand-new Harrigan and Braham song was pirated even before their first public performance of it. A crafty Italian bandleader eavesdropped on their rehearsals and used the number in a beer garden down the street from their theatre well in advance of their opening night. Harrigan, an unusually phlegmatic Irishman, was inclined to take a philosophical view of such infringements, but Hanley, who had a more conventionally excitable Celtic temperament, was not. When he heard that an outfit calling itself "Harrigan's Double Hibernian Irish and American Tourists' Company" was travelling out west with a repertory nearly indistinguishable from Harrigan and Hart's, Hanley had some letterheads printed up with "The Original Harrigan and Hart, Martin W. Hanley, Manager," inscribed on them, and on these he issued a flood of waspish communiqués denouncing the rival enterprise as, among other things, "an impudent and altogether unauthorized attempt to fraudulently trade upon the well-known name." The Tourists soon collapsed, but possibly no more from fear of retribution than from the burden of their weighty name.

While Harrigan and Hart were working for Josh Hart at the Theatre Comique, they became involved in one of the few instances of the era in which literary banditry was fought out in court. On November 14, 1874, Boucicault presented one of his most universally acclaimed plays, *The Shaughraun,* at Wallack's Theatre. It was an Irish drama starring the playwright himself, in the role of Conn, the Shaughraun, and featuring a dog of Conn's named Tatters, in whose honor, before the show's run ended, both a statue and a poem were to be created. The

title word was one Boucicault had invented, a noun derived from the Gaelic phrase "go a-shaughraun," or "go
a-wandering." The play's splendid reception was more
than a couple of envious variety-house managers could
bear. At the Olympic, on January 25th, John F. Poole
—who had the great gift, the *World* once facetiously declared, of being able to conceive and rehearse an entirely
original American drama backstage while Tony Pastor
was rendering a single comic song out front—unfurled a
remarkably similar production entitled *The Shockraun,* a
word that had no special meaning.

And at the Comique, the same day, Josh Hart came up
with a patently derivative afterpiece entitled "The Skibbeah"—the Gaelic for "hangman." This was billed as a
"new and beautiful Irish sketch," in twelve scenes, "arranged and directed by" George L. Stout, who was Josh
Hart's stage manager then and was to be Harrigan
and Hart's later on. Harrigan and Hart were in "The
Skibbeah," along with Wild and the other principal actors
of the house. Tony Hart played the leading part, Kerny
O'Leary, and he, too, had a dog, whose name was Rags.
The *Spirit of the Times,* in a discussion of the marked
resemblance of this production to *The Shaughraun,* said
it preferred Hart's performance to Boucicault's.

That was the last straw for Boucicault. It was bad
enough that he, a pioneer in the battle for authors' rights,
should have been twice plagiarized while his own play was
still on view; it was even worse that he himself should be
unfavorably compared to the star of one of these predatory
affronts. Boucicault wrote Josh Hart a bristling letter,
in which the word "pirate" was freely used. Hart replied
at once that when it came to piracy, he was under the im-

pression that *The Shaughraun* contained an entire speech, word for word, from something called *Hall's Ireland.* Furthermore, said Hart, he had asked Boucicault, through a couple of unimpugnable intermediaries, for permission to imitate *The Shaughraun,* and Boucicault had sent back word that he could do anything he wanted so long as he didn't appropriate its title. Boucicault retorted that this was nonsense, and he had his lawyer seek a court order enjoining both the Comique and the Olympic from continuing their variations on his theme any further. John Poole objected mildly to any such restraint. *The Shockraun,* he declared, was an original burlesque. But when Boucicault called the court's attention to the fact that there was no visible evidence of attempted burlesque in the Olympic's playbills or advertisements—indeed, they were almost exact duplicates of those at Wallack's— Poole's resistance ebbed. First he amended *The Shockraun* radically, and then he withdrew it altogether.

Josh Hart was not so easily intimidated. He had spent $5,000 on "The Skibbeah," he said, substantially more than a run-of-the-mill afterpiece cost to produce, and he had no intention of jettisoning this investment. He and his counsel stormed into court to argue against an injunction. The actors concerned in the dispute were not called upon to testify—which in some ways, considering their wealth of histrionic talent, was a shame—but they sat enthralled as spectators while Boucicault and Hart exchanged recriminations. Boucicault's lawyer started off briskly by repeating the charge that Hart was a pirate, and for good measure labelled him a pickpocket and thief as well. Hart's lawyer countered swiftly by shaking a finger at Boucicault and intoning, "Thou that sayest, 'Thou shalt not steal,' dost thou not steal thyself?" The plaintiff added that Hart had as much as admitted his felony by publishing as an advertisement for "The Skibbeah" a review in which the critic had flatly stated it was taken from *The Shaughraun.*

The defendant replied that, for one thing, Boucicault's play had been improperly registered with the Library of Congress, and that without a valid copyright, he owned nothing, so obviously nothing could have been stolen from him. Moreover, claimed Hart, there wasn't anything novel about *The Shaughraun* itself. To testify on this detail, Stout, the author of "The Skibbeah," was summoned as a witness. Stout, a plodding, heavy-set man, said he had never seen or read *The Shaughraun,* so he couldn't have copied it, and that his primary source for "The Skibbeah" had been a play produced in London in 1870, called *Pyke O'Callaghan, or The Irish Patriot.* He suggested that maybe Boucicault had been dipping into this, too, as well as into some of the secondary works he himself had consulted—*Peep O'Day* and *Kate O'Donohue,* to cite just two. Since both "The Skibbeah" and *The Shaughraun* probably stemmed in the main from *Pyke O'Callaghan* and were accordingly unoriginal, Stout declared imperturbably, what was all the fuss about? Boucicault had an answer for that. He swore he had never seen or heard of *Pyke O'Callaghan* in his life.

At this point Wybert Reeve, the author of *Pyke O'Callaghan,* was dragged into the proceedings. He had seen *everything.* He testified that *The Shaughraun* was quite unlike *Pyke* but that "The Skibbeah" was like both the others—although in his opinion more closely related to Boucicault's play than his own. This appraisal was confirmed by the prompter from Wallack's, in whose meticulous view "The Skibbeah" was a hybrid composed of four scenes from *Pyke* and eight from *The Shaughraun*. Josh Hart, who had no strong feelings about the Aristotelian unities, took his cue from this mathematical analysis and, to show his defiance of Boucicault, saucily eliminated from "The Skibbeah" the alleged *Pyke* scenes and retained only the *Shaughraun* scenes. This abridgment was explained in an interminable program note on the Comique's playbill the week of February 15th:

> NOTICE: As our patrons well know, we seldom represent one Piece for a greater length of time than one week, and never longer than two weeks. But by the action of the so-called author of *The Shaughraun*, in bringing us before the United States Circuit Court to answer a charge of infringement, we have been compelled to continue the performance of "The Skibbeah" for a much longer time, out of respect to the Court, because the withdrawal of our Piece might be interpreted by some as an indication of weakness, and because if we withdrew our Piece entire, Mr. Boucicault will make it an excuse to discontinue his suit and retire from the position he has taken, to avoid an adjudication of our respective rights, we are compelled to continue "The Skibbeah," or so much of it as Mr. Boucicault claims as his own. We therefore beg the indulgence of our patrons for a short time only, while we continue the representation of a portion of "The Skibbeah."

On February 16th, the court ordered the Comique to cease exhibiting the eight scenes of "The Skibbeah" that had been taken from *The Shaughraun*. Hart was almost, but not quite, licked. On March 22nd, he presented Harrigan and Hart in an abbreviated, two-man version of "the Sensational Irish Drama, from which the plot, action, and

characters of the Irish Drama performed in this house—
and also the plot, action, and characters from the Drama
(claimed under oath as original by the man up the street)
was taken—*Pyke O'Callaghan!*"

Undoubtedly impressed by all the importance they had
heard attached in Court to originality or the lack of it,
Harrigan and Hart took pains to bill themselves as "The
Great Originals" when, the following summer, they set
forth from New York on their first major road tour. Hanley arranged it for them, and it was a long one, lasting
from August, 1875, to June, 1876, and covering a good
part of the East and South. In the larger cities—Boston,
Philadelphia, Washington, Baltimore, and so on—they
generally played a week's engagement, but much of the
time they were doing one-night stands. Nearly every community that today has a movie theatre had a variety house
then. In New England, during one two-week stretch
in May of 1876, Harrigan and Hart's demanding itinerary
listed performances in Lawrence on the 14th, Manchester
the 15th, Concord the 16th, Nashua the 17th, Fitchburg
the 18th, Leominster the 19th, Norwich the 20th and 21st,
New London the 22nd, Meriden the 23rd, Waterbury
the 24th, Norwalk the 25th, and Danbury the 26th. Then
they got a day off.

This was no mere trek of a pair of song-and-dance
men. Hanley was shepherd of a company of thirty-seven,
which included a chorus of fifteen teen-age boys known as
"Harrigan and Hart's Original Miniature Sixty-ninth
Regiment." This was made up of fourteen white boys and
a colored target carrier. They did one number, "The
Gallant Sixty-ninth," in which Hart played the regi-

mental commander and Harrigan a doddering old man who kept trying to enlist in its youthful ranks. The diminutive soldiers had been well drilled for the stage, thanks to the patient pedagogy of Major Burk. Offstage, however, they constituted something of a disciplinary problem as they moved from town to town. "The regiment got me down and rolled and washed me with snow," Harrigan wrote to New York from one wintry stop. Two of them were so unmanageable that they had to be shipped home soon after the jaunt got under way. The survivors proved to be of great promotional value. They would participate nimbly in any parade that any community they passed through was putting on, and every Sunday Hanley would march them en masse, and in uniform, to church, where they caused quite a stir. "How's that for an advertisement?" wrote Harrigan in a letter home one Sunday night. "The Gallant Sixty-ninth singing hymns! Imagine that!"

Before Harrigan and Hart left New York, they had been advised by Tony Pastor to take a bunch of their standard musical sketches and incorporate these into a more or less cohesive production. As a suitable framework, they chose *The Doyle Brothers,* an old play by a man named John Woodward, whom Harrigan had met in California. Woodward, a veteran of the mining-camp circuit, had played at the Bella Union in the sixties, and for a while was a theatrical manager; when the Overland Circus, starring the Risarelli Brothers, came to San Francisco in 1870, he at once put on, after the peculiar fashion of the time, something called the Underland Circus, starring the Rise-er-early Brothers. His *Doyle Brothers* was a comedy about two improvident wild-catters—as actors were termed who rambled from town to town with no fixed schedule, much as Harrigan had done with Rickey and Burbank—whose specialties included parlor entertainments, gymnastic exploits, tricks of legerdemain, Shakespeare, and "other startling situations too numerous to mention." Harrigan rewrote *The Doyle Brothers,* and transplanted into it several of the sketches Hart and he had perfected at the Comique, among them "The Mulligan Guards," "The Little Frauds," "Patrick's Day Parade," "Slavery Days," and "Muldoon the Solid Man." By the time he was through, he had so many plays-within-plays crammed inside Woodward's vehicle that there were six roles in it for both principals. Harrigan portrayed, among other characters, a fine old Irish gentleman, a dear old maid, and an old Negro; among Hart's impersonations were a French flower girl, an Irish biddy, and a nine-year-old Negro girl.

When the performers got to New Orleans, Hanley suggested that they put on a Civil War sketch Harrigan had written, "The Blue and the Gray," which had gone exceedingly well back in New York. It related the melodramatic tale of how one of two brothers, Barney Reilly, a private in the Irish Brigade of the Union Army, had inadvertently shot his brother Dan, a Confederate soldier, on the battlefield; the grief this ill-fated coincidence aroused in their poor old mother was one of the action's highlights. "The Blue and the Gray," unlike many Harrigan and Hart concoctions, had a Message. This came at the end, when the Reilly brothers, marvelously reunited, were reminiscing fraternally, and Barney said, "Dan, we are two fools."

"How is that, Barney?" said Dan.

"For trying to break up a family that's lived one hundred years. There's Washington, Putnam, Daniel O'Connell, and all our great-grandfathers. If they lived today, 'twould break their hearts to see us making jackasses of ourselves."

This was the cue for a patriotic song, with the hymnsters of the Gallant Sixty-ninth joining in, that advocated unity and peace among all Americans.

Harrigan and Hart weren't sure how New Orleans audiences would go for the number. They had been told that no actor wearing hateful Yankee blue had been seen on any stage there since the end of the war. Ordinarily, in "The Blue and the Gray," Harrigan, as the Yankee, was the first of the Reillys to make an appearance. For New Orleans, the script was altered so that Hart, in Rebel gray, could lead off. At the sight of his nostalgic uniform, the audience bellowed with delight. In the wings, a stagehand grabbed Harrigan's blue-clad arm and said, "You're not going on in those clothes, are you? They'll kill you."

Harrigan took a deep breath and walked out on stage while the din Hart had evoked was still raging. At the sight of the newcomer, there was immediate and utter silence. Harrigan decided that Barney Reilly's lines could wait. He stepped to the apron of the stage and said, in his most beguiling brogue, "For the love of God, won't you give a poor Yank a hand, too?" The tense audience relaxed at that, and gave him a hand, and the sketch was well received. Harrigan and Hart were so grateful to emerge unscathed that, forgetting Hanley had got them into the fix in the first place, they went right out and bought him a five-hundred-dollar watch.

The tour was a big success. It was the habit then of
audiences to present actors whose efforts they admired
with medals symbolic of their agreeableness. By the time
Harrigan and Hart reached Pittsburgh, on their way back
north, the senior partner was writing to New York, "I
suppose we shall be covered like Marshal MacMahon before we get home." During the final phase of the tour,
Hanley went on ahead to see about winter bookings in
New York. He found confusion at the Comique. Josh
Hart had given up the theatre and moved to the Eagle.
The past season, the Comique had been run, and pretty
much run down, by a scenic artist named Matt Morgan,
who had begun by exhibiting living statues ("Magnificent Classical Tableaux—Startling Effects—Corps of
Ladies of Unrivalled Beauty"), and, when that immobile
display failed to catch on, had gone to the other extreme
and presented the can-can, which caught on all right but
was banned by the police. Morgan made a comeback a
few years later when billboard advertising was inaugurated.
The first large sheet poster of any kind was an ad for
Uncle Tom's Cabin put up in Cincinnati in 1878. It showed
Eliza crossing the ice, with such bloodcurdling blood-
hounds in graphic pursuit that a riot broke out. Morgan
and other artists outdid themselves to make their posters
more spectacular, if possible, than the stage spectacles
these publicized. One of the Reverend T. de Witt
Talmage's false assumptions about the wicked theatre
was that the scenes depicted on bill posters actually occurred on stages. Barnum & Bailey had many a squabble
over their display advertising. Bailey thought it should reveal everything in their circus, suitably exaggerated.
Barnum thought it should reveal merely one colossal act.

His view prevailed when it developed that whole families of thrifty Germans would go out on Sunday to stare at the signs Bailey advocated and then, satisfied they had seen all the circus had to offer, go home. Harrigan deemed lurid advertising an abominable innovation. In the eighties, he wrote a then-and-now poem, "The Stage Doorkeeper's Lament," in which his title character reminisced, "Then the performance took place on the stage, it couldn't be seen on a wall," and added, "Now . . . at talent they wink, it's all printer's ink."

The Comique was available, and Hanley rented it for Harrigan and Hart. Their proprietorship of the place began on August 7, 1876, and lasted for just under five years. The first thing the actor-managers did was to cut prices. To the joy of the newsboys, admission to the gallery was reduced from a quarter to fifteen cents. Minimum weekly expenses averaged slightly over $3,000, and the maximum weekly gross, at that price scale, was $5,000, but nonetheless Harrigan and Hart just about broke even that season. The following year, feeling surer of themselves, they began to experiment. One bold step they took was to lower a curtain between acts. Nobody had ever dared to do that in a variety house before, and skeptical old-timers warned them that if they did it, their audiences would surmise that the show was over and go home. But they took this chance—after minimizing the risk by plastering their advertisements and playbills with announcements of the new-fangled procedure—and they got away with it. Also, emboldened by their success on the road with *The Doyle Brothers,* they began concentrating on longer plays, some of which lasted nearly an hour. Most of these were amplifications of sketches that had run

around twenty minutes. These plays were loosely constructed affairs, but every one had a plot of sorts, and
every one had singing and dancing in it. They were neo-
lithic ancestors of the musical comedy of today.

That second season, too, Harrigan and Hart raised their
prices back to the Josh Hart level, and when Martin
Hanley totted up accounts in the spring, they found that
they had made a net profit of $40,000. They had come
along fast. The only theatre proprietor in New York
who did better financially that year was Boucicault, with
a $65,000 net. Their reputations were mushrooming out-
side of New York, too; that summer they played a successful five-week engagement in San Francisco.

There had been no Mulligans in "The Mulligan Guards,"
but the continuing popularity of the sketch gave Harrigan
the notion of capitalizing on the name and creating a
family to bear it. Between 1878 and 1881, accordingly, he
wrote—and, as he kept reviving and revising his work,
rewrote—*The Mulligan Guards' Picnic, The Mulligan
Guards' Ball, The Mulligan Guards' Chowder, The Mulligan Guards' Christmas, The Mulligan Guards' Surprise,
The Mulligan Guards' Nominee,* and *The Mulligans' Silver Wedding.* (By that time, it must have seemed to some
of his audience that the Mulligans had indeed been around
for twenty-five years.) The paterfamilias of the clan, Dan
Mulligan, became a character of such monumental, if tran-
sitory, fame, that the *Illustrated American* was moved to
say that he "has really had more influence in directing
the course of the contemporary stage than any fictitious
personage of his time." The unbridled Negro wench, Rebecca Allup, figured prominently in all of the Mulligans'
raffish adventures, and the Comique's regular patrons

were soon referring to its stars as "Rebecca Hart" and "Mulligan Harrigan." The *Herald* said, "Mr. Harrigan is so identified with Dan Mulligan that it is difficult to untangle their personalities. The public does not regard him in the light of playing a part at all, and for that matter it is not far wrong." This appraisal was, in a way, unfair to Harrigan. Dan Mulligan was his favorite character, but the playwright was not speaking for himself when he put into his hero's garrulous mouth such philosophical observations as "I fully believe 'twill not be many years before we'll be able to tow Ireland over and anchor that swept lump o' dirt off the Battery."

As the Harrigan and Hart plays began to grow in size, their audiences began to change, too. The gallery remained thronged with newsboys and their pals, but women and children invaded the orchestra in numbers theretofore unheard of at that theatre. The Comique was crowded at nearly every performance; in their fourth and fifth seasons there, Harrigan and Hart were regularly playing to 10,000 people a week. Martin Hanley said these audiences included the bonniest of the uptown bon ton, but a less partisan observer who looked one audience over carefully stated that he hadn't laid eyes on anyone bonnier than Tony Pastor.

In any event, the new plays were creating enough stir so that Harrigan and Hart felt safe in starting to eliminate the pedestrian variety acts with which they had prudently been prefacing their more ambitious productions. Gradually, they were bridging the gap between vaudeville and the legitimate theatre. They found this journey an extremely profitable one. In their five years at 514 Broadway, they cleared $200,000 between them.

Soon after that, Hart, who had spent most of his life in furnished rooms and cheap hotels, was ensconced in an opulently decorated private house on East 46th Street. It had mullioned windows with stained-glass panels, and it sheltered an imposing aggregation of livestock—three dogs, a flock of parrots and canaries, and a marmoset named Pat Rooney. Showing a friend around one day, Hart paused at a panelled wall on which were hanging two life-size oil paintings of Harrigan and himself. Between these richly framed portraits was tacked a small photograph of Harrigan and Hart that had been taken at the Winter Garden in Chicago. Hart pointed to the massive portraits. "All that," he said wonderingly, as his glance shifted to the puny tintype, "came from this."

8.

A NEW ORDER

of

LOCAL
DRAMA

Alexander Turney Stewart, an immigrant from Dublin who established the store that ultimately became Wanamaker's, was the first merchant prince of New York. In the mid-nineteenth century, no emporium in town could compare in size and in volume of business to A. T. Stewart & Co. Its proprietor liked to do all kinds of things in a big way. He founded the community of Garden City, in the hope of embellishing Long Island with a new-world facsimile of his beloved Dublin. He built himself a marble palace at Fifth Avenue and Thirty-Fourth Street, so spacious that after his death in 1876 even the Metropolitan Club felt inadequate to maintain it in proper style. In 1878, he achieved further unique notoriety when his corpse was stolen from the graveyard of St. Mark's in the Bowery.

Body-stealing occurred frequently in those days, and

193

it was the kind of enterprise that, inevitably, attracted Harrigan's wide-sweeping attention. He went into the grisly business at some length in *The Leather Patch,* where one of his characters, a Negro engaged full time in it, explained that he was "an agent for science" and was a refined type of corpse-snatcher, who robbed only the best private cemeteries and peddled his loot exclusively to high-class surgeons at Bellevue. This fellow looked down on lesser practitioners, who rifled paupers' graves and sold the contents to herb doctors. He objected strenuously to the announced intention of a newly bereaved widow of keeping her husband's ashes in a gin bottle on her mantelpiece. Cremation, he told her, was ruinous for his trade.

A. T. Stewart's corpse, from a necroscopic point of view, was worthless, since it had never been embalmed, but nonetheless a watchman at St. Mark's discovered on October 8, 1878, that his grave had been tampered with. This news brought quick action from Judge Henry Hilton, who had been Stewart's lawyer and closest friend, who had built himself a house right next door to Stewart's stately mansion, and who was one of his principal heirs and the executor of his sizable estate. Hilton threw an armed guard around the grave and, as a further precaution, had its identifying marker moved ten feet from the location of Stewart's body. On November 3rd, after four uneventful weeks, Hilton ordered the sentinels withdrawn. On November 7th, someone dug up the grave and lugged Stewart's remains away. The posthumous kidnapping created an uproar. The family of Commodore Vanderbilt at once posted a guard over his tomb on Staten Island. Hilton offered a $25,000 reward for the safe return of his benefactor's remains. In due course, he received a letter from Canada indicating that the body could be had for $250,000. For a year Hilton haggled fruitlessly with the thieves. He finally broke off negotiations, but in 1880 Stewart's widow—a self-effacing lady who, when asked once how it was that a woman in her position dressed as plainly as she did, answered "I can afford to"—took up the quest herself, and managed to retrieve her husband on payment of $20,000 ransom. By then, owing to the body's not having been embalmed, all she got back was a sack of bones. These were re-interred beneath the dome of the Garden City Cathedral, where they were secure from further molestation.

A project that Stewart conceived during his life, and that Hilton carried out after his patron's death, was the erection at Park Avenue and Thirty-third Street of a home for working girls, called the Park Avenue Hotel. Located on the site of what is now Two Park Avenue, it was never much esteemed by working girls, mainly because Stewart and Hilton appeared to have based their notions of how best to operate such an institution on a careful study of prison life. A particular working girl whose aspirations Stewart viewed more understandingly, however, was a beautiful, English-born young actress named Lucy Rushton, who as a child of seven had given Shakespearean readings for Queen Victoria and who may have taken Stewart's fancy because, in colorful contrast to his wife, she doted on the gaudiest outfits she could persuade anyone to drape around her. In 1865, Stewart bought the old Church of the Messiah, a Unitarian shrine at 728 Broadway, a block south of Astor Place and across Broadway from the New York Hotel, and had it converted into

Lucy Rushton's Theatre. The rear of the building abutted
the rear of LaGrange Terrace, a row of nine colonnaded
private homes on Lafayette Street that still survive;
Conte's Restaurant occupies one of them now.

Earlier in the nineteenth century, LaGrange Terrace
had been one of the city's most desirable addresses. John
Jacob Astor lived there. So did Julia Gardiner, President John Tyler's inamorata. The development had been
built in 1831 by Seth Geer, among whose other claims to
fame was an astonishing capacity for oysters. In the nineteenth century, the consumption of oysters, at all hours
of the day and night and in every conceivable manner of
preparation, was one of the wonders of New York. George
Templeton Strong noted in his diary for the year 1874
that during a three-week session in the city of the General
Convention of the Protestant Episcopal Church, the
delegates, who numbered three hundred odd, polished off
a total of 80,000 oysters. Seth Geer could average far
better than that even while slightly indisposed. He was so
inordinately fond of oysters that after gorging himself on
them at the Astor House Oyster Bar at Broadway and
Vesey Street, the entrance to which was a narrow basement doorway, he would sometimes get stuck in the door
on his way out.

Mr. Stewart's Miss Rushton tired of her theatre after
running it briefly, and during the next fifteen years it
changed hands, and changed names, more rapidly than
any other theatre ever had before, or has since. So many
managers foundered on its premises that it became known
as a hoodoo house. Some observers thought that its religious origins might have accounted for this run of bad

luck, a viewpoint that was propounded in couplet form by John Brougham soon after Lucy Rushton took over:

> You may paint, you may fresco the place as you will,
> But the scent of the church lingers about it still.

Miss Rushton was followed by three female proprietors, the celebrated Worrell Sisters—Jennie, Sophie, and Irene—a stout and swarthy trio who, singly or en masse, played a large number of the country's variety houses. They sometimes appeared in a complicated production entitled *The Three Sisters* that had eighteen parts—six for each Worrell. They renamed 728 Broadway the Worrell Sisters' Theatre. It was also known, up to 1881, under a fast-flowing succession of managers, as the Broadway Athenaeum, the New York, the Metropolitan, the Broadway, the National, the Globe (when Harrigan and Rickey appeared at it), Daly's New Fifth Avenue, Fox's Broadway, the American, the Manhattan, Bryant's Opera House, the New York Circus, and Heller's Wonder Theatre. In none of these guises did it shake its jinx, not even when Robert Heller, a magician and mentalist who claimed "Extra-ordinary Hypernatural Vision, or Second Sight Amplified and Made Still More Wondrous," advertised his tenancy by plastering billboards as far as twenty-five miles outside the city with the striking legend

---

GO TO HELL *er's Wonder Theatre*

Stewart's interest in the theatre waned when Lucy
Rushton gave it up, but he continued to own it, and after
his death Judge Hilton administered it for his estate. The
years from 1878 to 1881 were vexing ones for Hilton.
Not only was he plagued by his benefactor's bones, but
after he had transformed A. T. Stewart & Co. into Hilton,
Hughes & Co., he got into a jam there through his impetu-
ous management of still another of Stewart's legacies, the
Grand Union Hotel at Saratoga Springs. Hilton barred
Jews from the hotel, a policy decision that failed to take
into account the fact that Jews controlled much of the
merchandise that a department store needed to get along.
In retaliation for his restrictive edict, many Jewish manu-
facturers boycotted Hilton, Hughes & Co. The judge had
little time, with all his other troubles, to apportion to the
bothersome theatre, and in the winter of 1881 he was on the
verge of demolishing it when Harrigan and Hart, having
decided to follow the northward drift of the city's population and move up Broadway, called on him one day and
said they wanted to discuss a proposition.

What the two young men—Harrigan was still only
thirty-six, and Hart a mere twenty-five—had in mind was
to tear down all but the shell of the existing theatre,
and cause a shiny new pearl to grow within this rough
old oyster. The completed job would be known as Harrigan and Hart's Theatre Comique. They were prepared to
spend $30,000 apiece on the interior work if the Stewart
estate would spend another $30,000 refurbishing the ex-
terior. Moreover, they would commit themselves to $16,000
annual rental, for a minimum of seven years. Hilton was
aware how well they had done at the downtown Comique

—which closed for all time when Harrigan and Hart evacuated the premises—and he agreed to their proposal. It was his high hope that the evil spirit that had so long hovered over 728 Broadway would finally be laid to rest.

Hilton's optimism was not shared by many of Harrigan's and Hart's acquaintances. Theatre people have always been notoriously superstitious. Even Harrigan, a man whose attitude toward chance was usually as rational as a bookmaker's, felt acutely uncomfortable without a rabbit's foot in his dressing room, and, following the success of the Mulligan series, gave most of his ensuing plays titles beginning with the letter "M;" he and Hart prudently brought with them to their second Theatre Comique a pair of bronze statues that might just possibly have influenced their success when these were displayed at the first Comique. Most of their friends were of the gloomy conviction that even such propitiary gestures, while sensible enough, would prove unavailing, and that there was really nothing one could do about a hoodoo house except to shun it as if it were a play pirate, or the Reverend T. de Witt Talmage. Practically the only friend who consistently bucked up Harrigan and Hart, during the months they were plunging ahead with what was so widely considered their foolhardy venture, was the then boss of Tammany Hall, Honest John Kelly, who would wander over to the site from day to day, settle himself in a wheelbarrow, and, while a steady stream of ward-heelers and patronage-seekers poked their way gingerly through the litter of the half-finished structure to seek out his precious ear, warmly commend Ned and Tony on their sagacity as well as audacity.

Judge Hilton endowed the new Comique with a handsome façade of Philadelphia pressed brick, and within, Harrigan and Hart created what one admiring newspaper was to call "a shapely temple of comedy." Nearly all the theatres of that time were horseshoe-shaped; theirs was oval-shaped, with the result that the entire stage was visible from all the seats—450 of these in the parquet, 400 in the balcony, and, depending on how tightly its patrons could be packed in, between 800 and 1,000 in the gallery. The parquet seats were lavishly upholstered in tinselled raw silk. At each side of the stage were three elaborately canopied boxes, which not only had private staircases but private foyers. Overhead hung a splendid chandelier made up of 22,000 glass prisms, which reflected the gas lights in twinkling multiplicity. On the drop curtain, to reflect the confidence they had in their own staying powers, Harrigan and Hart instructed their scenic designer, Charles W. Witham, to boldly paint "To Be Continued."

Harrigan and Hart's Theatre Comique opened on August 29, 1881, with *The Major,* in which Harrigan played the scoundrelly title character, Mrs. Yeamans his gullible boarding-house keeper, and Hart a visiting Englishman. The public's response was exceedingly gratifying. So many more hundreds of people swarmed to the scene than could be accommodated that the police corralled the overflow and herded them across Broadway, where some of them camped in front of the New York Hotel throughout the performance, hoping at least to catch a vagrant strain or two of Dave Braham's songs. Judge Hilton beamed contentedly from the largest of the boxes, which had been reserved in perpetuity for the Stewart estate. At the insistence of the spectators who did get in, Harrigan repeatedly interrupted the performance to in-

troduce his cast, every principal in which made a speech
except John Wild, who contented himself with rolling his
eyes eloquently at the gallery. The audience was still not
satisfied, and Harrigan went on to present everybody who
had had a hand in erecting the shapely temple of comedy
—the architect, the building contractor, the decorator, the
scene-painter, the master carpenter, and Honest John
Kelly, among others. They all made speeches, too.

Harrigan and Hart brought with them to 728 Broadway most of the company they had assembled at the downtown Comique—Johnny Wild, Billy Gray, Annie
Yeamans, George Stout, and the Sparks Brothers. Another old standby of the Mulligan cycle to come along was
Harry Fisher, who specialized in German parts and always portrayed Gustave Lochmuller, Dan Mulligan's
Dutch rival. Still another familiar migrant was Annie
Mack, an ingenue whom Harrigan and Hart had admitted
to their entourage even though they thought her inex-
perienced; before joining them she had done little more
than to play Ophelia to Edwin Booth's Hamlet. With her
came her then husband, Ed Mack, because of whose limited
but effective histrionic range—he could play a policeman
with incomparable fidelity—Harrigan took pains to write
a cop into nearly every one of his early plays. Harrigan
was of the opinion that Ed Mack made such a splendid
policeman he really belonged on the force, but Mack preferred the stage. Then, too, there was Mike Bradley, an
angular, eccentric young man who was the troupe's best
dancer and its choreographer. Bradley, who created the
role of Walsingham McSweeny, Dan Mulligan's closest
crony, had one failing. He was so notorious a drunk that

one outspoken critic characterized him once as "thoroughly soaked in liquor." When Bradley's excesses led to his death, in 1888, at the age of twenty-nine, a writer for the magazine *Theatre* crowed cruelly, "I predicted an early death for him about a year ago, and I am surprised that he lasted so long."

With a few notable exceptions, such as Johnny Wild, most of Harrigan and Hart's actors were a high-living, devil-may-care crew. They were so improvident that Harrigan, to save a lot of last-minute inconvenience, had a standing arrangement with an undertaker to bury any of his cast who died insolvent and to send the bill to him. But they were an unusually loyal group of actors. There was, of course, no Actors' Equity in their day. Most managers didn't pay a penny's wages during rehearsals; Harrigan and Hart put their casts on half pay then. Moreover, the actors were sure of practically year-round employment. They became a close-knit unit, suspicious of newcomers, proud of their affiliation with Harrigan and Hart, and acutely responsive to Harrigan's lines and direction. "At short notice," the *Mirror* said of them, "they can become a band of darky serenaders, a mob of howling Irish, a party of exuberant Germans, or a Salvation Army. Long training has made them perfect in illustrating the humble side of New York." They were equally responsive to Harrigan's non-professional counsel. It became the tradition of the company that when a fight broke out between two of its members—somebody was always indulging in some such prank as pouring kerosene in somebody's else coffee—the dispute would be adjudicated at an arbitration hearing backstage, with Harrigan the sole arbiter.

Adept as the actors were, Harrigan never stopped trying to improve them. His appetite for perfectionism was
insatiable. If an actor was supposed to have brick dust on
his clothes, nothing would do but that he hunt up a mason
and get himself sprinkled with genuine brick dust. Harrigan was always polishing, always refining. Once he added
a new song to a show during the tenth week of a scheduled
eleven-week run. He kept telling his actors it was never
too late to learn, and he had a low opinion of actors who
he didn't think had learned enough. He brushed off one
veteran of sixty years' professional experience as "a very
excellent old amateur." When his son William was starting his drama career, Harrigan—who had already had
his wardrobe mistress sew up Bill's pockets, so the boy
would not be tempted to hide his hands in them on stage
—took him to see a reigning star of the theatre, and enjoined him to watch intently every move and every gesture
the fellow made. After the show, the boy announced that
he had complied with his instructions. "Good," said his
father. "Now I want you to remember everything he did,
and to be careful never to do anything like it your whole
life."

Upon the move to 728 Broadway, the company was
augmented, at Hart's urging, by a plump, pretty, curly-
haired soubrette named Gertie Granville. A smart, witty,
and sharp-tongued actress, she had been born in England
in 1851, and after coming to America had begun her
theatrical career, at nineteen, as a balloon ascensionist in
Barnum's circus. Not long after Hart had abruptly left
Madame Rentz's Female Minstrels, Gertie had toiled in
that troupe. She had twice been married and twice
divorced. Her first husband was a theatrical manager

named Charles E. Blanchard, and her second the well-known actor-manager William J. Fleming, who himself briefly ran the theatre at 728 Broadway, when it was known as the Broadway. Fleming, a distinguished interpreter of melodrama, played leads at the Bowery in the early seventies, and a few years after that made a memorable appearance at Niblo's Garden, where he starred in a timely opus entitled *Custer and His Avengers*. A tireless actor, Fleming played both Custer and, after the last stand, an avenger called Daring Bill.

For a while, too, Fleming was the leading man at one of New York's most singular theatres, the home playing field of one of the city's most singular actresses. This was Lena Aberle, a stage-struck young lady whose ambition to play romantic parts in the conventional theatre was thwarted by the awkward circumstance that she weighed somewhere between 250 and 300 pounds. Her indulgent father, a bartender, eventually set her up in a tiny playhouse at Astor Place called Lena Aberle's Theatre, where, being the boss, she could take any part she liked. Fleming once played Armand to Miss Aberle's bulging Camille. She was not unaware of her size—from time to time she would write fretfully to the papers, claiming they had maligned her and that she weighed hardly more than a healthy 150—and she always had the lights dimmed low during her romantic scenes. In consequence, her colleagues found it hard to concentrate on their lines, so preoccupied were they with refraining from bumping into her in the dark.

Gertie Granville was divorced from Fleming in 1878, and in the summer of 1879 she met Hart while both were on the West Coast. Hart was always attractive to women.

They liked to mother him, and although his intentions were usually anything but filial, he found his boyishness an estimable ice-breaker. Even though Nat Goodwin was his best friend and was forever getting married, Tony had never seriously contemplated matrimony; the only evidence that anyone got the impression he had ever even mentioned it is carved on the Brooklyn tombstone of a girl who died soon after a romance with him, and whose family had her commemorated on her grave as Tony Hart's fiancée. Gertie was four years older than Tony, but not much worldlier. He had become a familiar figure, and a big spender, at spots like Delmonico's and the St. James. He wore expensive clothes, embellished here and there with diamonds, had a gold-plated harness for his carriage horse, and sat in on after-theatre poker games where one contestant might lose as much as $3,000 in a night. Gertie domesticated him. In the summer of 1882, between seasons at the Comique, they sailed to England together, and they were married in London on July 15th. They never had any children, but a few months after their wedding they adopted Billy Gray's thirteen-year-old child, whose parents died penniless that year.

Harrigan, meanwhile, had been thoroughly domesticated by Dave Braham's young daughter. Ned and Annie bought a house in Greenwich Village at 14 Perry Street, and during an exceedingly happy marriage had ten children, three of whom died in infancy. The oldest, Edward, Jr., was born in 1878, when his mother was seventeen. Young Ned was widely regarded as the image of his father, in ability as well as appearance. He was Mike Bradley's most promising student as a dancer, had a pleasant singing voice, acted on his father's stage at twelve, and at fourteen began to write plays himself. The senior Harrigan, with his unflagging capacity for getting along with adolescents, consulted his son about his own plays and planned to collaborate with him when he got a little older.

Only one of the seven Harrigan children who grew up failed to go on the stage; he is Nolan, a banker. Another, Philip, had a brief fling at acting but gave it up for the coal business.* Ned's and Annie's second son, whom they named Anthony Hart Harrigan, made his stage debut at four, but his career, too, was short. It ended abruptly when his father told him sotto voce during a performance that he simply couldn't act. Tony walked off the stage at once, never returned to it, and became an eminent surgeon. He died in 1932. The first daughter, Adelaide, also appeared with her father as a child, but never took up acting as a career; she is now living in California. Both the remaining Harrigan children have been prominent stage figures. William became an actor at five, and has been one ever since, except for the First World War, when he was captain of the infantry company that rescued the Lost Battalion. The youngest of all the Harrigan children, Grace, changed her name to the patronymic Nedda when she went on the stage. Her first husband was the actor Walter Connolly, and after his death she married Joshua Logan, a man sometimes thought, because of his protean approach to all things theatrical, to be somewhat like Harrigan himself.

* Years after his father died, Philip Harrigan, as the spokesman for a coal company in some labor negotiations, was able to pry a major concession from a granitic old Irishman representing a trade union by first revealing his awesome lineage and then reducing the union man to a state of purring compliance by giving a concert, across the bargaining table, of some of the Harrigan and Hart songs.

Harrigan's off-stage life was much tamer than Hart's. Between his burgeoning family and the many facets of his stage work, he had little time for random diversions. He was rarely seen in the livelier night spots. After the theatre, he might stop in at a relatively sedate establishment like Trainor's, Scott and Earl's, or the Sinclair House for a supper of the inevitable oysters, or perhaps a helping of one popular dish that the stomachs of that rugged era could absorb—the slipover, which consisted of hot mince pie covered with Welsh rarebit. But mostly Harrigan was a homebody. His only hobby was buying land. When he and Hart started making big money, Tony promptly invested a good portion of his in diamonds. "I shall put mine in dirt," Harrigan said. At one point, he purchased a hundred-acre farm on the outskirts of Burlington, Iowa, for no other reason than that it struck him as a pleasant notion to own part of Iowa.

In the summer of 1882, Harrigan acquired a 125-acre tract on the shore of Schroon Lake, in the Adirondacks, and the following year built a summer home there. Characteristically, he left the supervision of its construction in his wife's hands. He was on the road much of the time the house was being built, and Annie kept him posted on its progress in business-like communiqués. "I have dispensed entirely with the idea of gas machine and electric lights," she wrote him one day, "as I think it is a little too much J. K. Emmett." It was a big house, three stories tall, with the two lower floors completely surrounded by wide porches, and it was commodious enough to sleep a couple of dozen relatives and guests, but she only had one bathroom installed in it. (Annie Harrigan called the place The Maples; her husband called it The Boulders.)

In the ensuing summers, when not on tour, Harrigan
spent a couple of months at Schroon Lake, theoretically
vacationing but always working on at least one new play.
Equipped with a welter of costly fishing tackle, he would
persuade one of his sons to take him out on the lake in one
of three family rowboats—these were called "Old Lavender," "Waddy Googan," and "Pete"—and he would drift
about for hours on end, but he was much more likely to
come back home with a new second-act curtain than a fish.

On stage and off, life was going smoothly for both Harrigan and Hart after they moved uptown. The maximum
the new Comique could gross was $9,000 a week, and
with *The Major* they hardly ever failed to hit that profitable figure. Their second production, *Squatter Sovereignty,* eclipsed even *The Major's* success, and the drama
critics began to lavish heady praise upon them. "At the
Comique," said Nym Crinkle in the *World,* "a new order
of local drama exists." The leading role in *Squatter Sovereignty,* played by Harrigan, was that of a frowzy sidewalk astronomer, a character the playwright based on a
pathetic old man he had once seen in Chicago—a fellow
who, during a pelting rainstorm, was dragging a telescope
through the streets and asking passers-by if they wouldn't
like to pay a dime for a peep at a patently invisible moon.
Tony Hart played a coarse Irish widow, and Gertie Granville, in a peculiar twist on real-life relationships, played
the widow's daughter. "You can charge to my account an
afternoon of fresh and unalloyed enjoyment," Augustin
Daly wrote Harrigan after taking in a matinee. "I don't
know when I shall be able to wipe off the score. Your
epic of Shantyville is . . . something all by itself. I think

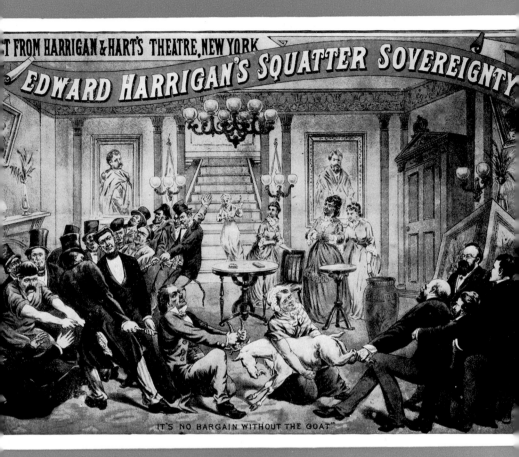

Scene from *Squatter Sovereignty*

A Contemporary Cartoon

JOHN HART   TONY HART   CHARLEY WHITE   GEO. S. KNIGHT   GUS WILLIAMS   BILLY BARRY   TONY PASTOR   BILLY GRAY
   JOHNY WILD   NED HARRIGAN   HARRY KERNELL

SOUVENIR

NED HARRIGAN CLUB

POPULARITY BEEFSTEAK DINNER

To our Commodore, Hon. Alfred E. Smith, October 26th, 1925

Nedda Harrigan Logan

Tony Hart in 1875

The Merry Partners in
"The Little Frauds"

Edward Harrigan in 1875

Old Lavender

Nedda Harrigan Logan

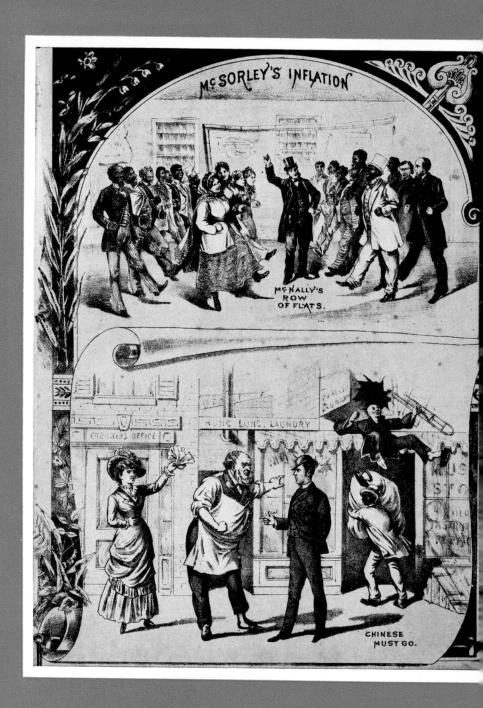

McSORLEY'S INFLATION

McNALLY'S ROW OF FLATS.

CHINESE MUST GO.

Five Scenes fro

CHARLESTON BLUES.

SALVATION ARMY.

WASHINGTON MARKET

Nedda Harrigan Logan

Sorley's Inflation

Harrigan's Park Theatre,
Herald Square at the Corner of Broadway and 35th Street, 1886

MR. HARRIGAN AND MRS. YEAMANS AS DAN AND CORDELIA MULLIGAN.

MR. HARRIGAN AS THE MAJOR.

MR. HARRIGAN AS WADDY GOOGE.

MR. HARRIGAN AS WILY REILLY.

MISS ADA LEWIS AS KITTIE LYNCH. "THE TOUGH GIRL."

MRS. ANNIE YEAMANS.

MR. JOHN WILD.

MISS ADA LEWIS.

Reproduction from *Harper's Weekly*

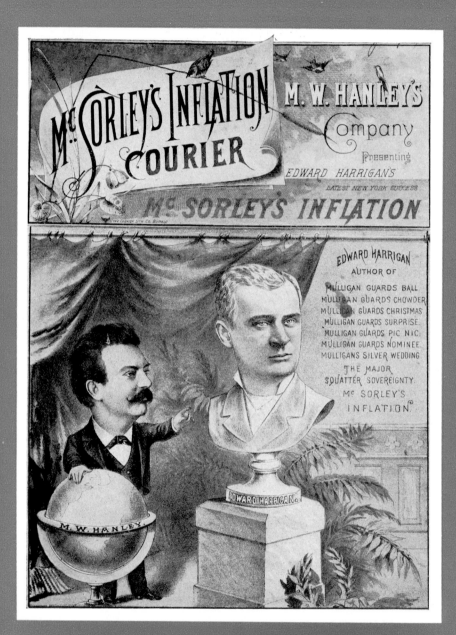

A Hanley Advertisement for a Harrigan Road Company

Nedda Harrigan Logan

Annie Braham Harrigan

Edward Harrigan and Mrs. Annie Yeamans
in Their Burlesque of *Romeo and Juliet*

Nedda Harrigan Logan

Exterior and Interior Views
of Harrigan's Theatre,
later The Garrick

INTERIOR OF HARRIGAN'S THEATRE.

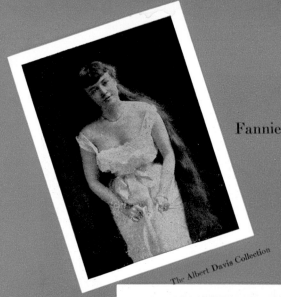

Fannie Batchelder

Mrs. Annie Yeamans
and Her Daughter Jennie

Marietta Ravel Hanley

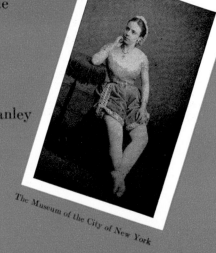

Tony Hart in *Donnybrook*—His Last Role

Scene from *Under Cover*, 1903,
the Last Play by Harrigan Produced in New York

it is the best of your series. But why not—every new step
you have taken in your little dramas has been a step above
the previous one. I think Mr. Hart surpasses himself as
the Widdy Nolan. I know no 'leading woman' who could
touch even the hem of his petticoat in the part, and as
for yourself you're a living chromo."

Squatter Sovereignty was mainly concerned with the
kind of life led by the inhabitants of the city's many
shanty-towns. In the eighteen-seventies and eighties, thousands of poor families with no other place to live moved
to the desolate, rocky flanks of Central Park—the city
would not permit them to settle in the park itself—and
fashioned crude homes for themselves out of packing
boxes, stove pipe, sewer tile, and any other building materials they could get their hands on. As often as not, they
were camped on privately-owned property, but they didn't
care. They just squatted there, in a crazy jumble of huts
that were soon plastered, as were the rocks on which
these perched, with advertising sheets for patent medi-
cines, porous plasters, nostrums, spavin cures, and theatrical productions. Dogs, geese, and goats roamed all over
the shanty areas, and they lived with the squatters in
their huts. Harlem used to be full of such settlements,
and was known for years as Goatville. When a sinning
policeman was banished to that remote beat, he was said
to have been sent to the goats. So intimately did these
animals co-exist with their human neighbors that they were
sometimes thought to harbor human emotions. When
cholera broke out in one shanty-town, a newspaper report
on the epidemic stated, "The whole neighborhood was
soon seized with a panic, even the goats showing fear."
In a short story Harrigan wrote about a shanty-town

boy lying deathly ill in his miserable bed, there was a goat in the bed with him. Harrigan's insistence on realism made it necessary to have a live goat on stage during *Squatter Sovereignty*, naturally, and when the animal originally cast in this part choked to death on a sharp-edged tomato can, the gallery was as saddened as if a soubrette had been skulled with a sandbag.

Harrigan was a rapid writer, and considering that he generally put on two or three new plays a year, plus perhaps a couple of revised old ones—for the 1882 season, he wrote four new full-length plays—he had to be. He had dashed off some of the early Mulligan shows in two weeks. He was so facile that it was occasionally bruited about, quite erroneously, that he was not really the author of all the works attributed to him. For a while, the finger of suspicion pointed at George Stout, who was in the Harrigan and Hart company and whose playwriting was so derivative that he had no ascertainable style of his own. Another candidate sometimes put forward was Edmund E. Price, a criminal lawyer who moved in theatrical circles; he had written a couple of plays himself and for twenty-five years had his office on the ground floor of the *Clipper* building. But although Price was a friend of Harrigan's, the closest bond between them was John L. Sullivan, whom the lawyer managed when the fighter went on the stage after winning the championship, and whose picture was displayed in Harrigan's otherwise undecorated dressing rooms backstage.

Still another man rumored to have written a few Harrigan plays was George W. H. Griffin, an ex-law clerk who demonstrated a gift—while simultaneously serving as the choirmaster of a Brooklyn church and as a professional minstrel—for composing with equal ease both sacred and profane music. Griffin, known as an intellectual among minstrels, was for a while stage manager of the downtown Comique when Harrigan and Hart were its proprietors, but he died in 1879, with no perceptible effect on Harrigan's subsequent output. Notwithstanding, the town gossips kept insinuating that *somebody* must be writing Harrigan's plays for him, and this supposition was so regularly aired that *Turf, Field & Farm,* always ready to strike a blow for its favorite, was moved to declare heatedly that there was nothing more to all this tawdry speculation than there was to the Baconian theory about the authenticity of Shakespeare.

Harrigan did spend a long time on some of his scripts, writing as many as a half dozen complete drafts of them, but as a rule he could turn out an entire play in six weeks, in addition to acting, writing song lyrics, and running his theatre. It was his custom, before writing a word of dialogue, to have models made of the sets he planned to use. One time, after the models had been completed, he made a bet with Witham, his scene designer, and William Vail, his master mechanic. Harrigan wagered $200 that he could write the play faster than they could build the sets for it. Martin Hanley held the stakes, and both sides went furiously to work. Exactly one month later, the script was finished, and since a few dabs of paint were still missing from one of Witham's and Vail's backdrops, Hanley declared Harrigan the winner. Harrigan treated the company to a banquet with the proceeds. In those days, you could throw a banquet for $200.

Harrigan wrote with particular actors in mind for the

characters he was creating. He always thought the player
was the thing. "You can buy the text of *Hamlet* for fifteen cents," he once said, "but you must look long and
far for your Hamlet." (One time, after Harrigan had
told an interviewer, "I believe I could pick out the best
cast for *Hamlet* ever seen in this country," he was asked
which, if any, part he would assign to himself. "One of
the gravediggers," he said.) When his casts changed,
he changed his lines to suit. Except on matinee days, he
usually wrote for four or five hours daily, beginning at
noon. He would sit down at a desk with a line of cigars
neatly ranged across it. When he had worked his way
through the cigars, he would quit and take a nap. By then,
the floor of his study would be littered with paper, which
some member of his household would gather and give to
an amanuensis for copying. Harrigan felt that violent
action on stage could be achieved only by complementarily
agitated composition. "The man who can tear up paper
and trample it under foot is the best writer," he said.
Asked once how he was coming along with a script, he
replied cheerfully, "I am still treading foolscap."

Harrigan's plays make labored reading today. "They
lived on the stage; the library would be fatal to them," one
drama student has accurately observed. Harrigan was
inordinately addicted to puns of the most primitive quality, and so were his audiences. They were convulsed with
laughter when the old astronomer in *Squatter Sovereignty*
began lecturing the shanty-town widow on the planet
Jupiter, and she thought he was talking about a rogue
in Sing Sing named "Jew-Peter." They could hardly contain themselves on being exposed to the following piscine
colloquy between a character named Ellen and her hus-

band, Michael, who had a fish tied to his back on April
Fool's Day and didn't realize it until his wife spotted it:

> MICHAEL: Be heavens, that's a haddock.
>
> ELLEN: 'Tis and was hanging to a sucker.
>
> MICHAEL: You're only codding me.
>
> ELLEN: What eels you?
>
> MICHAEL: I've smelt that before.

Let one Harrigan character say, "I was saved by Providence," and another was certain to parry with, "I'm here
by de way of Fall River." Let one state that he was paying
a fine under protest, and the response would surely be,
"I don't care what you pay it under as long as you pay
it over." Fast-paced dialogue like that would inspire cries
of admiration from the gallery. "Good old Ned!" a grateful auditor would shout. "You've hit it on the button!"
And sew it seamed to go on and on, with the audience alternately on pins and needles and in stitches.

For their next production after *Squatter Sovereignty,*
Harrigan and Hart departed from their habitual pre-
occupation with New York low life. They decided not
to do a Harrigan farce but a full-blown melodrama, *The
Blackbird,* written by the eclectic Stout. Harrigan would
merely direct and act in it; Hart would essay the unusual
role, for him, of an idiot boy; Braham would content himself with re-arranging some old Scottish and Irish airs;
and Johnny Wild and Billy Gray would be given novel
dignity by being listed on the program as "Mr." Another
innovation was the inclusion in the cast of a rank outsider,
De Wolf Hopper. Then a twenty-three-year-old ex-law
clerk who had squandered a $50,000 inheritance as an ill-
starred theatrical producer, Hopper was making his first

appearance on Broadway as an actor. His debut was inauspicious; his mother suggested after the opening night that he give up the stage entirely and return to the law. Hopper compromised; he gave up Harrigan and Hart.

Stout's play, laid in England in the early eighteenth century, had been written after his usual fashion. The *Times* thought it had been mostly culled from *The Shaughraun,* which apparently had an irresistible appeal for him whenever he poised pen over paper, and from another Boucicault opus, *The Colleen Bawn.* The *Spirit of the Times* found traces of no fewer than five old plays in it. But this paper had probably examined it more carefully, since on the eve of *The Blackbird's* opening it had shown a strong interest in the new play:

> Everybody will go to the Theatre Comique, early next week, expecting to see a great success. The public argue that, when a shrewd and clever manager like Mr. Harrigan changes the entire policy of his successful theatre; breaks away from all the traditions of his management; takes down his own name as author from the bills where it has stood for so many years; puts up the hitherto unknown name of George L. Stout, the prompter; transforms his entertainment from gay vaudeville to grave drama; discards the new tunes to which Dave Braham, the American Offenbach, can make the whole town keep time; substitutes the Jacobite period and the adventures of the Pretender for local hits at the present day, and engages De Wolf Hopper, the tallest actor in the business, as his leading man—the public argue, we say, when such facts are revealed to them, that Mr. Harrigan must have got hold of the best play ever written since Shakespeare tackled the historical drama and cut the chronicles of Hollingshead into blank verse. We should not be surprised to see, on Monday, a startling revelation in dramatic art. Nothing

less than this will excuse the revolution in the policy of the
Comique and the public's deprivation of our only local,
original, vaudeville, American theatre.

The Blackbird was not an utter flop, mainly because
of the electrifying waterfall-and-whirlpool scene that
Witham had created, during which Stout's second-hand
dialogue was mercifully inaudible. But there had been
trouble backstage. Tony and Gertie had returned from
Europe, as newlyweds, just before the play went into rehearsal, and when Harrigan began casting the show,
Gertie marched in, swathed in sealskins and accompanied
by a pug dog in matching furs, and demanded a large part
—that of the girl who fell into the whirlpool. Annie Harrigan, without whose consent her husband would never
cast a part, balked at this. Dave Braham sided with his
daughter. But Tony was for letting Gertie have whatever
she wanted, and Harrigan, to keep peace, persuaded his
wife and his father-in-law to withdraw their objections.
Harrigan got a measure of revenge on opening night.
After the scene in which he had fished Gertie out of the
water, there were four curtain calls. Harrigan took the
first two alone. The audience yelled for Gertie. Harrigan
took the third one alone. The demands for Gertie became
louder. Harrigan took the fourth call alone, and, while the
petulant Miss Granville stood dripping in the wings, he
directed that the play proceed.

The new Mrs. Hart was by no means the only relative
to affect Harrigan's and Hart's fortunes. From the first
moment they began to prosper, assorted kin could be found
buzzing about their hive. A writer for the *World* thought
that an appropriate motto for them to adopt might be
"Keep the money in the family." While Harrigan and

Hart were touring in 1876, their second violinist took sick. Martin Hanley, Harrigan's wife's uncle, thereupon asked his own brother-in-law, Dave Braham, to find a replacement. Dave wired to New York for his cousin Harry Braham to come on, but in the confusion Harry's brother John arrived instead. Nobody minded; John could play the violin just as well as Harry and needed a job anyway. As new generations of the family grew up, they joined in the fun. When a road company took to the hinterlands one winter in the early nineties with a repertoire of Harrigan and Hart material, Harrigan's son Eddie was in it, and Dave Braham's son George, and Annie Yeamans' daughter Lydia. The accompanying xylophonist was Eddie King, Jr., whose father was the xylophonist at the Comique. Hanley's son Willie, inevitably, became a manager. He showed more independence and initiative than some of the gang. In addition to following his father's footsteps, Willie Hanley edited a Chinese newspaper in New York and took a circus to Europe, where, when the troupe went broke, he obtained return fare for it by selling a surplus elephant to a French farmer, who was persuaded by Willie that it was just what he needed to pull his plow.

As soon as Ned Harrigan demonstrated that the theatre was a paying proposition, moreover, his father abandoned ships and prevailed on his son to install him as his box-office man. William Harrigan never entirely overcame his distaste for the stage, however; while selling tickets his attitude toward would-be purchasers was so unbendingly chilly that it has been suggested he may have been the model after whom all subsequent box-office men have molded their personalities. Once he got his foot in the box-office door, he ushered through it, to assist him, his son Warren, Ned's half-brother; and also Ned's older brother William. The younger William in particular needed a helping hand. He had been a prisoner of the Confederates during the Civil War and had never amounted to much afterward. He did love to tell, though, how he had been standing only ten feet away from General Philip Kearny on the night of September 1, 1862, when that dashing soldier, a one-armed veteran of the Mexican War, had been shot and killed by the Rebels. It was William Harrigan's sole claim to distinction. Some faithful patrons of his brother's theatre thought they must have heard the story of Phil Kearny's last breaths almost as often as they had "The Mulligan Guards."

In sheer numbers, Harrigan's relatives swamped Hart's. But Tony's family did their best. A brother-in-law of his was night watchman at the uptown Comique, and a nephew played child parts in the company. (Years later, two other nephews went on the stage, and adopted their uncle's adopted name, one calling himself Mark Hart and the other Tony Hart, Jr.) Tony's brother, John E. Cannon, for a while served as manager of both Comiques, and another brother-in-law, James A. Athy, later a prominent undertaker in Worcester, also had a whack at the box office. When the Hart clan occupied this citadel, the unemployment rate in Harrigan's family would sharply rise. But then the Harrigans would regain control, and Tony's relatives would have to tighten their belts. For several years, the box office changed hands regularly; a hasty reader of some of the contemporary newspaper accounts of the struggle to dominate this

stronghold might have inferred that the Civil War had
broken out anew.

After the apathetic reception accorded Stout's *Blackbird,* Harrigan resolved never again to produce a
play written by anyone else. The next offering at the
Comique, however, was still, for the patrons of that house,
somewhat radical. This was *Mordecai Lyons,* a play with
nothing but Jewish characters in it. Harrigan, as a pawnbroker, and Hart, as his son, managed to assume Jewish
accents with passable conviction, but for some of the company, the unaccustomed dialect proved hard to master.
One actor, Charles Coffey, had a brogue so thick and in-
eradicable that at the last moment Harrigan reluctantly
changed his part from that of a Jew to that of an Irishman. The others did better, but not sensationally so. The
Spirit of the Times observed that the best that could be
said for *Mordecai Lyons* was that Harrigan had contrived
to play a jew's-harp and make it sound like an Irish harp.
The Giddy Gusher thought Harrigan was a silly goose.

Prior to *The Blackbird,* nine consecutive Harrigan and
Hart shows had achieved runs of at least 100 performances
apiece. *The Blackbird* ran for only two months, and *Mordecai* for only one month. Impressed by these gloomy sta-
tistics, Harrigan and Hart beat a retreat to more secure
ground. They brought forth *McSorley's Inflation,* a re-
soundingly Hibernian production that satirized the Salvation Army and that was named in honor of a long-time
admirer of theirs, John McSorley, the legendary saloon-
keeper. Their fans were much relieved by this reassuring
return to orthodoxy. When the next show at the Comique,
The Muddy Day, seemed relatively humdrum, the worst

that the usually acerb *Spirit of the Times* could bring itself to say of it was: "Jove nods occasionally, and so does
Edward Harrigan." In the daily papers, *The Muddy Day*
drew such wildly conflicting notices that the *Spirit,* which
had a low opinion of the critical faculties of all other pub-
lications, mischievously took the opportunity to splice into
a single review some phrases from the conspicuously dissimilar appraisals the play had received from the *Herald*
and the *Telegram.* "Now, here is a play that is not up the
mark;" the hybrid began, "but bids fair to become even
more popular than its predecessors. It has less than the
usual amount of fun; but the spirit of fun and the genius
of drollery presided over the proceedings. Its weak puns
take the place of racy satire; but its dialogue is witty and
brilliant, rich in aphorisms and similes. Its life on the stage
will be brief; but Mr. Harrigan wove a spell over the audience that will draw them and their friends to the house
again."

After that, Harrigan and Hart played it even safer.
They went back to the Mulligan family. Harrigan came
up with *Cordelia's Aspirations.* The resurrection of Dan
Mulligan and his cronies was the occasion for civic rejoic-
ing. The pallor that had crept into the cheeks of some of
the galleryites gave way to a ruddy glow, as if they had
just gorged themselves on an exceptionally tonic barrel of
oysters. The Mulligans, to be sure, had been uprooted
from Mulligan Alley and planted on Madison Avenue—
Dan's wife Cordelia had decided they should invade high
society—but this gave Harrigan, as Dan, a chance to sat-
irize many an upper-class affectation. For instance, urged
by his social-climbing wife to take up the gentlemanly pas-
time of painting, he obliged by adding a mustache to a

portrait of George Washington, to make him resemble
Daniel O'Connell. And when his brother-in-law objected,
"You've mutilated the father of his country," Mulligan
replied, "I used red, white, and blue. His favorite colors."
The scene that really got the audiences, though, was one
in which Mrs. Yeamans, as a momentarily despondent
Cordelia, swallowed a vial of whiskey under the misapprehension that it was poison, and thus got the opportunity to
portray an uproarious drunk. This was nearly identical
with a drunk scene Mrs. Yeamans had had two years before in *The Mulligans' Silver Wedding,* but Harrigan had
no compunctions about plagiarizing himself, and his audience was too pleased to have the Mulligans back to care.

Harrigan's research for Mrs. Yeaman's drunk scenes
had been, for him, unusually effortless. On New Year's
Day in 1880, she and her daughters Jennie and Emily had
conspired in one of those backstage tricks that actors perpetually like to play on one another. First the girls had
come in and begun wailing, within Harrigan's earshot,
that poor Mama had got dreadfully tipsy during holiday
calls that afternoon, and however would she manage to
keep erect, much less say her lines? Then Mrs. Yeamans
tottered in, insisted thickly that she felt perfectly fine, and
reeled toward the stage, where, a second before the curtain
went up, she stopped pretending and revealed herself as
cold sober. Harrigan was so impressed by her counterfeiting that he resolved instantly to put it to profitable use.

In *Dan's Tribulations,* the play that followed *Cordelia's
Aspirations,* Harrigan shunted the Mulligans back downtown to their original haunts. There was supposed to be
nothing symbolic in the choice or juxtaposition of this sequence of titles. But with the extraordinary success of

Cordelia's Aspirations, the aspirations of the merry partners were fulfilled as they never had been before. And not
long after the production of *Dan's Tribulations,* Harrigan
and Hart began to have great tribulations of their own.

9.

A Pair of Scissors

BURST ASUNDER

Nowadays, firemen are far more conspicuous in New York theatres than at most public gathering places. This is not out of any special love they bear the stage, although safeguarding Shuberts indoors is probably a good deal less taxing than scaling ladders in the open. It is, rather, a vestigial reflection of the universally held nineteenth-century belief that every theatre in town was in constant danger of bursting into flames. As a further memorial to this morbid conviction, the theatres of New York, located in a city where acreage is precious and skyscrapers abound, are today uniformly squat, earth-hugging structures. The ceilings of their auditoriums, instead of supporting towers full of rentable floor space, are surmounted by empty sky. The reason for this is that the municipal building code decrees that nothing may be set atop a theatre, and the reason for *this* is the persistence of the age-old fear that stage folk are no more trustworthy, when it comes to playing with fire, than are children with matches.

The current caution rests on a firm foundation of historical precedent. In the last century, most theatres were tightly sandwiched between neighboring buildings and thus had no side exits. There were pitifully few stairways connecting the balcony with the main floor, but the upstairs customers were expected to take greater risks, since they paid less admission. The combination, not to mention the proximity, of gas lights and inflammable scenery was frightening, and frequently it had frightful consequences. "One of the pleasures of old-time theatre-going," a historian of the eighties has reminisced sentimentally, "was speculating on the chances of being incinerated before the close of the performance."

The odds of survival were even calculated, in a rough way. A couple of surveys made in 1878 and in 1882 revealed that one out of every four theatres burned within the first four years of its construction, and that the average flame-free life expectancy of any theatre was a mere twelve years. Lillie Langtry's American debut in 1882 had to be postponed when the theatre she was supposed to appear in flared up the very night of her first scheduled appearance while she looked on, appalled, from a hotel across the street. Oscar Wilde, whose approach to fires was aesthetic rather than statistical, was another witness. "It was a beautiful fire," he said. P. T. Barnum was burnt out twice in three years. In the summer of 1865 his museum at Broadway and Ann Street was destroyed; Barnum lost two valuable white whales that had been quartered in the basement, and a volunteer fireman named Johnny Denham became a municipal hero when he felled a loose tiger with an axe.

Barnum gamely fixed up another museum a little farther north on Broadway, at Spring Street. This one came a flaming cropper during the winter of 1868, in what proved to be one of the city's most colorful blazes. The fire began in the bird section of the menagerie, and spread rapidly to where the monkeys, bears, boars, lions, tigers, seals, and other larger fauna were housed. The weather was so cold that the hydrants froze. At that, many of the animals might have been saved if a panicky giraffe hadn't blocked a main stairway. This time, too, a tiger got away, leaping half-crazed from a second-story window to Broadway, where a policeman managed to shoot it. A quick-thinking gang of ruffians looted a nearby Knox hat store during the height of the excitement and sold their plunder to chilled spectators. The Circassian girl was rescued by one fireman, and the fat boy by four firemen. The next day, the ruins were completely sheathed in silvery ice, and many people thought this inadvertent spectacle was one of Barnum's best ever. Barnum switched to circuses.

Some New Yorkers did not much care whether or not places of entertainment went up in smoke, and a few of them actively espoused this. "We who are called Puritans hate the theatre in our hearts and would like to see them all burned down in a single night," Dr. Wendell Prime, a clergyman who thought along the Reverend Talmage's uncompromising lines, told a Y.M.C.A. audience one night, with little grammar but much feeling. Such forthright exhortations made an impression; when a minstrel hall that had formerly been a church burned in 1872, a writer in the

World, who obviously preferred ministers to minstrels, said that "the vengeance of heaven, which for some unaccountable reason had spared them before, descended upon them." Some other lay citizens felt the same way. One of them asserted that every theatre fire was a public blessing, since it reduced the potential number of public ovens. His viewpoint, however, was something less than dispassionate, since he was the manufacturer of an allegedly fireproof paint with which he hoped to have all new theatres daubed.

The majority of New Yorkers, though, were in favor of keeping reasonably intact the theatres they had, and to that end many schemes were proposed. Dion Boucicault, in an attempt to dramatize the effectiveness of fire-proofing scenery, invited some friends to Wallack's Theatre in 1876 to watch him scorch, with a flame equal in intensity to 150 gas jets, a canvas backdrop treated with fire-resistant chemicals. The canvas crumbled, but it didn't blaze. Despite the success of this experiment, Boucicault's example was not widely copied for many years afterward. One idea—it was aired long before Winston Churchill used the phrase in a different context—was that all theatres should be equipped with an iron curtain, separating stage from audience. This notion was dismissed as impractical, but in the eighties the asbestos curtain did come into use. Theatre managers were as proud of their new asbestos curtains as they would have been of a two-headed end man. They had artists paint "Fire Proof Asbestos Curtain" on these novelties in the fanciest letters at their command, and before each performance the curtains would be run up and down, at top speed, a half dozen times, to make sure everybody present was aware of them. Some theatres, disturbed by a falling-off in attendance that followed every fire, began devoting a large part of their advertising budgets to their supposed incombustibility. "Practically Fire Proof," boasted the Broadway. "Main Auditorium on Ground Floor. Large Exits to Street. The Only Theatre that Stands Alone and has Exits on Four Sides. The Lobbies Sufficiently Large to Hold Entire Audience." Two and a half square feet of lobby space were guaranteed each patron.

Quite a few theatres burned down, fortunately, when they were empty, but there were heavy casualties all over the world. Within a six-year stretch of the eighties, 450 people perished in one theatre fire in Vienna, 300 in Paris, 200 in Exeter, England, and 150 in Nice. The worst toll exacted by any New York theatre fire occurred on December 6, 1876, when the Brooklyn Theatre, then barely five years old, burned. *The Two Orphans* was playing there, having moved across the river after a lucrative stand at the Union Square. Twelve hundred people were in the audience that night, and the play had nearly ended, when fire broke out in the fly gallery. At first the flames were visible only to the cast and backstage crew, and the actors, after hesitating momentarily, went on with their lines, while the stagehands tried ineffectually to stop the blaze. Since there were neither hoses nor buckets on hand, there wasn't much they could do. Then the audience spotted the fire, and a stir of apprehension swept through it. Kate Claxton, an actress famed for her tear-jerking portrayal of a blind orphan in the show, stepped quickly out of character. She strode to the footlights, gazed compellingly at the audience, and shouted, "Be quiet! We are between you and the fire, the front door is open, and the passages are clear."

But Miss Claxton had scarcely finished when she and the other actors on stage had to dodge fiery timbers that came crashing down upon them. The fire spread along a canvas dome that stretched across the ceiling, and clouds of choking smoke filled the gallery. The spectators downstairs bolted for the exits, and the actors dived into the orchestra pit, which was connected with an underground corridor that led to the street. At first it was thought that almost everyone had been safely evacuated from the building, but after the ashes cooled, searching firemen came unexpectedly upon a heap of charred bodies—auditors in the gallery who had suffocated before they could escape. In all, there were 289 deaths. Miss Claxton toured in *The Two Orphans* for twenty years after that, and she achieved still further fame as a jinx when a half dozen theatres along her route caught fire during her tenancy. In time, she herself became so pyrophobic that she would never ascend more than one flight up in any structure anywhere.

Harrigan and Hart's new Comique was adjudged one of the safest theatres in the world when it was opened. There were no fewer than five exits from the gallery. There were hydrants on stage, and special pumps backstage, and fireproof doors between the stage and the dressing rooms, which looked out on a wing of the Colonnade Hotel—an establishment, also owned by the A. T. Stewart estate, that had its main entrance on Broadway just south of the theatre, and that ran through to Lafayette Street and occupied part of the old LaGrange Terrace. Despite all these estimable precautions, nobody in town was very much surprised when, on the morning of Tuesday, December 23, 1884, the three-year-old Comique burned to a crisp. The *Sun's* account of the tragedy was matter-of-factly headlined "Good-bye to the Comique. Harrigan and Hart's Turn to Be Burned Out Arrives."

The company had just swung into the seventeenth week of a scheduled nineteen-week run of *Investigation*. For the new year, Harrigan had a new play on tap, *McAllister's Legacy,* in which he expected to dazzle his audiences by reproducing on stage the floor of the New York Stock Exchange. (In his Exchange scene, the floor was invaded by a riotous band of Negroes, led by Johnny Wild, who wanted the brokers there to reimburse them after they had been fleeced by some curbstone salesman of phony securities.) The opening of *McAllister's Legacy* had been set for January 5th, and with only two more weeks to go, Harrigan called a rehearsal on Monday night, December 22nd, following the evening performance of *Investigation*. It was three o'clock in the morning before he dismissed his weary troupe. No one remained in the theatre except the night watchman, Hart's brother-in-law, Austin Heffern. When no trace of Heffern's body could be found on the premises after the fire, it was assumed he was done for. Hart sent the fourteen-year-old boy he had adopted, Billy Gray's son, to break the news to the watchman's family, who lived in Brooklyn. Billy, Jr., walked grimly across the Brooklyn Bridge, and found Heffern at home, sipping a mid-morning beer. He said he had left the Comique shortly after six o'clock, and that everything had been shipshape then.

The theatre apparently remained vacant between Heffern's departure and the arrival, about an hour and a half later, of a cleaning woman, whose name is remembered merely as Maggie. At seven-forty-five, Maggie was changing into her work clothes in a closet off one of the foyers

when she heard a banging noise. She opened a door to the
main auditorium and was horrified to see flames dancing
about the stage. Maggie rushed screaming into the street,
where she ran head-on into an equally agitated porter from
the Colonnade, who had spotted the blaze through a window and was on his way to a fire box to turn in an alarm.
Already flustered, and further shaken up by the collision,
the porter pawed ineffectually at the fire box for a moment,
and then sprinted toward Great Jones Street, where Engine Company No. 33 was located. Meanwhile, Patrolman
Patrick Clune of the Fifteenth Precinct, walking his
beat a block north of the Comique, saw flames jumping
from a second-story window. This was the headquarters
of the Actors' Fund of America, which had been founded
three years before. (Harrigan was one of its seventeen original trustees—on the board with him were Henry E.
Abbey, P. T. Barnum, Edwin Booth, J. K. Emmett,
Joseph Jefferson, John F. Poole, and Lester Wallack—
and Harrigan and Hart had given the fledgling organization office space in their building.) Patrolman Clune turned
in an alarm, and within a few minutes thirteen engines
were on the scene. By that time, a column of flame fifty
feet high was pouring through a hole in the roof.

The firemen concluded at once that the theatre was
doomed, so they concentrated on saving the adjoining
buildings. The Colonnade Hotel was most seriously imperilled. It had 150 guests registered. One of them who
was in a room facing the theatre, Dr. F. R. Alexander,
was getting dressed at around seven-thirty when he heard
a muffled explosion across the way, and soon he saw flames.
He watched them calmly for ten minutes. Then the window shutters in his room caught fire. The doctor packed

two valises, strolled to the reception desk, and said he wanted to check out. His serenity was unique. The other guests were scrambling to and fro, in various stages of dishabille. Mr. F. W. Klein, a transient from Detroit, was observed charging down a flight of steps with his suspenders dangling. The stairways were littered with clothing dropped there by people who had been trying inexpertly to dress in flight. Looters from the street trooped merrily into abandoned rooms, improvised sacks out of bedsheets, and toted off a rich haul. The Colonnade was spared, but it was damaged to the extent of $8,000, not counting stolen goods. The building immediately to the north of the Comique, occupied by Mundorff & Moench's saloon, also escaped destruction. It was damaged to the extent of $1,000, by smoke and water, but the bar was so feverishly patronized during the day that the net loss was trivial.

At eight-thirty, the Comique was racked by a blast, and the roof caved in. By ten o'clock, all but the stone walls of the old Unitarian Church had collapsed. Judge Hilton's fancy pressed-brick façade tumbled to the ground and almost crushed a steam engine. The judge himself had turned up by that time, and he revealed that the Stewart estate had no insurance on the place. (Fire-insurance rates were so high then that many property owners felt they would rather trust to luck than to coverage.) Harrigan and Hart, arriving from their respective homes after only a few hours' sleep, watched the fire glumly from a window of the New York Hotel across Broadway. They had carried $30,000 worth of fire insurance, but were surprised to learn, as they looked hollow-eyed at the havoc, that their policy had lapsed several days before. It seemed that Har-

rigan's father, whose responsibility it was to take care of
the premiums, had absent-mindedly omitted to pay the last
one. Hart was not altogether pleased at the news of this
remissness. Harrigan, in his turn, thought it was strange
that Tony's brother-in-law should have quit his watchman's post as early as he did. Before the morning was over,
various sorrowing relatives of both had drifted in, and
charges and countercharges of negligence were briskly
batted back and forth between the groups.

Judge Hilton estimated that the Stewart estate had
lost $50,000. Harrigan and Hart were hit even harder.
The $60,000 they had invested in the theatre was gone, and
along with it a host of lesser assets. There had been $1,150
in cash locked in the box office, all but fifty of this representing advance receipts for a Christmas Day performance. The remainder, ironically, was an as yet unmailed
contribution Harrigan and Hart had made to a fund being
raised to rebuild St. John's Asylum, an orphanage recently levelled by fire. Scenery and props that the team
valued at $30,000 had vanished, along with an $8,000
hoard of costumes. What was worse, most of the latter
were irreplaceable, being garments Harrigan and Hart,
with much patience and some risk, had cajoled off the
frames of chance acquaintances. Harrigan lost the only
script he had of *Dan's Tribulations* (later he rewrote it
from memory), and George Stout lost the only scripts he
had for two of his plays—a deprivation that, however
salubrious it might have seemed to some of this playwright's critics, was devastating to Stout. Annie Yeamans
lost a packet of jewelry, and Johnny Wild a stage wardrobe he had been painstakingly accumulating for twenty

years. Dave Braham lost a stack of arrangements, as well as a 300-year-old Stradivarius violin, which he customarily carried everywhere with him but had left at the theatre overnight owing to the lateness of the rehearsal. One of the high spots of the Comique fire, from the point of view of detached spectators, was the frenzied arrival of Braham. His ordinary composure completely forsaken, the conductor scurried from fireman to fireman, yelling "Save my fiddle! Save my fiddle!"

Nothing was saved, but as the wretched day progressed, and word of the disaster spread rapidly around town, theatre people began to rally to Harrigan and Hart's side. Colonel William E. Sinn, who operated Brooklyn's showiest theatre, the Park, gallantly volunteered to serve as chairman of a committee to solicit funds to rebuild the Comique. One of the most grandiose gestures was made by Frank W. Sanger, a managerial associate of the playwright Charles Hoyt. Years before, Hoyt and Sanger had been in a fix; they were broke and had to move an ailing road show from one town to another. They had turned everywhere for help, and everywhere had been turned down. Finally they had appealed to Harrigan and Hart, who had bailed them out. Hoyt and Sanger had since become wealthy, and a few hours after the downfall of the Comique, Sanger showed up at the site with a blank check dramatically outthrust in his hand. But Harrigan and Hart declined his and the other offers. They said that although they had had quite a blow they were still better off than if their banks had burned down; and besides, they weren't sure they wanted a third Theatre Comique.

The immediate problem was to get *McAllister's Legacy* on the boards. Harrigan and Hart were too preoccupied

with this challenge to pursue, for the time being, any debate about culpability for the fire. (No one ever did find
out how it started.) By ten-fifteen, the night of the tragedy, they obtained a six-week lease on the New Park Theatre, at the northwest corner of Broadway and Thirty-fifth
Street. This was a cavernous structure, and to its new tenants' distress, it didn't have a gallery. It had once been
an aquarium, and, after a fire of its own in 1883, had been
rebuilt. Some of the materials used in this re-construction,
including the boxes, had been salvaged from the demoli-
tion of Booth's Theatre. At the end of 1884, the Park was
serving as a dime museum and menagerie. "We shall move
out the monkeys and begin work at once," Harrigan announced.

While the monkeys were being lassoed, Tony Pastor
offered to let Harrigan and Hart rehearse at his theatre.
On December 24th, twenty-four hours after the fire, their
company gathered at Pastor's. The actors were as down-
cast as if attending a wake. George Stout and Harry
Fisher were in tears, and they only stopped bawling when
a fellow performer observed that it was senseless to waste
such snuffling histrionics on a tiny audience of compara-
tively unimpressionable professionals. And then, as often
happens at a wake, the atmosphere began to brighten. One
of the actors broke into a clog dance, and another joined
in. Somebody sat down at a piano and rattled off a medley
of Braham's liveliest tunes, and soon the whole assemblage
was singing cheerfully. By dusk, that Christmas Eve, the
party was nearly as merry as any in town.

It still seemed unlikely, notwithstanding the availabil-
ity of a theatre, that *McAllister's Legacy* could open on
time. But it did. Almost every scene painter and costume

designer in town pitched in, and by New Year's Day the
vanished sets and wardrobes had been magically replaced.
The play itself drew mixed notices. The Stock Exchange
scene, as Harrigan had anticipated, was its most provoca-
tive element, but although the *Spirit of the Times* dubbed
this "a miracle of stage management," not all of the per-
snickety daily reviewers agreed. The *Times* thought the
scene "an excrescence," and its critic went on to say, "The
personal appearance of most of the brokers suggests the
ravages of a more protracted financial panic than has yet
been known." But the reaction to the opening night itself
—as an exhibition of an unshakably devout following's
worship of its idols—was unanimously one of awe. An hour
before curtain time, Broadway was jammed by what even
the *Times* admitted was "a huge and enthusiastic mass
meeting. . . . a great family party." The Seventh Regiment,
as a token of its abiding affection, sent a delegation of 250
of its loudest-lunged militiamen. As the orchestra seated
itself for the overture, a voice cried out, "Who is Dave
Braham?" and from the Seventh's massed throats thundered the answer: "First in war, first in peace, and first in
the hearts of his countrymen!" Lawyer Abe Hummel
thereupon hunched himself onto the stage and presented
Braham with a 1690 Guarnerius violin that friends of his
had covertly arranged to give him. Harrigan, Hart, Mrs.
Yeamans, and Wild, it goes without saying, were called
upon for speeches. And amid lusty cries of "We're with
you still, Harrigan!" and "How are you, Mr. Hart?" the
show went on.

Despite that flattering reception, Harrigan and Hart
were dissatisfied with the Park. Not only did it seem too

vast an auditorium to them, but the rent they had been obliged to pay to get it in the first place struck them, on reflection, as absurdly high. Scouting around, they discovered that the Fourteenth Street Theatre, a much less spacious arena, was available at more modest terms. On March 2nd, they shunted *McAllister's Legacy* down there. It got off to an inauspicious start. The premiere coincided with Grover Cleveland's inauguration in Washington, and the politicians who could always be counted on for shrill attendance at a Harrigan and Hart opening were thus unavoidably absent. Even after the Tammany Braves returned from the capital, though, business failed to pick up much. Harrigan and Hart took off *McAllister's Legacy* after two lacklustre weeks and revived *The Major*. Business picked up a little, but not enough to please them, and a month later they took off *The Major* and revived *Cordelia's Aspirations*.

Nothing seemed to be going right. To all outward appearances, Harrigan and Hart ought to have been able to survive the fire. They had enough money left to carry on in their accustomed fashion. They were still young; Tony had not quite reached the age of thirty, and Ned was barely forty. On stage, they made a superb team, each skillfully complementing the talents of the other. But their off-stage associations were growing increasingly tense. Left alone, they would undoubtedly have got on fine, but the relatives who had latched onto them were becoming intolerably burdensome. It was scarcely possible for a member of Harrigan's family to confront a member of Hart's without recriminations being exchanged about responsibility for the fire. Ned's father and Tony's brother wouldn't speak to each other. And even before the fire, Annie Harrigan and

Gertie Hart had been at odds. Annie had given grudging consent to Gertie's getting juicy parts in the plays, but for this concession she had exacted heavy vengeance; she refused to admit Gertie to her home and would not treat her as a social equal anywhere. Gertie did not take this snub lying down. She told Tony he was worth two of Ned Harrigan, that his stubborn adherence to Harrigan was hamstringing his career, and that it was high time he went on his own or paired up with somebody else—Nat Goodwin, say. Goodwin might have a lot of wives, she pointed out, but he only had them one at a time, and it would be a blessed relief for Tony to be rid of all those infernal cousins and in-laws of Harrigan's and Braham's who were forever underfoot.

Harrigan was under similar pressures. Annie preserved a queenly reticence, but others of his relatives muttered that Gertie was becoming impossibly uppity, that the next thing anyone knew she would be wanting to change "Harrigan and Hart" to "Harrigan, Hart, and Granville," and that Tony was dispensable anyway. Did Hart write the plays? Did he direct them? Did he help write the songs? Of course not; he was just a passably talented kid whom Ned had been decent enough to pick up when he was down and out, and perhaps the moment had come to send him packing. Ned and Tony tried gamely to hang on together. If the box-office receipts at the Fourteenth Street Theatre had been more robust than they were, the partners might have been able to ignore the constant hammering of their querulous families. But business was so bad that Harrigan felt they had to get out of the theatre in mid-May, a whole month before their New York season normally ended, and take to the road. Tony didn't feel like travelling. But he

acquiesced when Martin Hanley booked a spring and summer tour for them—Newark, Jersey City, Brooklyn, Philadelphia, Boston, and many New England towns. Meanwhile, Harrigan knocked out a play to be put on by some
second-stringers in the company on Fourteenth Street.
Called *Are You Insured?*, it was to open there Monday,
May 11th, the same night that Harrigan and Hart were
due in Newark with *Cordelia's Aspirations.*

The public was largely unaware of the backstage bickering that had been going on. Therefore, when, on May
3rd, word got out that the day before Tony had sent Ned
a curt note stating that he had resolved not to go on tour
after all, and was severing his partnership with Harrigan
as of Saturday, May 9th, the news had the effect of a
bombshell. There are octogenarians around today who can
still vividly recall their dismay. "You could hardly exag-
gerate the reaction," one eighty-five-year-older said recently. "I could cry right now if I allowed myself to think
about it very much." Harrigan and Hart to separate! A
delegation of politicians called upon Mayor William R.
Grace and asked him, as a civic service, to heal the breach.
The mayor dutifully tried, but got nowhere. Reverbera-
tions of the split were felt as far off as Chicago. "A pair
of scissors burst asunder, a turtle dove bereft of its mate,
Damon without Pythias—none of these examples of ruptured union serve adequately to express the state of deso-
lation . . ." mourned the Chicago *Herald.* Reporters
camped on Harrigan's doorstep, and on Hart's, seeking
elucidation. Tony wouldn't comment, except to say that
his feelings for Ned hadn't changed. The most anyone
could get out of Harrigan was a restrained "Well, I suppose it all came about through the women."

The contracts that Hanley had signed for the road tour had specified the personal appearance of both Harrigan and Hart. Ned wanted to make the tour with or without Tony, and Hanley began to get in touch with all the theatre managers concerned, to find out if they would accept Harrigan in his plays without a co-star. Meanwhile, Harrigan engaged Richard Quilter, a veteran minstrel who had been with the company at the old Comique, to take over Hart's parts. It was a nerve-shattering week for Harrigan. On Wednesday, May 6th, while the press was still badgering him for comment, his youngest child, an infant boy, took suddenly ill, and two days later the baby died. The day after that, Saturday, Harrigan and Hart made their farewell appearance at the Fourteenth Street. That night, the house was brim full. After the final curtain fell, there were incessant calls for both men. Harrigan and Hart took them hand in hand, with tears streaming down their faces. Long after they had retired to the wings, much of the audience stayed in place, shouting "Ned!" ... "Tony!" ... "Ned!" ... "Tony!" ... "Ned!" ... "Tony!" ... "More!" ... "More!" ... "More!"

Harrigan didn't have much chance on Sunday to brood about the previous evening. There was his baby's funeral to attend. Richard Quilter had to be rehearsed, in Newark, for the following day's opening there of *Cordelia's Aspirations*. And, on Fourteenth Street, there was a dress rehearsal of *Are You Insured?* (It would have been astonishing if this play, a warmed-over and expanded version of an 1878 sketch called "Love vs. Insurance," had amounted to much, considering the circumstances under which it was conceived. *Are You Insured?*, to no one's great surprise,

lasted only a week.) On top of everything else, Martin
Hanley came up with a ticklish report: he had heard from
all the out-of-town managers, and all but one had agreed
to take Harrigan *sans* Hart. The holdout, Colonel Sinn
of the Brooklyn Park, was adamant. He had a signed
contract guaranteeing the presence on his stage for two
weeks, beginning June 1st and ending June 13th, of Harrigan *and* Hart, and however inconvenient it might be for
them to fulfill this commitment, he was prepared to make
trouble if they reneged.

In the theatre, nobody takes farewell appearances seriously. Sir Harry Lauder lived off them for years. The
clink of a single coin against a box-office till has proved
enough of a spur to cause actors to gallop snortingly out
of the pasture of retirement. Harrigan and Hart, though,
had honestly thought their collaboration was over. Quite
apart from their personal feelings in the matter, as actors
they sensed that it would be a sour anticlimax, and bad
timing, too, for them to turn up together again after a
mere three-week hiatus. But as businessmen they both
respected Colonel Sinn's position. Besides, Brooklyn was
not the same as New York. Hart agreed to go through
with the engagement. When the momentarily reconsti-
tuted team appeared there—they did *The Major* one week
and *Investigation* the other—partisans of both men flocked
to the Park for every performance. Every time Hart
moved on or off the stage, his devotées shook the rafters.
Every time Harrigan moved on or off stage, *his* devotées
tried to top the Hart fans' din. Compared to the efforts
of these spontaneous factions, the heaviest-handed paid
claque would have been drowned out. Thanks to these
raucous expressions of favoritism, a fair portion of every

performance was utterly inaudible. In the view of detached observers, the result was a standoff: Harrigan's fanciers were thought to be a mite more numerous, Hart's a mite more clamorous. That was really the end of the team. "Good-bye Mulligan," the *Dramatic Mirror* headed its elegy on the separation, and the title was prophetic. Harrigan subsequently revived a couple of the Mulligan plays, but after the split-up he never wrote another one. And Hart, in the few unhappy years that remained to him, never again acted in a Harrigan play. The Giddy Gusher, who had a pipeline to Hart's inner feelings, revealed that the two men were "so welded that when they parted every fiber of Tony's anatomy felt the wrench." And Tony himself, in a self-analytical mood not long afterward, was heard to lament, "Who is Tony Hart? Everybody knew Harrigan and Hart. Nobody knows Harrigan or Hart."

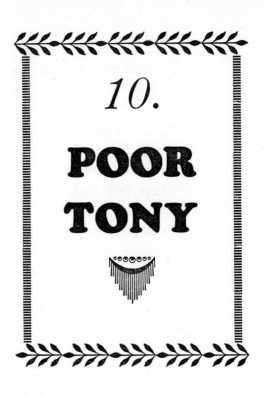

10.

POOR TONY

The Victorian era, for all its legendary prudishness, spawned some breaches of taste that would make even a twentieth-century gossip columnist blink. It tickled the fancy of one New York newspaperman in 1892, for instance, to publish a wholly fabricated yarn to the effect that the following theatrical season would be highlighted by the joint tour of two celebrated Irish comedians, Harry Kernell and William J. Scanlan, under the management of Max Clayton. This combination would be a most appropriate one, the item stated, inasmuch as all three men were patients at the Bloomingdale Insane Asylum, where they shared the common bond of being afflicted with paresis. Nobody in the nineteenth century would have presumed to make public mention of syphilis, but when it came to paresis, the dread advanced phase of that then still in-

243

curable disease, the same squeamishness did not apply, especially if someone connected with the theatre happened to be the victim. Syphilis and its ravaging consequences laid low many hapless citizens who weren't actors, too, in the days before penicillin was discovered, but the democratic nature of the scourge was rarely stressed. When stage folk lost first their health and then their minds to the pesky spirochete, it was regarded as a kind of joke. Actors themselves—at least those enjoying *mens sana* in *corpore sano*—were not above adopting this callous attitude, also. Shortly after John McCullough, the famous tragedian, was disclosed to be suffering from paresis, variety-house audiences all over the country were regaled with a sordid sketch entitled "The Ravings of John McCullough."

And so it went with Tony Hart. On Sunday, December 15, 1887, what many actors had been privately whispering about him for a couple of years was revealed in print by the scandal-loving New York *Herald,* under the heading:

THAT TELLTALE LISP

Tony Hart's Trouble Begins Like
That of John McCullough

ALL THE SYMPTOMS OF PARESIS

Why Ned Harrigan's Former Partner
Has Been Forced to Leave the Stage

The symptoms that the *Herald* proceeded to enumerate were a sad catalogue. Tony's once clear and bell-like voice, it seemed, was rough and raspy. Sometimes he lisped, sometimes he stuttered. His memory was faltering. His eyes looked odd, his gait was unsteady, and he had fearful tantrums, during which he couldn't articulate coherently. He had even struck his wife while temporarily deranged. The *Herald* had been told by Tony's friends, to be sure, that he was merely suffering from a sore throat, but it was, notwithstanding, the paper's hunch that he might soon have to be committed to an institution and that his days on earth were numbered.

The story did not go unanswered. "Newspapers like the *Herald*," sputtered the *Spirit of the Times,* "which ought to be as magnanimous as they are mighty, should be taught that there are some subjects outside the pale of legitimate journalism, some tactics that are reprehensible, and some rights that actors and every other class of people inalienably possess." The Giddy Gusher spoke her piece, too. "Confound the idiotic prints!" she erupted. "The man has sat and brushed the fast-gathering tears as he read the heartless summing up of his life's work and its end —and cried out in bitter agony against the vivisection of the press. In all the books of martyrs I believe Tony Hart's experience is not far exceeded. . . . For Heaven's sake, daily journals, with weakly [*sic*] Sunday editions, forbear. Don't print obituary notices, and then when your victims visit you and beg of you to believe they are still above ground, take back the fact of the burial but insist the hearse is yet in the street."

But, alas, the *Herald* story was substantially correct.

Even before his sickness became a matter of public debate, Hart had been having rough going. While Harrigan went off on his own, following the break-up, Tony and Gertie had recruited a rival company, with Tony's brother John Cannon and brother-in-law James Athy handling the business end of things. Only a month after the final farewell appearance at Colonel Sinn's theatre in Brooklyn, a notice had appeared in the *Clipper* heralding the advent, for the 1885-1886 theatrical season, of "The Inimitable Comedian, Mr. Tony Hart, assisted by the Charming Soubrette, Mrs. Tony Hart, and his own Grand New York Company, in an entirely new and original play." The play was *Buttons,* written by a journeyman dramatist named William Gill and tailor-made for Tony and Gertie; he had seven parts in it and she had five. They tried it out that August in Burlington, Vermont, and in Tony's home town, Worcester. Then, beginning on September 21st, Cannon booked a long and far-ranging tour for them. It was to start at Buffalo, to last eight months, and to cover practically the entire United States, including engagements in New York and San Francisco.

From the first, things went awry. Gertie took ill during the summer and there was day-to-day uncertainty, as the Harts set out on their trek, as to whether she would be able to perform any given evening. Two days after the tour got under way, Tony inadvertently gouged a hole in one of their supporting actors with a pitchfork. The play itself was so universally condemned by the critics whose path it crossed that in Youngstown, Ohio, on October 2nd, Tony threw out the whole last act and substituted a new one. Three days after that, in Columbus, Gertie fainted between the first and second acts, and, after being revived, was injured in the third act when a crank flew out of a stagehand's grip and struck her on the elbow.

In Cincinnati, the company grossed a feeble $700 in a whole week, a dismal record that was to stand until, seven years later, Julie Marlowe matched it. (Miss Marlowe had just married her first husband, a relatively obscure actor named Robert Taber, and had sentimentally insisted that she and her groom be billed, on a tour they made, solely as Mr. and Mrs. Taber. To many Julia Marlowe fans Mrs. Robert Taber was unknown, but although the bride's purse-pinched manager pleaded with her to give him, and herself, a break, she wouldn't budge. She clung to her conjugal anonymity and consented to use her own magnetic name only after the aggrieved manager got a court order insisting that she do so.) In Iowa City, Gertie was so indisposed she had to be left behind a couple of days while the rest of the company moved forward. On November 4th, after a dragging matinee in Minneapolis, Billy Gray, Jr., who was accompanying his foster parents and who recounted some of their woes in a diary he kept, made the terse, rueful entry, *"Buttons* must go!" Five days later, in St. Paul, Tony and Gertie cancelled the remainder of their tour, and they returned to Worcester to lick their wounds.

Buttons never did reach New York, but a couple of months after it folded, Tony returned to the city in another Gill opus, a farce called *The Toy Pistol,* which marked the debut as a Broadway producer of Charles Frohman, who as a young man had faithfully visited the old Comique every Saturday night, and used to entertain his family on Sundays with adoring imitations of Harrigan and Hart. There was not much to the play. In fact, it was almost identical with one that Gill and a collaborator had put on just a year previous. But it did give Tony a chance to demonstrate his virtuosity. In the third act alone, he appeared in three male characterizations—an Italian, a Jew, and a Chinese—and also as an Irish woman. And it did give him a chance to reappraise his personal popularity. The ovation he got on opening night—the Seventh Regiment turned out 450 strong—was something memorable. E. A. Dithmar, the *Times'* critic, who in keeping with the dignity of that journal habitually referred to Tony as Anthony Hart, had never seen anything quite like it. "The greatest dramatic artist the world ever saw could not hope for a tribute or greeting more spontaneous or emphatic than that given to Mr. Anthony Hart when he stepped upon the stage at the Comedy Theatre last evening," Dithmar wrote. "Our Booths and Jeffersons, Bernhardts and Modjeskas are rarely received with such demonstrative applause." Flowers by the basketful were propelled at the stage, and in addition to routine manual applause, there was much shouting, stamping of feet, and thumping of canes. But despite this promising getaway, the show's New York run lasted only two months, possibly because the Seventh was only a regiment and not a brigade. And to make matters worse, Harrigan was simultaneously appearing in *The Leather Patch,* which opened six days before *The Toy Pistol* and ran to brimming houses throughout that season, achieving such *éclat* that the Broadway streetcar conductors, a normally laconic tribe, took to alerting their passengers, as they neared the theatre that harbored it, with reverent shouts of "Harrigan's!"

Gertie Granville stayed out of *The Toy Pistol,* but there was another Miss Granville in the cast—Evelyn, or Eva, a

comely and amiable young woman who was to become one
of the most notorious members of the acting profession
and to earn the sobriquet, "Fair Evelyn of the Tenderloin." Her life was relatively tranquil up to the time she
played with Hart. Born in Chicago as Evelyn Post, she
later took her mother's maiden name and called herself
Evelyn Green, and still later adopted the name of Granville, quite probably hoping to capitalize thereby on
Gertie Granville's success. Evelyn went to a convent
school, whose curriculum appears to have left her sensationally unaffected, and graduated from there into the
chorus line of the Casino Theatre. She became a versatile
woman. She was an expert poker player. She once had
a short story published about a man who had unwittingly
married his own daughter; in an accompanying author's
note she swore that she knew this to be a true incident.
She achieved the distinction of being barred from Philadelphia, where the police got tired of hearing complaints
about her from wealthy philanderers who, after dallying
with her, would find themselves accused of stealing jewels
she had never owned and threatened with blackmail unless they made good. Before her career was over, it was to
be said of her that no greater argument for Prohibition
had ever lived. While still in her twenties, she served five
terms in the workhouse as a common drunk, and after she
was thirty, she was reputed to subsist on an exclusive diet
—the allegation was perhaps somewhat fanciful—of
whiskey, chloral, morphine, and opium.

Evelyn Granville had an exciting social life. One man
she lived with for a while, a lawyer who decided to run
for political office, concluded that her presence might be
detrimental to an orderly campaign, so he gave her $10,000

and packed her off to London, a municipality she presently
enlivened by grinding a champagne glass into the face of
a rather stuffy Britisher during a dinner party. Her most
renowned lover was Burton C. Webster, a New York
bookmaker, who was tried in 1892 for the first-degree
murder of Charles E. Goodwin, a dry-goods man who
had been competing with his slayer for Evelyn's fair
favors. Howe & Hummel represented Webster—ultimately they got him off with a ten-year sentence—and
when the case came into court, Evelyn Granville figured
importantly in the tactics of the defense. While Webster
was in the Tombs awaiting trial, she had borne a child
of his, and William F. Howe had her lug the infant into
court each day, so that its cries could continually assault
the jury's ears. During the trial, a district attorney, in
the course of a rather lengthy dissertation on Miss Granville's moral fiber, commented offhandedly that she was
"only an actress," and this implied disparagement of a
species enraged actors all over the country. They cited the
remark long afterward as an example of the kind of in-
dignity that their honorable profession had to put up
with. Fair Evelyn, despite the rigors of her youth, lived
until 1938, when she was close to seventy. At her death,
she was employed on a W.P.A. sewing project.

There was a line in *Old Lavender,* uttered by Harrigan
in the title role to Hart as the wharf rat, that went, "Keep
your voice and you'll always have company." Tony must
have been reminded of that when his next theatrical venture got under way, because it was during this show, a
comedy with music entitled *The Maid and the Moon-
shiner,* that he began to be seriously plagued with the

enunciative difficulty that was the first symptom of his ailment. Hart was co-starred in this play, written by Charles
Hoyt, with Lillian Russell, but even this combination of
local favorites couldn't keep the show running more than
two weeks. On the opening night, Hart, whose memory
had theretofore always been keen, blew up on his lines,
and the ones he did recall came out rather blurred. A few
days later he went to see his physician, Dr. Thomas S.
Robertson, who was both doctor and friend to a galaxy
of stage folk. Robertson's relationship with his patients
was so unconventional that he sometimes sent flowers to
their funerals. The doctor had his home and office at 28
East 20th Street, the birthplace of Theodore Roosevelt,
and he would receive callers there while seated, theatri-
cally, in an elegant Italian armchair on a raised dais.
Behind this throne stood a glass-faced cabinet on the
shelves of which were arrayed various jewels and other
gifts from stage people. Some of these presents had been
pressed on him by patients unable to meet his bills with
cash. When one actress not only paid the doctor in money,
but paid him promptly, he sent her a flowery letter of
astonished acknowledgment.

Dr. Robertson regretfully identified Hart's ailment as
paresis, but Tony and his family were reluctant to believe
this harsh verdict. Hart went to a couple of specialists,
hoping for some contrary word. They confirmed Robertson's diagnosis. Tony returned dejectedly to Worcester,
but in a few months he felt well enough again to have another stab at acting. This time, with Gertie playing opposite him again, he climbed aboard a vehicle called
Donnybrook, which had a brief run in New York in the
closing days of 1886 and then took to the road. *Donny-*

brook was not much more of a success than *Buttons* had
been, and moreover, Tony's condition got increasingly
worse as he traipsed around the country. But he kept the
show going until May of 1887, when he appeared on the
stage for the last time at the Howard Athenaeum in
Boston, where Harrigan and he had scored their first real
triumph.

Hart went back to Worcester once more, and soon, as if
he didn't already have trouble enough, he found himself
pestered by various petty law suits—one brought against
him by a printer who claimed the Harts owed him $2,000
for lithographs, another by an actor who had been fired
from *Donnybrook* and maintained that his professional
standing had thus been severely jeopardized, and still another by somebody who thought he had been bitten by
the Harts' dog. Then the nature of Tony's illness became
generally known. A spate of commiserating publicity followed, most of it referring to "poor Tony." A Worcester
paper, in one lugubrious account of Hart's rise and fall,
led off with "Poor Tony Hart!" and ended with it, too.
The phrase was apt in more than one respect; Hart by
then was nearly broke. Accordingly, some of his friends
in New York resolved to give him a benefit.

Prior to the formation of the Actors' Fund, which looks
after down-and-out performers and has its coffers periodically replenished by the proceeds from special performances of Broadway productions, benefits for individuals
were commonplace. The beneficiaries didn't even have to
be hard up. In lieu of extra salary, it was stipulated in
most actors' contracts that they were entitled to one benefit a year, and the custom extended to behind-the-scenes

folk, too. In May, 1872, the Howard Athenaeum had a solid week of benefits—six evening performances and two matinees—in honor of, among others, its box-office man, its orchestra leader, and its stagehands. Once an individual had agreed to take his benefit on a certain night, it was his good fortune if the house was full and his tough luck if business was slack. One time an actor who had prevailed on Edwin Booth to be an extra added attraction at his benefit learned, after he had tentatively settled on a date with his manager, that Booth couldn't make it that night. The actor tried to squirm out of his agreement, but the manager was firm. Then the actor realized something both he and his manager had overlooked: the date in question was a holiday, and the prospects for a sellout were rosy, Booth or no Booth. The manager realized this also, soon afterward, but by then it was too late for *him* to welsh, for in the meantime the actor had cagily inserted ads in the newspapers proclaiming the holiday performance as his very own.

Being speculative entities, benefits were often traded in, like securities. An actor who didn't want to risk having his benefit could sell his rights back to his employer, or even to an outside party. Lester Wallack once made a blanket offer to one of his casts; he proposed buying back all their benefit rights, and suggested as a fair price the average gross of the three most lucrative benefits of the season before. (There were fake benefits, too. Lola Montez, an actress who had some startling ups and downs— she was born in Ireland as Eliza Gilbert, functioned for a time as the mistress of and chief adviser to the King of Bavaria, and died a near pauper—had an ad published in the papers one time announcing her *real* benefit for that year. Previous benefits for her that had taken place in New York, Washington, and Philadelphia were phonies, she said; they were nothing but ordinary performances thus publicized by her manager in the hope of increasing his take.) Around 1870, just about one out of every three theatrical performances in the country either was or was represented as somebody or other's benefit. The calendar often got so crowded that on one occasion Dave Braham and John Cannon, despite a feud then raging between Harrigan's and Hart's kin, agreed to share a benefit.

In addition to benefit performances of regular shows, there were many special all-star benefits on Sunday evenings, Thursday matinees, and at other times when actors from a number of theatres could be herded together under a single roof. (They were even herded out of doors. A benefit was once held at the Polo Grounds for the playwright Bartley Campbell, who was languishing in a sanitarium; two teams called Tragedy and Comedy played a game of baseball in the author's behalf. Alexander Salvini starred for Tragedy and Nat Goodwin and De Wolf Hopper for Comedy.) Some actors got fed up with performing free to line other actors' pockets, a viewpoint that a player-within-the-play in *The Mulligans' Silver Wedding* expressed when he exclaimed, "Between benefits and subscriptions for indigent actors, I am impoverished."

Tony Hart's benefit was of the all-star variety. Nat Goodwin and George W. Floyd, at the time Goodwin's manager, were the principal instigators of it. They organized a sponsoring committee from among Hart's friends that included Dr. Robertson; managers Albert M. Palmer and Frank Sanger; and comedians Stuart Robson, William H. Crane, and William J. Florence. A

"Grand Testimonial Benefit" was scheduled for March 10, 1888, at the Academy of Music, but it had to be postponed for five days because some of the artists who had volunteered to take part—among them were a lady whistler, a boy cornettist, and a flock of minstrels—were out of town. The misfortune that had been dogging Hart's shaky footsteps still pursued him. The benefit had to be pushed ahead again when, four days before the second scheduled date, the Blizzard of '88 blanketed the city.

Even so, when the Grand Testimonial Benefit finally came off, on March 22nd, it was an imposing affair. The proceeds totalled close to $14,000—more than any such event had ever reaped before, and more than enough, it was expected, to keep Tony going for whatever time he had left. The *pièce de résistance* was the assassination scene from *Julius Caesar,* enacted exclusively by comedians. Goodwin was Marc Antony, Robson Brutus, and Crane Cassius. Such luminaries of the stage as Steele Mackaye, Frank Mayo, and Francis Wilson were assigned walk-on roles. All the comedians planned in advance to play their parts straight, but as soon as Robson, who had a squeaky, laugh-provoking voice, opened his mouth, the audience began to titter. He began to yell his lines, and the audience guffawed, and finally the audience was screaming with mirth and Robson was cursing. Toward the end of the scene, a sharp-eyed observer in the gallery spotted a familiar, slight figure, wearing the toga of a Roman senator, who was standing silently in a mob. It was Hart. A whisper ran through the gallery, and soon Robson's shrill protests and the attempts of his fellow comedians to strut their tragic stuff were engulfed by a roar of acclamation for poor, poor Tony.

Almost every theatrical personage of consequence in town showed up for Hart's benefit, with one exception— Edward Harrigan. Harrigan was then enjoying a successful New York run in his play *Pete*. When he first heard of the impending testimonial, he volunteered to bring his entire company to the Academy of Music and put on the second act of *Pete*. But he never did show up, and the only excuse given for his conspicuous absence was that he had already played ten benefits that season and was tired of them. Nobody believed that. Later it came out that Harrigan had changed his mind on being told that somebody had heard that Hart had told somebody else in a fit of petulance that he would accept no benefit at which Ned Harrigan appeared.

In June, 1888, Hart became unmanageable and was committed to the Worcester insane asylum. Gertie thereupon went back to work, as a featured performer in *The Paymaster,* whose author, Duncan B. Harrison, was a long-time friend of Tony's and hers. (Harrigan starred in the play, and created for himself a breath-taking scene in which he leapt from a prison tower, landed in a pool of water, and, as far as the audience was concerned, drowned. The tank was only four feet deep except in its center, where Harrison was supposed to land. He misjudged his aim one night, and caught his chin on a ledge at the four-foot mark. While a prison sentry solemnly announced his fictional death on stage, Harrison almost drowned in fact, having laid his jaw open to the bone and knocked himself cold. He was saved by a hastily lowered curtain, following which the sentry who had just pro-

claimed his demise fished him out. Then the ubiquitous
Dr. Robertson arrived and patched him up.)

By the start of 1889, Hart's condition seemed so much
improved that he was released from the insane asylum.
He stayed out for seven months. In February, he spent
some time in New York, and one night was taken by
John Cannon to see a performance of *Pete,* which Harrigan had revived. Hart and Cannon sat in a box, and nobody realized they were present until the curtain went up
and Harrigan's eye, roving casually over the house, fo-
cussed on them. Harrigan stopped dead in the middle of a
speech and stared as if he had seen a ghost, which in a sense
he had. Later Hart and Cannon went backstage and had a
brief, not unfriendly chat with Harrigan and Martin
Hanley. By a number of optimistic journalists around
town, this reunion was interpreted as a sign that the old
team was going to pair up again, but actually it was the
last time Harrigan and Hart ever met.

Tony was too far gone to act again with Ned or anybody
else. During the summer of 1889, while watching a baseball game, Hart got so excited that he became violent,
and he had to be sent back to the asylum. He left it after
that only to attend two funerals—that of one of his sisters
and that of Gertie, who died in March, 1890. Tony followed her casket down the aisle of St. John's Roman
Catholic Church in Worcester, sobbing like a child. He
grew sicker and sicker, and on November 4, 1891, hope-
lessly paralyzed, he died in the asylum, three months after
his thirty-sixth birthday. He left an estate later ap-
praised at eighty cents. During his last weeks at the
asylum, he had only one visitor, a retired prizefighter, but
his funeral, on November 6th, was attended by many old

acquaintances, including Annie Harrigan and two of her sons, Martin Hanley, and Dave Braham. The actors then in Harrigan's company sent a floral harp. Hanley sent a harp with a broken string. And from Harrigan—who could not attend because he was playing in a show—there was a huge floral pillow of orchids, bride roses, carnations, and tuberoses. In the center of it, on a field of pure white roses, was spelled out, in bright red carnations, the single word "Partner."

11.

Holding the Mirror Up to Nature

In 1848, a troupe of Parisian actors crossed the English Channel and, in London, announced that they would shortly appear in an all-French production of *Monte Cristo,* a dramatization of the Dumas novel. The reaction was crackling. A group of English actors and their friends, incensed at what they considered usurpation of their rightful domain by a band of pushy foreigners, bought out the entire house for the opening night and carried on so boisterously that not a single word uttered on the stage was audible off it. The French retreated in dismay—"unheard and insulted," one chronicle has it—and the incident became known as "The Monte Cristo Riot."

Among American actors, similarly, there was to be considerable resentment against invading aliens. Here the animus was directed chiefly against Britishers, many of

whom had adopted the rewarding course of playing engagements in the United States and departing these shores with
fistfuls of money that local actors felt had been more or less
wrenched from their proprietary hands. The situation was
not smoothed over any by the attitude of the British.
In 1888, for instance, taking note of a series of complaints from unemployed American actors, one English
theatrical agent cabled the *Herald* that the reason for his
countrymen's domination of the American stage was plain
enough. "They speak English," he said, "while the average
American actor does not." The *Herald* delightedly published this goading communiqué, and asked a number of
Americans for their comments, which it correctly anticipated would be sulphuric. Harrigan's was among the
milder responses. "I don't think I'll go to England to
learn English," he said. "I've been talking English, and
Irish, too, for that matter, on Broadway for a number of
years."

The *Herald* did not let the controversial matter rest. It
next proposed that American actors be sent abroad, prin-
cipally to London, for post-graduate training in correct
stage deportment. Martin Hanley, always glad to have his
name in print, swiftly furnished the paper with an all-star
committee that he thought would be ideal for passing on
candidates for such a finishing school. It should consist,
he declared, of Ada Rehan, Mrs. John Drew, Mrs. Emma
Waller, Edwin Booth, Joseph Jefferson, Dion Boucicault, and Edward Harrigan. Nothing ever came of the
notion, but enough of a stir was aroused to prompt Boucicault, in association with Albert M. Palmer, to start up a
finishing school for actors in New York. "As though we
had no mint here to stamp a value on our coin!" exclaimed
Boucicault.

But the transatlantic feud continued—indeed it persists today, as the restrictive regulations of both the American and English Actors' Equity organizations attest—and periodically, on one side of the ocean or the other, a plaintive cry would be heard. Harrigan, though the sympathetic chronicler of immigrants and the head of a stock company that included many foreign-born actors, was, curiously, usually in the forefront of the Buy American forces. In one bitter public statement, he pointed out that the theatregoing public had become such a sucker for imported wares that a $15-a-week American chorus girl, who could only sing three notes, had vaulted into the $1,750-a-week salary bracket by the simple expedient of making a round trip to England. Harrigan thought that $583.33 a note was excessive remuneration for her talents. Moreover, he said, the American craze for foreign-language entertainment was a ridiculous affectation. "The nasty songs of Anna Held, Yvette Guilbert, and others of their ilk are raved over by people who couldn't order a dinner in a Parisian café," said Harrigan, whose own French by then was quite fluent. "But Buggins pays his money, goes to the theatre, laughs immoderately at the wrong time, punches Muggins in the ribs, and, not to be outdone, Muggins laughs, too. And there you are!"

There was international bickering about plays as well as players. To the despair and envy of American playwrights, American producers had fallen into the habit of disdaining their works and presenting imported ones instead. However lamentable the lot of the actors might be, the authors had it worse. When, in 1887, a whole dozen new plays by American writers were unveiled in New York, the statistic elicited yips of astonishment. And three

years after that, commenting on the news that a Society
of American Dramatic Authors was in process of formation, a writer for the conservative magazine *Lippincott's*
pronounced himself incredulous, and said the public would
be, too. "That there are Americans who wrote for the
stage could be inferred from the presence of their names,
now and then, upon play-bills," the *Lippincott's* man said,
"but that there was more than a baker's dozen of them,
or that their calling justified even the doubtful honor of
organization, no one would be likely to imagine."

At about the same time, over in London, Henry James
was giving contemporary British dramatists *their* come-
uppance by asserting that the way things were going,
England seemed fated never to produce a native Aristophanes, which James presumably thought any self-respecting culture ought to do or throw in the towel. It was while
such gloomy analyses of the state of playwriting were
being tossed about that William Dean Howells put the
theatrical career of Edward Harrigan in a somewhat new
light by suggesting that maybe Harrigan was an American Aristophanes and that, in any event, he was perhaps
the most important playwright in the United States, and
certainly the most *American* American playwright.
Howells was, of course, the nation's foremost apostle of
literary realism, and he found irresistibly fascinating not
only the Harrigan plays themselves but also such state-
ments of their author's as: "The secret of success in playwriting lies largely in fidelity to nature. A play succeeds
when the spectator can put himself in the place of a leading part and see himself doing what is being done." Howells launched the forerunner of what was to become a
fleet of effusive testimonials to Harrigan in the July,

1886, issue of *Harper's Monthly Magazine,* describing his plays as "the joyous yet conscientious art of the true dramatist in all times who loves the life he observes. . . . the spring of a true American comedy, the beginning of things which may be great things," and the playwright himself as "a man in whom the instincts of the author combat the theatre's traditions, and the actor's experience censures the author's literary vanity." Howells threw in a few flattering allusions to the Dickensian nature of Harrigan's work and concluded, "In his province, we think he cannot be surpassed."

Howells' rating touched off a lively debate that went on sporadically for a couple of years, until it petered out for want of further fuel. Harrigan himself participated in it, even though, as one observer of the time put it, "I am sure that no one was quite as surprised to learn how great he was as Harrigan himself." A. M. Palmer emerged as the principal disputant of Howells' thesis. "A national drama must be reflective, and, to be reflective, it must have something to reflect," said Palmer. "I am aware that in some very minor instances our local stage has of late found something to reflect, and in this fact certain people fancy they discover the commencement of a national drama. The clever Mr. Harrigan, going down among the humble and degraded for his subjects, has produced plays whose claim to the attention of serious minds lies in the fact that they put before us types of character with vivid faithfulness. But what are these types?" Mostly imported Germans or imported Irish or Negroes, Palmer said, none of whom he would categorize as being American. Harrigan was ready with a patriotic rebuttal. "Whoever votes the Republican or Democratic ticket in these United

States," he said, possibly giving his Tammany Hall
cronies a slight twinge by putting them second, "must be
an American, no matter what may be his mother tongue or
color. So I class my works as American, and the greatest
compliment paid to my plays by foreigners is that they
do not understand them."

Palmer had other arrows in his quiver. For one thing,
he said that it was silly to argue about whether or not
Harrigan was a playwright, inasmuch as Harrigan's concoctions could not truly be called plays, but were rather
merely "a prolongation of sketches." What was *Hamlet,*
retorted Howells, when you came right down to it, but
a prolongation of sketches itself? Harrigan's reply to this
charge of Palmer's was, in keeping with his usual manner,
extravagantly prolix. "The phrase 'a prolongation of
sketches,' coined by Mr. A. M. Palmer, is not well put
regarding my plays," he said. "I would say 'a continuity
of incidents,' with some simple reason for their dovetail-
ing, and each link on the string sustained by some natural
motive that calls for the building of the entire stage structure. In this principle of playmaking, or sketch-prolong-
ing, we find reason for the character-drawing which should
be the one great aim of the dramatist. The plays that have
lived the longest have been poor in plot but rich in character. Unpretentious dramatic works, with one touch of
nature pervading them, are always welcome to the people.
But that one touch is so rarely found in the intricate plot-
production." Palmer's reservations about Harrigan's work
did not, however, preclude him from asking Harrigan to
be a featured speaker, along with Mark Twain, Chauncey
M. Depew, Lawrence Barrett, and other eminent citizens,

at a testimonial dinner for Edwin Booth that Palmer organized at Delmonico's in 1889.

Harrigan continually professed not to give a hang about plots. "I wish a fellow could make a play without a plot," he once said. "They are nightmares to me. When I find a bit of poor human nature and place it among its lowly surroundings, it grieves me to make him talk plot, yet I know that my work, let it be filled with the richest kind of character drawing, would fail with the audience that heard no plot, so I endeavor to find simple stories to serve as a gateway for my characters to enter, and I admit that my plots will never pass down into history as complex studies." Ideally, he thought, a good play should more or less follow the pattern of a good dinner-table conversation—gaiety over little jokes one minute, gravity at the recital of some misfortune the next. "Laughter and tears should be the component parts," he said. "The sunshine is not appreciated without the shade."

Harrigan's impatience with plots won some recognition, if not altogether the kind he hoped for. One time, a critic dubbed a play of his a classic example of "incomprehensibility absolute." There were some plays, the reviewer said, of which it could definitely be ascertained that they had a plot, but you couldn't figure out just what the plot was. This state of affairs the critic would describe as "incomprehensibility relative." In Harrigan's case, however, the man said, it was impossible to deduce for sure whether or not any plot had been intended. In the main, however, drifting in practice far from his own theory about dining-room chit-chat, Harrigan came up with some of the most cumbersome and complex plots ever devised. In this respect at least his comedies certainly deserve to be ranked with Shakespeare's. Mistaken identities and misconstrued letters were the foundations on which the majority of Harrigan's plays were ponderously built. The kind of device he frequently employed in his comedies of error was exemplified in *The Last of the Hogans,* where a welter of incident was based on a lady poet's innocent misreading of a letter she came upon that was intended for someone else. The letter had to do with a forthcoming prizefight, but because one of the contestants was called "The Parson," and because the text was full of references to a ring and gloves and a jewelled belt, the woman took it to be a proposal of marriage from a swain too shy to speak up. The complications that ensued from this misinterpretation were interminable. There were so many plots and subplots in the standard Harrigan play that the actors themselves sometimes failed to grasp them all. An actress who had had a protracted run in *The Leather Patch* was asked not long after this engagement for her views on its dramatic structure. "I never fully understood what it was all about," she confessed.

The object of Howells' affection and Palmer's disaffection had been turning out prolongations of sketches, or continuities of incidents, or whatever they were, at a brisk clip since his separation from Hart. In the fall of 1885, Harrigan had gone back to the Park Theatre, which he transformed into, to quote one of his own advertisements, "Harrigan's Park Theatre, the only theatre in America producing original comedy and local drama, all written, directed, and the principal characters impersonated by the author, Mr. Edward Harrigan." Harrigan spent close to $15,000 refurbishing the place, and had the last few rows of orchestra seats ripped out to make its size less overwhelming. The lack of a gallery still bothered him, but it was the best house he could get in a hurry, even though the rental terms—twenty per cent of the gross— seemed exorbitant. On some interior scrollwork, he had inscribed a phrase from *Hamlet* that he had come to think of as a suitable motto for his operations: "to hold, as 'twere, the mirror up to nature."

Martin Hanley, who had been relatively dormant in Harrigan and Hart's affairs while these were *in extremis,* came back as Harrigan's business manager, and soon earned new tributes to his imagination and acumen by initiating the custom of outfitting theatre ushers—the Park had eight of them—with pseudo-military uniforms. Up to then, ushers had been garbed in evening dress, to the occasional discomfiture of identically clad patrons who found it embarrassing to be asked to escort a gentleman to his seat or remove a spitball from a lady's hair. Hanley costumed his octet in bright blue jackets with brass buttons and black pants with bright red stripes. So dashingly identifiable a crew of ushers had never been seen before, and the admiring audiences began referring to them as "Father Hanley's Flying Artillery," which gratified Hanley enormously. What the ushers thought has not been recorded.

The first production at Harrigan's Park was a considerably expanded version of *Old Lavender,* which had been a modest afterpiece when Harrigan wrote it for Hart and himself in 1877, had been amplified in 1878, and was now a grandiose production with a cast of sixty-seven. Big casts always appealed to Harrigan. The late George C. D. Odell,

a valiant historian of the nineteenth-century theatre without whose meticulous and methodical researches latter-day
dabblers in the field would be mightily handicapped, con-
scientiously recorded the names of every member of every
cast of every play that came within his purview. In his
Annals of the New York Stage, Odell once mused, wist-
fully, "I wonder if Harrigan could have written a straight-
forward play involving not more than eight characters?"

Old Lavender, probably Harrigan's most famous play,
was a nicely balanced blend of the sunshine and shade its
author espoused. For shady pathos, there was Harrigan's
portrayal of Old Lavender, a man named George Coggswell who, early in the action, was fired from his job as
cashier in his brother's bank when, failing to hear the
brother's warning that a certain check was no good, he
went ahead and cashed it. He became a courtly, philosophical alcoholic (one of his lines, anticipating W. C.
Fields, was "I've been imposed upon by water"), and at
the end saved his brother's tottering bank by means of
some previously worthless mining-stock certificates that
suddenly turned valuable. For sunshiny mirth there was,
among other risibilities, John Wild's portrayal of Smoke,
a colored dog thief, whose favorite phrase, "Anybody
want to buy a dog?," was as widely quoted around town
as was to be Joe Penner's much later "Wanna buy a
duck?"

Old Lavender had been popular in its early, abbreviated
versions, but as a full-blown drama it attained far greater
renown. William Winter, the *Tribune's* highly respected
critic, said there was "no more thoroughly finished char-
acterization on the American stage than Mr. Harrigan's
Coggswell. It ranks with the few great creations of the
last twenty years and is in its way as entirely an artistic

performance as Mr. Jefferson's Rip Van Winkle."
Matthew Arnold was impressed with *Old Lavender,* and
so was the visiting Sir Arthur Pinero, who shortly after
seeing it wrote, not entirely to Harrigan's pleasure, a
comedy of his own called *Sweet Lavender.* Another touring Englishman who saw the play, Frederick Wedmore,
the London *Academy's* drama critic, did not much care
for its ethics—in Harrigan's eyes, it seemed to Wedmore,
all besotted bums were to be revered, and all men of
wealth were automatically villainous—but he felt that the
play had more vitality than just about any other in town,
and he declared, "In New York today Mr. Harrigan shows
to a third-class audience, presumably yearning for sensation, the virtues of restraint and reticence, the delightful-
ness of artistic delicacy."

All over New York, various broken-down citizens
claimed the dubious honor of being the real-life prototype
of Harrigan's artistry. One elderly bachelor who was
thrown into the Tombs in 1893 for blacking his landlady's
eye said, in justification of the blow, that he was constantly
being picked on by his fellow tenants and having his hat,
a high, spotlessly white one, knocked off by neighborhood
children, merely because he tried to behave and dress—
as more or less did the fictional Old Lavender—with the
fastidiousness and dignity appropriate to a gentleman
who had known better days. Could a body be expected
to maintain his composure forever, the defendant asked
the judge, if, every time he went out for a walk, he was
trailed by a pack of ill-mannered boys, shouting, "There
goes Old Lav! Let's block his dicer!"?

In four seasons at the Park Theatre, Harrigan indus-
triously wrote, produced, directed, and starred in eight

new plays, and, furthermore, sandwiched in among them nine revivals of his earlier works. The second new play, following *Old Lav*, was *The Grip*, the intricate plot of which involved a secret handclasp and a profusion of mistaken-identity episodes. Harrigan played a sergeant who was confused with a colonel. The play opened at a time when there was considerable public agitation about a gadget on the two-year-old Brooklyn Bridge, known as a grip, which was used to haul streetcars across the structure. The bridge grip was held to be unreliable, and the city's concern about it provided Harrigan with a fine publicity break—the kind that plays with names like *Hamlet* or *Macbeth* could never hope for. "Why do not the Brooklyn Bridge managers secure *The Grip* of Edward Harrigan's?" inquired the Yonkers *Gazette*, for instance. "That never gives way."

Harrigan's *Grip* did give way, after a two-and-a-half-month run, to *The Leather Patch*, his treatise on body-stealing, in which he played an undertaker and Mrs. Yeamans a lady undertaker. One notable night soon after it opened, 110 members of the New York Undertakers Association attended in, as the saying goes, a body, accompanied by the coroners of New York and Hoboken. This excursion engendered some fraternal dissension. The mortuarian delegation was headed by the vice-president of the association, since the president had refused to have any part of it, being of the unalterable opinion that it was unseemly for members of his stony-faced vocation to be seen laughing in public. The remaining new plays that Harrigan presented between 1885 and 1888 were *The O'Reagans, McNooney's Visit, Pete, Waddy Googan,* and *The Lorgaire.* Benoit Constant Coquelin, the celebrated interpreter of Cyrano and Tartuffe, was in New York during *Waddy Googan's* run, and Brander Matthews took him around to see it. Matthews was astounded when, on escorting Coquelin backstage after the performance, Harrigan conversed with him in rippling French. Coquelin, for his part, was astounded by the singular goings-on he had witnessed during the performance. *"C'est quelque chose de très particulier,"* he told Matthews.

The Lorgaire was an innovation for Harrigan. A Boucicault-like melodrama laid in a fishing village on the west coast of Ireland, it was the first full-length play of his authorship to take place anywhere but New York. "Lorgaire" is Gaelic for "detective," and as an Irish sleuth Harrigan contrived to don five disguises, which in effect gave him a chance to play six parts. Besides being a detective, he was on view as a commercial traveller, a French smuggler, a sailor, a schoolmaster, and a fiddler. The *Spirit of the Times* sent a man up into the balcony one night to find out which of the six Harrigans was the favorite there.

"We like Harrigan best when he's himself," was the reported consensus.

"And which roles are those?" pursued the *Spirit's* surveyor.

"Why, sor, every one of them," was the reply.

Harrigan's stay at the Park was prosperous. Despite the high rent he had to pay—it averaged around $40,000 a year, or nearly twice the going rate—he made a clear profit of around $50,000 each of his four seasons there. Satisfied that he had nothing to worry about without a co-star, but dissatisfied with the terms of his lease, he resolved to build a theatre of his own. Several of his friends pitched in to help with the financing, pre-eminent among them Austin Corbin, the president of the Long Island Rail Road and the boss also of a 28,000-acre estate in New Hampshire where he kept a pet herd of buffalo. On West 35th Street, just east of Sixth Avenue, Harrigan found a promising spot, the site once more of a derelict church, this time an African Methodist one. While plans for the new theatre were being drawn, Harrigan decided to go on the road for a season. He had not missed a winter in New York for twelve years, and at the news that he proposed to skip the city entirely for two years, a few of the old hands in his company—notably Annie Yeamans and John Wild—balked. Harrigan's mind was set, though, and, while some of his fans wondered how he would ever manage without garrulous Annie and gallery-eyed Johnny, Harrigan let them go.

Many stars of Harrigan's era, when they went on tour, took with them only a handful of featured players, and filled the gaps in their ranks with inexpensive local talent recruited along the way. Harrigan preferred to be surrounded by actors familiar with his *très particulier* methods. Sometimes he would hire a few bucolic extras to stand around in mob scenes, but for the most part he stuck with his New York company. When he set forth in June, 1889, on a junket to the West Coast, he took with him a retinue of fifty people, including his wife and his two oldest children. The principals rode in a Pullman car, and the chorus men and women in day coaches. Scenery, wooden chests crammed with props, and can-

vas hampers full of costumes occupied two baggage cars.
A notable feature of this trip was the only appearance on
stage, during her long association with her husband's ventures, of Annie Harrigan. At Leadville, Colorado, one
young actress took ill shortly before a scheduled performance of *Waddy Googan*. Annie, who knew practically
all the plays by heart, stepped nimbly into the breach—a
challenging one, since she had by then borne seven children and the actress she replaced was a tender ingenue
whom one goggle-eyed critic had called "willowy as a
tulip stem and with lips as red and moist as the heart of
a watermelon"—and gave a polished performance.

While Harrigan was travelling, his new theatre was
taking shape. As his architect, he had picked F.
H. Kimball, the designer of the second Comique, and
Kimball evoked a small, cozy theatre that just suited his
client's tastes. It had a seating capacity of not quite 1,000,
and a separate gallery. Harrigan's Theatre, as the structure was named, was an Italian-Renaissance building,
the exterior finished in white terra cotta, and the interior
panelled in black oak. Here the only evidence that the site
had once had religious connotations was provided by a
stained-glass portrait of Dan Mulligan, which was fitted
into one of the windows, much as a patron saint might
be honored by a church. Taking frank recognition of the
fact that his wife, sooner or later, assumed control over
most of his financial affairs, Harrigan made her nominal
owner of the theatre right off, and he had her initials, encircled by a stone wreath, carved on the front of the
building.

Harrigan's Theatre opened on December 29, 1890, with
Reilly and the Four Hundred. Harrigan had been writing

this play for months, hoping to inaugurate the house with a thoroughly polished piece of work, and had originally intended to call it something like *Moses and the Four Hundred,* since its leading character was to be a Jewish pawnbroker who made a safari into high society. But Annie demurred. She said his public doted on him as an Irishman, and that he would be foolish to risk disappointing them.

"I'm tired of being an Irishman," Harrigan replied. "Ned Booth said I made a great Jew in *Mordecai.* He told me I ought to do Shylock some time."

"Write it any way you like," replied his wife, tactfully omitting to remind him that, however bracing Edwin Booth's opinion of *Mordecai Lyons* might have been, it constituted a minority view, "but you'd better be an Irishman if you want to play it in your theatre, because I own it."

Harrigan played an Irish pawnbroker named Wily Reilly.

Reilly and the Four Hundred was a smash hit. It ran for 202 successive performances that first season. (Six weeks after its première, George Stout, who by then had left the Harrigan company, paid it his own special form of compliment by coming up with a play about a pawnbroker and high society.) Several factors contributed to *Reilly's* success. The return of Harrigan to New York after his unaccustomed absence was, of course, one. Another was that John Wild, after flopping badly in a show of his own called *Running Wild,* was back in the Harrigan fold. Another was the song "Maggie Murphy's Home," which was fetchingly rendered by Emma Pollock in her debut with the company. She was only fifteen but had got herself hired by auditioning in her older sister

Evelyn's clothes. But the most talked-about aspect of the production was Harrigan's unveiling in it of a type of low-life character novel to the stage—the Tough Girl.

In San Francisco, during his latest transcontinental tour, Harrigan had hired several indigenous young women as supernumeraries, paying them fifty cents a performance each. One of them was a seventeen-year-old fish-cannery worker named Ada Lewis. Backstage, Harrigan overheard her telling stories in a beguilingly hard-boiled accent, and he asked her to come east with the company, at $15 a week, and take a speaking part in his forthcoming play. The role of the Tough Girl that he conceived for her didn't offer much in the way of dialogue. It was that of a saucy, self-assured, hard-shelled, worldly girl who affected a mannish walk, talked in low-class slang, and wore a seedy get-up consisting of a brown jersey that was too short at the wrists, a ragged brown dress, a shabby straw hat, and ill-fitting gaiters. Her like had not been on the stage before, and since her costume provided the added attraction of being corsetless—she was the sweater girl of her day—Harrigan hoped that the characterization would be effective. It was. On the opening night of *Reilly*, Miss Lewis had but to saunter on stage and in her peculiar fashion utter two words—they were "Sa-a-y, Reilly"—to be greeted by a shout of acclamation. While the ovation continued, Harrigan, who up to that instant had been apprehensive about the entire enterprise, whispered to her to stay where she was, and he sidled toward the wings, where his wife was standing.

"Annie, your money's safe," he whispered, and then ambled back to the side of the Tough Girl.

Ada Lewis was not supposed to re-appear after that

scene, but Harrigan was so impressed with her reception
that between the first and second acts he decided to work
her into an upper-class ballroom scene that occurred in
Act III. During the intermission after the second act, he
dashed off a couple of lines of dialogue for her, and, while
Miss Lewis was memorizing these and a wardrobe mistress
was feverishly pinning an evening gown on her, Annie
Harrigan and Marietta Ravel Hanley, who were dressed
in their finest for the big occasion, peeled off all their personal jewelry and decked the dazed young actress with it.
Ada Lewis became famous overnight, and from then on
was nationally recognized as an expert on the tough-girl
species. Years later, she was giving interviews, as an authority on raffish slang, to the *Literary Digest.*

Harrigan had never been sitting prettier. He moved his
family to a spacious brownstone on West 44th Street,
to be nearer his theatre. The children were growing up.
Ned, Jr., had made his stage debut in San Francisco the
year before, and his brothers were begging for a chance
to emulate him. Acclaimed as playwright and actor,
prospering as a theatre proprietor, and with the city
singing his and Braham's songs as contentedly as ever,
Harrigan looked as though he could go on for years with
no more perturbing headaches than those foisted on him
by the ever-watchful Society for the Prevention of Cruelty
to Children, or, as it was commonly known, the Gerry
Society. This organization was an outgrowth of the
S.P.C.A., with whose founder, the scrappy Henry
Bergh, Harrigan had repeatedly tangled. Once, while
Bergh had looked on disapprovingly from an orchestra
seat, a horse playing a minor role in one Harrigan pro-

duction had plunged through a weak spot in the stage flooring, and had had to be hoisted out with a derrick before the performance could continue. Harrigan treated the animals in his shows humanely enough, and on the whole they were less rarely injured by the spirited demands of his direction than were their human colleagues, but on Bergh's next visit, as it happened, a cat leaping from a pot of chowder—in a Harrigan play, there was always apt to be a cat in the chowder—inadvertently brushed against a gas footlight and singed some of its hair off.

The S.P.C.A.'s growing suspicions that Harrigan merited special scrutiny had darkened still further when *Pete* opened in 1887. This play called for the presence of a jackass, and Harrigan, anxious to avoid reproof from Bergh's outfit if he could, planned originally to have two human actors impersonate the animal. But immediately after the dress rehearsal, which finished at two o'clock in the morning, Harrigan's passion for realism got the better of him. Nothing but a genuine jackass would do, he decided. He thought at once of a nocturnal fellow he knew named Paddy Campbell, who prowled the city collecting fat, in the wake of a splendidly dilapidated jackass with whom Harrigan was also acquainted. After hastily downing an oyster supper, Harrigan set off in search of Campbell, and caught up with him at five in the morning. The fat collector was perfectly willing to let his jackass go on stage that night, but only on condition that he himself go on, too. Adding an extra face to one of his bulging casts was not a terribly difficult feat, so Harrigan consented to these terms. The beast and his escort dutifully reported to the theatre at dusk. So, alas, did the S.P.C.A. When the jackass, fidgety despite its master's proximity,

kicked Harrigan toward the beginning of things, and
Harrigan, no man to miss an opportunity like that, spon-
taneously kicked the animal right back, most of the audience chortled gleefully, but the S.P.C.A. agent merely
took notes. The script subsequently required the jackass
to die on stage, in a fall through a trap-door. Harrigan
had considerately placed a heavily padded stall beneath
the spot, so the animal wouldn't be hurt, but a mis-
chievous super sneaked in there and began tickling the
jackass with a feather. During the following scene, the air
was rent with hideous, ghostlike braying, and the S.P.C.A.
man came close to braying himself with indignation.

The chief counsel to the S.P.C.A. was Elbridge T.
Gerry, a distinguished lawyer, yachtsman, and civic
leader. Gerry had been responsible for the founding of the
S.P.C.C. when, in 1874, he had established that the
municipal courts could be as hospitable to complaints of
child-beating as of horse-beating. That same year, he
started up the S.P.C.C., and he was soon trying philan-
thropically to rid the streets of *padrones* and their en-
slaved juvenile musicians, and to rid the stage of youthful
opera troupes and such aggregations as Harrigan and
Hart's pint-sized Sixty-ninth Regiment. Gerry became
so vigilant a guardian angel for child actors, and so un-
remitting a gadfly to their employers, that when, in 1892,
he made a $50 contribution to a Santa Claus fund being
collected for stage children, the *Dramatic Mirror,* which
reflected their employers' viewpoint, expressed wonder
that the soliciting committee should have accepted such
tainted money.

In the fall of 1893, one of Harrigan's young sons
persuaded his father that it was high time he launched

his theatrical career. Harrigan indulgently gave him a bit part in a revival of *Dan's Tribulations* that was then in rehearsal. All the boy had to do was carry a growler of beer across the stage and say a couple of words, a scene that took place well before nine o'clock, by which hour kids under sixteen, in keeping with a statute Gerry had got enacted, were supposed to be tucked in bed, or at any rate tucked out of sight. Even before curfew time, youngsters were supposed to have a permit issued by the mayor's office before they could act. Martin Hanley had applied for one of these for the boy, but it hadn't yet arrived when the play opened, and he went on without it. This was what Bergh and Gerry had long been waiting for. Elated at having a chance finally to prevent Harrigan from being cruel to something, even if it was his own son, the S.P.C.C. demanded that the unlicensed boy be kept off the stage, and until the situation could be straightened out by City Hall, he was. "It would be more for the public interest," fumed the partisan *Spirit of the Times,* "if Commodore Gerry were to concentrate his attention upon the defenders of the America Cup and leave Harrigan's jug severely alone. If Lord Dunraven should capture the cup, as now seems probable, the tribulations of the Commodore who lost the cup will surpass those of Dan Mulligan." Everything ultimately worked out all right, however, since Harrigan's influence at the mayor's office easily equalled, if it did not surpass, Gerry's. After a couple of suspenseful days, Harrigan's son was granted his working papers, and, despite the *Spirit's* misgivings, Commodore Gerry's boat, the aptly named *Vigilant,* trounced Lord Dunraven's *Valkyrie II,* three races to none.

Of all the young folk who appeared on Harrigan's stage—in some New York circles it was thought that, the Boucicault-Palmer training program notwithstanding, there was no better finishing school in town for actors than the Harrigan company—none had a more diverting personality than Fannie Batchelder, who was enrolled in the cast of *Reilly and the Four Hundred* in May, 1891, when she was twenty-four years old. Known as "the girl with the wondrous locks," she had an enormous mane of reddish-brown hair that fell well below her waist and that endeared her to contemporary photographers. Her picture was frequently taken, with her massive tresses in one captivating arrangement or another, by the elegant Fifth Avenue photographer Sarony, who conducted his sittings attired in a velveteen jacket and a velveteen fez with a velveteen tassel, which he directed his subjects to watch instead of a birdie. Miss Batchelder had an unusual background for a member of Harrigan's retinue. She was a Boston girl, the daughter of a railroad official whose ancestors had settled there in 1632, and she was raised under the shadow of Bunker Hill, which a forebear of hers, Colonel William Prescott, had commanded in the perilous days when it was Breed's Hill. She moved in the most refined social circles (the elder J. P. Morgan was a pal of hers), and as a debutante went out exclusively with Harvard men. Few old grads have ever loved Harvard more fiercely than did she. "Harvard's Fair Champion" was her favorite appellation for herself. When a bunch of Yale undergraduates left a posy of violets backstage for her one evening, along with a note inviting her to sup with them, she declined brusquely. Her reason, she later explained, was that "These boys did not know the song in my heart:

'Harvard will be Harvard as Harvard was old Harvard when Yale was but a pup.' "

Harvard's fair champion was a writer as well as an actress, and the university was her favorite theme. A collection of light verse she composed, entitled *Sons of Harvard,* contained poetic tributes to, among other landmarks of the Cambridge campus, such institutions as the Hemenway Gymnasium, Memorial Hall, and the College Library, along with a testimonial quatrain to the football team that went:

> Give three cheers—'Cheer-cheer-cheer'—
> And one cheer more
> For Harvard's true champions.
> *Je vous adore.*

Miss Batchelder made her stage debut in 1885, when she was eighteen, and her infatuation with Harvard soon got her into an extraordinary row. She was playing in *A Tin Soldier,* by Charles Hoyt, at the Standard Theatre in New York when, on the night of May 28, 1886, 500 Columbia students attended en masse. Most of them were sophomores, but in honor of this class other undergraduate luminaries turned out: the varsity crew occupied one box, for instance, and the varsity baseball team another. By way of expressing appreciation of this lavish patronage, Hoyt instructed all the women in his cast to affix to their bosoms blue and white satin rosettes, with satin streamers in the same colors dangling beneath. Fannie was appalled. "I pinned the rosette over my heart," she subsequently recounted, "but I was sure Columbia could not be as fair a college as Harvard." This loyal reflection prompted her to action. On top of her Columbia rosette, she defiantly

pinned a ribbon in Harvard crimson, and around her
wondrous locks, which were braided, she tied a second
piece of crimson.

The Columbia boys acknowledged the testimonial
rosettes, as a couple of actresses made their entrances, with
resounding cheers. Then Fannie Batchelder came on. At
first, she, too, was acclaimed. Then the audience spotted
the insolent crimson superimposed on her blue. Boos,
hisses, and shouts of "Take it off!" supplanted the applause. Hoyt, wondering what on earth had happened,
rushed to the edge of the stage, and saw red. He began
yelling at the ingenue from there. A crew man leaned
precariously out of his box, threatening, in real or simu-
lated rage, to jump onto the stage and remove the crimson himself, but he was restrained by two fellow oars
from proceeding further. Fannie simply curtsied. Hoyt
beckoned her to the wings and told her sharply that if
she didn't mend her ways, and amend her costume, she'd
be fired that instant.

"Now take it off!" bellowed the playwright.

"No I will not," she declared firmly. "I shall wear this
little bit of crimson or, as you say, I shall not go on the
stage any more tonight!"

"Take it off!" thundered Hoyt.

"I love Harvard!" she retorted. "Take off the crimson?
Never!"

By then she was crying so hard, with rage and emotion,
that all her colors were wet with tears. But Hoyt couldn't
budge her, and she departed damply from the stage and
from the show.

The doughty Miss Batchelder was brought to Harrigan's attention, a few years later, by Joseph Howard,

Jr., a journalist, a biographer of Henry Ward Beecher, and the one-time perpetrator of a hoax that had nearly caused a major New York riot—a story he invented for the *World* one otherwise dull day in 1864 to the effect that President Lincoln planned to draft an additional 400,000 residents of the city for military service that year. Harrigan hired Miss Batchelder, although the closest he had ever come to Harvard had been when he and Hart, during their engagement at the Howard Athenaeum in 1872, had taken part in an antic regatta on the Charles River; they had entered a race in which each contestant rode in a washtub hitched behind six geese. (Neither man won, but four years later, in a New Orleans variation of this bygone sport, Harrigan took the first-prize medal in a washtub hauled by eight ducks.) Fannie's allegiance to Harvard hadn't wavered. One of her costumes in *Reilly* included a sailor hat, and she swiftly girded it with a crimson band. By then, Harvard had begun to reciprocate her affection. Just before curtain time on May 26, 1891, she received several dozen crimson roses from the Harvard class of '88; the accompanying card said the flowers were to commemorate the fifth anniversary of her gallantry at the Standard Theatre. In her second year with the Harrigan company, Miss Batchelder was wed to Charles Montagu Ward, a socially prominent banker, a cousin of Julia Ward Howe, and the man who had singlehandedly broken a horsecar-drivers' strike a few years earlier by piloting a vehicle down Third Avenue through a shower of missiles, while unarmed save for a gold-headed cane. For a couple of years their marriage was kept secret—ostensibly because it was considered bad business for young actresses to be known as wives (most managers customarily cut a

single woman's pay the moment she admitted to matrimony), but possibly because the bride was reluctant to
confess that her spouse was, of all unlikely people, a
Columbia man.

The eventual revelation of Miss Batchelder's marital
status was heralded by a telltale dedication page in a
paper-bound book of hers that was published early in 1894,
entitled—rather incongruously, in the circumstances—
Why Men Like Married Women. The page said, "To
Charles Montagu Ward, *Mon Ami Le Plus Devoué.*"
The book was a potpourri of poems and essays, most of
which she had previously had printed here and there
under the by-line "Ingenue," and one chapter of it created
a furor backstage at Harrigan's Theatre. Fannie had already ruffled the feelings of some of the other ladies there.
For one thing, Harrigan permitted her to wear her own
jewelry, of which she had a twinkling amount, on stage;
for another, the gentlemen who came around to court her
were the envy of her less socially endowed colleagues. The
controversial chapter purported to be a letter from the
maid of an actress to a friend, and there were several
easily identifiable characters delineated in it with what one
newspaper described as "a pen dipped in gall"—among
them a theatrical manager who was the smiling, ruddy,
pompadoured, and pompous image of Martin Hanley.

The principal targets of Miss Batchelder's pen were
"The Racy Four," a quartette of actresses dubbed "The
Hoodlum," "The Human Fly," "The Bleached Poll," and
"La Sale." There could be little doubt in the minds of any
knowledgeable readers of the work that these stood, re-
spectively, for Ada Lewis, Emma Pollock, Emma's sister
Evelyn, and another young actress named Margery Teal.

It was to be deduced from the text that these girls had been teasing Fannie Batchelder. Miss Teal, it seemed, had once impishly chalked a large star on Fannie's dressing-table mirror, by way of accusing her of a swelled head, and had then called the rest of the company's attention to her art work by marching up and down the corridor outside chanting the "Star-Spangled Banner." Miss Lewis, in mockery of Fannie's beloved hair, had bought a long, coarse switch and roguishly informed Miss Batchelder one day that she planned to wear it thenceforth. And some one of the four tormentors, it appeared, had poked out the eyes of a photograph of Fannie that hung in the property room. In retribution, the author made her Racy Four out to be ninnies of little charm and less culture. The Human Fly was depicted, for example, as childishly prone to jealous tantrums, La Sale as a spiteful gossip, and the Hoodlum as so woefully ignorant that when an admirer presented her with some sterling silver she had been obliged sheepishly to ask Fannie Batchelder what "sterling" meant.

Both Harrigan and Hanley tried to keep calm about the book, and to ignore it. But their actors were not similarly disposed. Backstage, the air sizzled with vengeful talk nightly until the author walked in, at which point, according to the *Advertiser,* "the atmospheric change is so rapid within a few moments that every one is obliged to put on her heaviest wraps and the water pipes freeze solid." Ada Lewis said the book was absurd, and Emma Pollock, while insisting that she could surely not have inspired any of it, denounced it as scurrilous. "The boot pinches only those who wear it," retorted the irrepressible author. Prodded by the newspapers, Hanley finally expressed himself. He said that while he hadn't read *Why Men Like Married Women,* he had heard enough about it to deem it regrettable, and that as a matter of fact when the company moved from New York to Boston, as it was planning to at the start of a road tour in a couple of weeks' time, Miss Batchelder would be leaving. "After our engagement there, I shall have to fall back on my old standbys, Mrs. Yeamans, Mr. Wild, and Mr. Harrigan," continued Hanley sarcastically. "We shall try to worry along somehow and give a performance every night. Miss Batchelder does not care to travel. She's quite right. Many actresses have found the provinces malarial before this. On the road one has to put up with so many inconveniences and such second-rate cabs. Of course, with Mr. Harrigan, Mrs. Yeamans and myself, it's different. We're tough and well seasoned. If the provincial cabs don't suit us, we can walk, or, if the worst comes to the worst, we can hail a streetcar. But then, you know, we're born actors; the manufactured article has to be dealt with more tenderly."

Fannie was not abashed. The following day, she declared that Hanley was mistaken and that she was not quitting the company. At that, Harrigan felt compelled to speak up. He was not certain how soon it would happen, he said, but there was no doubt in his mind that Fannie Batchelder's days with his company were numbered. A month later, she did leave it, and not long afterward retired permanently from what had been a brief, but stimulating, stage career. Upon immersing herself contentedly in private life—she lived until 1954, when she died at the age of eighty-seven—she made an unsolicited gift of her collection of theatrical photographs, a large one, to Harvard University.

12.

HOW CAN MY VOGUE HAVE PASSED?

Early in 1895, Harrigan, just turned fifty, announced his intention of taking his company to London and, perhaps, to Australia. Some of his early sketches had been done abroad in variety halls, but none of the full-length plays had ever been exported. His most recent plays—*The Last of the Hogans, The Woolen Stocking,* and *Notoriety*— had done fairly well at home, but he sensed a gradual diminishing of the New York public's appetite for his peculiar fare. One thing that pleased him, however, was that his oldest son had almost reached the age of eighteen, had become a full-fledged member of the Harrigan company, and would soon, his father hoped, figure as importantly in its destiny as Tony Hart once had. The boy had already set some sort of theatrical record. At the age of fourteen, he had manned his father's box office, thus

becoming the third successive generation of his family—
his grandfather and uncle had preceded him—to occupy
that trusted post. Then, early in February, 1895, young
Ned fell ill with what was at first thought to be a re-
currence of an attack of typhoid fever he had suffered at
nine. He had severe abdominal pains, for which the attending physicians prescribed hot flaxseed poultices. By the
time specialists were called in and correctly diagnosed his
trouble as appendicitis, his appendix had ruptured, and on
February 17th, after belated and unavailing surgery, he
died of peritonitis.

The boy's father, then appearing in a revival of *The
Major,* was shattered. For a few days, he kept on performing, but it was painful for him and painful for his audiences. On February 23rd, too dispirited to continue any
further, he dismissed his company and closed the theatre
doors. He was never to set foot on that stage again. A
month later, Harrigan's Theatre was leased to Richard
Mansfield, who renamed it the Garrick—a choice that
enabled him, when he changed the carved inscription on
the theatre's façade, to make use of the existing letters
"ARRI." Mansfield, after having the place fumigated,
which may have been a routine sanitary measure rather
than a token of his estimate of Harrigan's clientele,
made several fancy alterations. In the basement, he set up
a lounge called the Pompeian Room, where coffee and ices
were served in front of a marble fountain and where, Mansfield thought, theatregoers who had journeyed to the city
from remote environs like Staten Island could rest for an
hour or so before curtain time.

Mansfield couldn't make a go of operating the theatre,
and he abandoned it after a costly eight-month occupancy,

but it remained known as the Garrick up to the time it
was torn down in 1932. Until Harrigan died in 1911, and
until his wife died seven years after that, their principal
source of income was the rental they got from a variety
of tenants, including the proprietors of a burlesque outfit,
the Joyland Girls Company, who inhabited the place for
a spell in 1915 and, to the Harrigan family's dismay, contrived to have it raided on grounds of immorality. In 1919,
a year after Annie Harrigan's death, the premises became the first home of the newly formed Theatre Guild.
Many people who nowadays look back nostalgically upon
the Guild's *Garrick Gaieties* are unaware that the ghost
of Harrigan's gaieties hovered above them.

Grief made Harrigan sick himself, and after ailing the
rest of the winter of 1895, he set off for Europe, with
Dave Braham, Jr., as a companion, to convalesce. He
returned markedly refreshed, having enjoyed his first
glimpse of Ireland and having been further perked up,
while in Paris, by the tonic presence of his old friend Tony
Pastor. Harrigan and Pastor were sharing a horse-drawn
cab on the Champs Elysées one afternoon when Pastor,
whose command of French was rudimentary, got into a
wrangle with the driver about the fare. Harrigan, by then
a recognized expert among his American acquaintances
not only on the French language but on the French
mode d'être, told Pastor gravely that an argument like
that could be satisfactorily resolved, in Paris, solely by
a duel. When the driver, to Harrigan's surprise, echoed
this imaginative sentiment, the party repaired to the Bois
de Boulogne. Inasmuch as no one present had any other
weapons, fists were agreed upon. Only one blow was

struck; the driver swung first and busted Pastor's dental plate. Then the adversaries embraced and adjourned, with Harrigan, to the nearest bistro. This was as close as Harrigan ever got to having any of his shows, or what could readily have been an episode in many of them, produced abroad.

Back home, Harrigan quickly ground out a new play, *My Son Dan,* in which he toured the provinces during the following season. By the end of the summer of 1896, he felt up to acting in New York again, and, renting the Bijou Theatre, he put on another fresh work, *Marty Malone.* Like *Reilly and the Four Hundred,* it was a play that skipped from salon to saloon, and to appear in it with him Harrigan re-assembled a number of his old supporting players. Wild and Mrs. Yeamans had gone their own ways—they were in vaudeville, and Harrigan, after viewing Mrs. Yeamans in a monologue act, sandwiched between a Dutch comedian and some trained dogs, said he had never seen a more pathetic spectacle—but Harry Fisher, Ed Mack, and Charles Coffey rallied to the familiar standard, and so did George Merritt, who had introduced *Paddy Duffy's Cart,* and Dan Collyer, who had joined Harrigan in 1885 and filled many a Tony Hart role. But while Harrigan scored a personal triumph, his audiences seemed less eager than theretofore to swallow his hearty doses of turmoil. Knockdown and slapbang were beginning to pall. "Does this excellent actor think the public is turning from him because he doesn't hit them hard enough?" mused one critic. "It is not that. It is because he has broken heads and gouged eyes and battered teeth; and the public turns whither it may get love taps instead of lambastings." Harrigan himself was more dis-

turbed than he had ever been before by dissident criticism.
"They have almost got Harrigan frightened this time," he
declared.

He was determined nonetheless to push on. But he was
finding it increasingly difficult to write with his usual
facility, and after months of wrestling with unyielding
scripts he wanly accepted an offer, in the spring of 1897,
to make a tour of the Keith & Proctor vaudeville circuit.
"A wanderer over the face of the earth playing in continuous shows," as one sorrowing admirer described him
then, Harrigan, supported by what was for him a dreadfully austere cast of ten, appeared in a succession of "petite
plays"—half-hour condensations of *The Grip, McSorley's
Inflation, The Mulligan Guards' Ball,* and other items
from his repertoire. One week in 1899 he found himself
on the same bill at Proctor's 23rd Street in New York with
another falling idol, Isabelle Urquhart, who not so long
before, in light opera at the Casino, had been a star of a
magnitude almost rivalling Lillian Russell's, and who had
achieved immortality there one night when her dress split
in two, exposing to her breathless auditors a pair of legs
that, one stupefied witness babbled when he recovered himself, seemed massive enough to support the Brooklyn
Bridge, or at any rate the Equitable Building. Still, Miss
Urquhart's ownership of two such showy underpinnings,
one visitor to Proctor's reflected afterward, had proved no
more sturdy a foundation for lasting success in the unpredictable world of entertainment than Harrigan's ownership of two substantial theatres.

Pared down though his petite plays were, compared to
the unabridged versions, Harrigan yet found himself
obliged, every so often, to make room in them for the

specialty act of someone or other whom his vaudeville employers asked him to accommodate. One time it was a professional mesmerist named Salvation Jones. Another time it was Bob Fitzsimmons, who, to capitalize on his recently acquired heavyweight championship, had gone into vaudeville himself and, in *The Mulligan Guards' Ball,* gave an exhibition of bag-punching and later went three rounds with a sparring partner named Yank Kenny.

Fitzsimmons had appeared at the Metropolitan Opera House, too. Immediately after the Met opened, in 1883, its sponsors needed money desperately, and to help raise it made the place available for all kinds of non-operatic events—prizefights, wrestling matches, flower shows, and so on. Fitzsimmons was seconding a wrestler named Ernest Roeber at the opera house one night when Roeber's opponent, a fellow called the Terrible Turk, began to get the upper hand. Fitzsimmons leaped into the ring to aid his man, and precipitated a melée that the police had to stop. The Turk was declared the victor, but his purse proved to be his downfall. Distrusting paper money and banks, he converted his winnings into gold coins and stuffed them into a money belt. Not long afterward, when a ship on which he was returning to Europe sank, most of the passengers were rescued—nearly all, in fact, but the Terrible Turk, who was so weighted down he plummeted toward the bottom as soon as he hit water.

Harrigan didn't mind too much joining forces with Fitzsimmons, for the champion was a friend of his and, what was more, had a few months earlier given an exhibition of impromptu acting that Harrigan admired. On that occasion, Harrigan had been strolling on Broadway when the boxer spotted him, prankishly clouted him across the back, and sent him sprawling. At first mildly annoyed, Harrigan pretended to be murderously angry when he recognized his assailant—who, though approximately his equal in weight, was almost twenty years younger, let alone being the established superior of James J. Corbett— and, brandishing a cane in mock rage, Harrigan turned on him. Fitzsimmons, happy to play along, feigned abject terror and, with Harrigan on his heels, ran into a cigar shop, vaulted the counter, and cowered there begging for mercy, while Harrigan bellowed, "Lemme at him!" The shopkeeper, who knew both celebrities and was puzzled at the improbable course their combat seemed to have taken, was nevertheless momentarily persuaded that it was genuine, and was on the point of summoning the police when Harrigan and Fitzsimmons abruptly stopped play-acting and, arm in arm, made their exit.

But despite the warmth of their personal relations, it was a blow to Harrigan's professional pride when not only did Fitzsimmons' billing in *The Mulligan Guards' Ball* eclipse his own, but so did that of Fitz's sparring partner.

Harrigan remained on the vaudeville circuit for two years, well enough received for the most part, but unable to figure out how he had got into that particular rut. By now he had heard from many a source that he was passé, that New York had progressed beyond him, that the Irish and German immigrants dear to his creative heart had been overwhelmed by Jews and Italians, that the flavor of fresh topicality in his work was widely thought to have soured into faded antiquity, and that the question of whether he was or wasn't a great playwright

seemed to most people academic. He found all this hard
to believe. "How can my vogue have passed when I am
all alone in my field," he lamented to one interviewer,
"when I have no competitors and stand on a reputation of
years?" As if seeking reassurance from the record, he
stopped acting entirely for a year and devoted himself to
the writing of a reminiscent book, which was published
in 1901. Called *The Mulligans,* it was theoretically a novel,
but actually it was little more than a stringing together
of incidents from the Mulligan plays. There was one man
at least, the author reminded himself while writing it, to
whom the Mulligans and their escapades would never seem
dated! And so he dedicated the book to the memory of
Tony Hart.

The Mulligans contained large chunks of dialogue from
the old plays that Harrigan transplanted virtually un-
changed into his narrative, and it also contained a hint of
his feelings about the latter-day theatre when he had a
playwright in it say to Dan Mulligan, while describing
a drama he was writing, "It is a burlesque of the modern
type, extremely exaggerated, but really a perfect carica-
ture of human nature, and, I tell you, Mr. Mulligan, that
the time's ripe for the work! The public demand it. They
are bored by witnessing our great actors, who, with con-
summate art, hold, as 'twere, the mirror up to nature.
They desire the gross and sensual! Give them a bevy of
youthful beauties formed like Venuses, jingling melodies
tied to doggerel rhyme containing the slang of the day,
backed up by shapely costumes and magnificent scenery,
all of which, I confess, panders to a taste which is de-
praved and vulgar, but, when you are in Rome, do as
Rome does! . . . Our people have become luxurious from

the immense increase of wealth which begets lasciviousness, and is being augmented, year after year, by the concentration of capital inculcating the disease called 'Greed'; and remember, sir, greed is the Nero that makes a clown of Art!'"

But if Harrigan the writer was unappreciated and perplexed, Harrigan the actor was still a drawing card. "The fashion he created was discarded," one contemporary declared, "but not Harrigan." In 1901, he played Uncle Tom in a William A. Brady production of Mrs. Stowe's perennial, and at the start of 1903 played an Irish labor leader in Clyde Fitch's *The Bird in the Cage,* a comedy starring Nat Goodwin. Harrigan's performance was widely conceded to be just about the only saving grace the play had. "Hurrah for Harrigan!" wrote one critic. "He has had more downs than ups of late years, but he knows how to live on the stage, and a man who can blow the breath of life into such an artificial, impossible, and limp affair as *The Bird in the Cage* ought to be grappled to Broadway so securely that he can never escape again."

Harrigan was immensely bucked up by such encomiums. At once he began to write a new play, *Under Cover,* which he envisioned as a merry romp in his old tradition. It became more than that; it was practically a family reunion. George Braham wrote the music, and George's sister Ida was in the cast. John Wild had died in 1898, but his daughter Alice was in the show. So was Annie Yeamans, and so was her daughter Jennie, for whom Harrigan conceived a bedraggled character called Boozie Susie, a somewhat modernized version of his Tough Girl.

Boozie Susie, who appeared also to have been patterned on the notorious Evelyn Granville, was a slatternly, sloppy

drunkard who had just been released from the jail on
Blackwell's Island and was living in a Bowery flophouse.
When *Under Cover* opened, the character was unwaver-
ingly intoxicated throughout the action, much to the satisfaction of Miss Yeamans, who, like many other actresses
before and after her, loved to play drunk scenes. But
within a few days of the première, letters began to pour
in, mostly from advocates of teetotalism, begging that
this wretched creature be reformed. Harrigan thereupon
rewrote the play. The renovated Boozie Susie was handed
some money, urged to clean herself up, and did; in the last
act she not only appeared in decent clothes, but ostentatiously declined a proffered drink. The prohibitionists were
delighted, but Jennie Yeamans was furious. She thought
her part had been ruined and declared, furthermore, that
if anyone were to give a real Boozie Susie a handout, she
would spend it not on finery but on gin.

Joseph Sparks, Harry Fisher, Dan Collyer, and
Maurice Drew, who had been in the company at Harrigan's Theatre, were added to the roster. George Stout
was the stage manager. Instead of producing *Under
Cover* himself, though, Harrigan turned this chore over
to the firm of Liebler & Company, which booked the
show into the Murray Hill Theatre, on Lexington Avenue.
Annie Harrigan had had her doubts about the whole venture, and when her husband told her he would be at the
Murray Hill, she burst into tears.

"The Murray Hill?" she exclaimed. "Ned Harrigan not
on Broadway?"

Harrigan tried to soothe her by expounding on the
glories of the East Side, where he asserted there was a
virtually untapped mine of cultural opportunities.

"Lexington Avenue!" she went on, bitterly. "You might as well be in Kansas."

Harrigan's New York fans would perhaps not have followed him from Broadway to Topeka, but they demonstrated that, despite Annie's misgivings, they were perfectly willing to make a cross-town trek for him. The opening of *Under Cover,* on September 14, 1903, was described by the *Times* as "one continuous love feast." But it was not the new play itself—a tangled, awkward story involving politics, horse-racing, and the relocation of a graveyard—that evoked this emotion. It was, rather, when Mrs. Yeamans turned to Harrigan and said, "Do you remember that old thing that you and I used to sing when we were kids—how does it go now?—Oh, yes!" and with that the two of them began to march, march, march in the Mulligan Guards. The audience made them sing the song six times.

Under Cover achieved a creditable ninety performances, but its reception was not enough to convince Harrigan that he was once more securely grappled to Broadway, or even to Lexington Avenue. After it closed, he took to the road again, and for the next four seasons trudged wearily around the country doing skeletonized versions of *Old Lavender, Squatter Sovereignty, Waddy Googan,* and some of his other mainstays. He had seen *Old Lavender* grow from an afterpiece to an extravaganza; now it shrank again, until he was playing it with a cast of nine or ten, who—aside from his son Bill, who joined him on tour in 1904—would like as not be a ragtag crew of actors recruited in the hinterlands, unacquainted with and indif-

ferent to the perfectionist standards he had always set
himself.

Harrigan's final appearance in a Broadway show was
in the fall of 1908, when he took a small part in *His Wife's
Family,* an Irish comedy starring Arnold Daly. On opening night, he got his usual rousing ovation. His fans demanded noisily that he sing "Paddy Duffy's Cart." In one
of his own theatres, he would unquestionably have dropped
everything else and have done so, but now he was only
a minor member of someone's else cast, and all he felt he
could do was to make an embarrassed, apologetic speech
—he had to do something to quiet the audience so the play
could proceed—regretting his inability to oblige. Later
that fall, he toured the Midwest briefly in *Cameo Kirby,*
written by Booth Tarkington and Harry Leon Wilson.
Again he had a bit part; he played a hypochondriac
Negro servant named Croup who shuffled about complaining, at intervals, "I'se a very sick man," and who had
little else to do.

Harrigan himself was far from being a well man. For
several years, he had been suffering from respiratory ail-
ments, and his heart had been acting up, too. Now and
then, while touring in *Old Lavender* with his son, he had
found the pace too gruelling and had let Bill fill in for him
in the title role. (It had been Harrigan's fixed rule in
earlier days that nobody but himself could ever play Old
Lav—not even Joseph Sparks, who understudied him as
Dan Mulligan and in his other roles.) In the spring of
1909, Bill Harrigan agreed to appear in the annual Gambol of the Lambs Club, but then learned that a play he
had signed up for was going to be out of town at Gambol time. The Lambs' show, which had been held at the

Metropolitan Opera House since 1898, was a big event of
the theatrical year.

(An especially noteworthy Gambol was that of 1889,
in the course of which one of the performers, a famous
mindreader named Washington Irving Bishop, suddenly
and unaccountably dropped dead. After an autopsy was
performed on his corpse, his mother sued the officiating
doctor, claiming that her son had probably not died at
all but had merely fallen into a state of suspended anima-
tion. She said this often happened and that Bishop always
carried a note on his person warning strangers under no
circumstances to cut him up if he seemed lifeless. A
coroner's jury exonerated the doctor when no further evidence of the existence of any such note could be found.)

Although Ned Harrigan had been one of 140 original
members of the Players Club when Edwin Booth founded
that organization in 1888, he had never joined the Lambs
and had never set foot in their clubhouse. But, disturbed
that a Harrigan was evidently going to have to renege
on a promise, Ned telephoned Victor Herbert, who was
supervising the Gambol, and asked if he could understudy
his son. Herbert was overjoyed. He had assumed, along
with the rest of the stage world, that Edward Harrigan
would probably never perform again anywhere. He invited Harrigan down to the clubhouse on West 44th
Street, and, convening the Lambs who were present,
shouted, "I nominate Mr. Edward Harrigan for member-
ship!" By acclamation, Harrigan at once became a Lamb.

A distinguished cast including Weber and Fields,
DeWolf Hopper, and Eddie Foy had already been lined
up for the 1909 Gambol, but when Harrigan was added
to the group the program was amended to include a big

production number featuring a medley of his best-known songs. To an announcement of his impending participation that a reporter for the *Telegraph* wrote, the paper's copy editor had the urge to append a few subjective words of his own. This postscript, which was published along with the basic story, went, "I'd rather hear Ned Harrigan sing one verse of the Mulligan Guards than Caruso warble his entire repertoire."

On May 9, 1909, when the Gambol opened at the Metropolitan, Harrigan received a ten-minute ovation at his first entrance. The finale was to be an old-fashioned minstrel walkaround, and Harrigan, his face blackened by burnt cork just as it had been in his youthful days of minstrelsy, was sitting in the wings, waiting to go on, when he suddenly clutched his side and said to Eddie Foy, "I can't get up." He was removed from the opera house in a wheelchair, and spent the rest of his life in one.

White-haired, emaciated, and feeble, Harrigan lived as an invalid for two more years. Aside from his immediate family, he led a lonely existence. To the general public, a non-acting actor might as well be dead, and many of Harrigan's fans, on the few occasions when anybody bothered to mention him, were surprised to hear that he was still breathing. Most of his former associates had passed away—first Hart, then Wild, then Hanley, then Dave Braham. Annie Yeamans was one of the few old-timers around, and occasionally she would call on him and, with one or two of his sons pitching in, re-enact for him some of his favorite scenes. He asked most frequently for something from *Old Lavender,* and he had become pretty much of an Old Lavender himself, constantly brooding about bygone and better days—an example of nature, as 'twere, holding the mirror up to art. He wrote a couple of plays, to pass the time, but he never seriously contemplated producing either of them, nor did anyone else. On June 5, 1911, he asked his wife to fetch him the manuscript of *The Mulligan Guards' Picnic.* The following day, he gave it back to her. On the margin of the first page he had scribbled, "My dear Annie: My ambition is satisfied. We own a beautiful theatre which brought to us a home for ourselves and children. Ned." Minutes later, he died.

A few days before his death, Harrigan had complained to Annie Yeamans how tragic it was to have once been so universally beloved and then suddenly to have become so utterly forgotten. His funeral proved him wrong. More than a thousand mourners showed up for it, including actors and theatrical managers, grown-up newsboys, politicians and crooks, judges and prizefighters, and an unidentified blind old Irishman from Yonkers, who insisted tremulously on being led to the coffin, so he could kiss it.

In an editorial upon Harrigan's death, the *Times* said that he "served his era well, and helped to lighten the cares of life." It was Harrigan's misfortune that, although far from superannuated—he was only sixty-seven when he died—he outlived the era he served. Not long before the end, while meditating on his lapse into relative obscurity, he remarked that in the seventies and eighties people had cared far more deeply about the theatre than they appeared to in the baffling twentieth century. When he and Hart were at the height of their career, he observed, their audiences would customarily leave the theatre humming Dave Braham's latest tunes, would stop at a street-corner oyster stand for a quick snack, and then, still blissfully humming, would sensibly go on home. It was to be deplored, Harrigan declared, that all this had changed. Oysters, he sighed, weren't considered good enough any more. Now audiences, instead of sitting alertly on the edges of their seats during a performance, would slump back droolingly conjuring up images of the lobsters they were going to eat in some fancy restaurant after the theatre. What could you expect of folks who were too busy thinking about those damned lobsters while in the theatre to concentrate on the tunes, and too busy afterward cracking the damned claws on those lobsters in those restaurants to hum the tunes even if they did somehow manage to remember them? "I guess Tony and I were lucky," Harrigan concluded. "In the old days, we didn't have to reckon with the lobster."

ABOUT THE AUTHOR

Readers of *The New Yorker* are acquainted with E. J. Kahn, Jr., as the writer of many articles of fact and fancy that have appeared in that magazine over an eighteen-year stretch. He has also contributed to various other national magazines, and is the author of a half dozen books, among them *The Army Life, G.I. Jungle, Who, Me?* and *The Peculiar War.* He served as a correspondent for *The New Yorker* from the Southwest Pacific during the Second World War, from Berlin during the Airlift, and from Korea during the war there. With his wife and their three young sons, he divides his time between homes at Scarborough, New York, and Truro, Massachusetts.